When Things Went Right

To Breck,

with all best wishes.

[signature]

2015

Publication of this book is generously supported by
a gift from David C. Lindsey, a member of the Texas
A&M University Press Advancement Board, in honor
of his parents, John H. and Sara Lindsey.

When Things Went Right

The Dawn of the
Reagan-Bush Administration

Chase Untermeyer

Texas A&M University Press · College Station

Unless otherwise noted, all images are courtesy of the George Bush
Presidential Library and Museum, College Station, Texas.

This paper meets the requirements of ANSI / NISO Z39.48—1992
(Permanence of Paper).
Binding materials have been chosen for durability.

Library of Congress Cataloging-in-Publication Data

Untermeyer, Charles G. (Charles Graves), 1946–
When things went right : the dawn of the Reagan-Bush
administration / Chase Untermeyer. — 1st ed.
p. cm.
Includes index.
ISBN 978-1-62349-013-3 (cloth : alk. paper) — ISBN 978-1-62349-102-4 (e-book)
1. United States—Politics and government—1981–1989. 2. Conservatism—United
States—History—20th century. 3. Untermeyer, Charles G. (Charles Graves), 1946–
Diaries. 4. Presidents—United States—Staff—Diaries. 5. Bush, George, 1924–
6. Reagan, Ronald. I. Title.
E876.U847 2013
973.927—dc23
2013008688

The author is directing any royalties he may receive from this book to the Bush School of
Government and Public Service at Texas A&M University, in gratitude for the kindness of
George and Barbara Bush.

Frontispiece: President Ronald Reagan and Vice President George Bush outside the
Oval Office, 1981. (White House photo)

To Diana and our Elly

Bliss was it in that dawn to be alive,
But to be young was very heaven!

William Wordsworth, "The Prelude" (1805)

There should be a flat rule that no one be permitted to enter the gates of the White House until he is at least forty and has suffered major disappointments in life.

George Reedy, *The Twilight of the Presidency* (1970)

Stunned by [the Kennedy people's] glamor and intellect, Lyndon Johnson had rushed back to tell Sam Rayburn, his great and crafty mentor about them. . . ."Well, Lyndon, you may be right, and they may be every bit as intelligent as you say," said Rayburn. "But I'd feel a whole lot better about them if just one of them had run for sheriff once."

David Halberstam, *The Best and the Brightest* (1972)

Contents

Preface
Crossing the Potomac

In the genre of coming-to-Washington literature, no one wrote better than the late lawyer-lobbyist Harry McPherson. In his memoir, *A Political Education*, Harry lyrically described the night in 1956 that he and his wife arrived in the nation's capital after a long journey from Texas:

> I slow the car to cross Memorial Bridge. I want to remember this time, this shifting of our lives. We are crossing the wide, black Potomac River, mythic in the January night, leaving the South and its easy permissiveness, its flattering affirmations. . . . We are entering the North, where one must be astute as well as compassionate. It is a solemn moment. The smell of power hangs over this city like cordite.

My arrival, as described in the pages of a personal journal, was less lyrical but equally excited. Poetically as well as automotively, I arrived in daylight, the veritable dawn of the era of Ronald Reagan. It was 4 January 1981, a little over two weeks before Reagan's inauguration as the fortieth president of the United States. For me and so many others already in the city or shortly to arrive, this was a dramatic moment both for our nation and for ourselves. We were like the eager youth who flocked to town in March 1933 to join Franklin Delano Roosevelt's New Deal or those who, twenty-eight years later, came to be part of John F. Kennedy's New Frontier. We probably would have come just as enthusiastically at the start of any president's administration, but these three moments proved of particular consequence to the country. We would brag to the youngsters who followed us, with a mixture of nostalgia and pride, that we were there *then*.

Significantly for this narrative, I did not arrive as a committed Reaganite. Instead, I came to Washington to work for the new vice president, George Bush, another Texan who bestrode national government in the twentieth century. A member of the centrist or "moderate" wing of the Republican Party, Bush had been Reagan's main opponent for the GOP presidential nomination in 1979–80. Unlike the two Texans who preceded him, John

Nance Garner and Lyndon Johnson (vice presidents to the aforementioned Roosevelt and Kennedy), Bush's challenge to Reagan was no tardy push at the national party convention. Instead, it was a long, tough, and often bitter battle fought across the map of primaries and caucuses in the opening months of 1980. Bush won some, Reagan won more, and it was for reasons of party unity, not fondness or comradeship, that Reagan put Bush on his ticket. In so doing, he planted the seeds of a famous victory in November and two more after that.

Although Reagan and Bush were partners in that triumph, it was far from clear as I arrived in Washington that the new VP—and, by extension, I—would have an easy time of it in the White House. Viewed with suspicion and no little hostility by those who had supported Reagan's presidential hopes as far back as 1968, Bush may well have been isolated and ignored as vice president. After all, the previous Republican vice president, Nelson Rockefeller, had been politically emasculated by President Gerald Ford's two chiefs of staff, Donald Rumsfeld and Dick Cheney, if not by Ford himself, despite having been supreme lord of New York State for fifteen years—and a Rockefeller to boot.

This possibility (even prospect) greatly concerned someone who was not among the many arriving in Washington during those frigid days at the start of 1981. He was already there: Vice President Walter F. Mondale. A devout liberal Democrat who had gone down in political flames with Jimmy Carter in November, Mondale did not care about George Bush so much as the modern American vice presidency, an institution he had forged. In 1976, with the fate of then–Vice President Rockefeller vividly in mind, Mondale consented to go on the Democratic ticket with Carter only if Carter agreed that as president he would do four things: give Mondale an office in the West Wing of the White House; allow him access to the same policy papers and intelligence that Carter himself saw; give him a standing invitation to any meeting in the Oval Office except those of a personal nature for Carter; and have a weekly luncheon, with no one's staff present, to guarantee that the VP would see the president regularly and privately. Carter assented to all of Mondale's conditions, and one of the most important developments in American government became, not statute or constitutional amendment, but the accepted practice of all subsequent presidential–vice presidential partners.

Viewed from our time, when Vice President Dick Cheney loomed powerfully in the administration of the second George Bush, the Carter-Mondale agreement seems obvious, even quaint. We think, *of course* the vice president will see all important papers and attend all important meetings; and *of course* he not only will be in the fabled West Wing but will always have the final and most impactful access to the presidential ear. Yet this was not the presumption in January 1981. How George Bush became a solid and substantive member of the Reagan team is a theme of this book. In short, it occurred because of the immense capacity for friendship that each man had had all his life; because of Bush's earnest and energetic devotion to the man he was invited to join in July 1980; his selfless conduct in the aftermath of the attempted assassination of Reagan in March 1981; and because as one of the most experienced governmental and political figures of his day, Bush's talents were simply too vital and too valuable not to utilize to the fullest.

I had first worked for George Bush as a volunteer in his 1966 campaign for a new Republican congressional seat on the west side of Houston. In the forty-two-year-old oilman I saw not only an exciting new leader for the Lone Star State and its fledgling Republican Party but my own chance to enter the national government that I as a college student was then studying so intently. Bush won, and not long after his victory he sent a letter suggesting that I might become an intern in his House office. It was a moment of immense delight and excitement, to be surpassed only on the evening fourteen years later when Vice President–elect Bush would invite me to join his White House staff.

I worked two summers during Bush's freshman term in Congress (1967 and 1968), happily answering letters, giving Capitol tours for his constituents, and writing policy memos. There followed for me, during the 1970s, an ever-expanding life of serving in the Navy, globe-trotting, working as a newspaper reporter and county official, and eventually entering politics for myself as holder of Houston's silk-stocking seat in the Texas House of Representatives. Though separated from George and Barbara Bush in these years, we remained in touch by occasional visits and by the brief personal notes (typically on blue-bordered cards) which he sent to his myriad friends and supporters and on which he figuratively climbed to the presidency.

As the recipient over time of a sheaf of such communications, it was my particular assignment during his 1979–80 campaign for the GOP presidential nomination to draft faultlessly Bush-like answers to the personal mail that flooded into his Houston headquarters. I was not more active because for me the most important election in 1980 was not for the White House but for my third term in the Texas Legislature. Bush understood, as a fellow politician (albeit on a loftier scale), and respected my priority. This put me out of sight—and, I feared, out of mind—but in his wonderful way, George Bush remembered.

If I did not come to Washington in January 1981 as a committed Reaganite, neither did I come as a committed conservative. As a Texas Republican, I had a basic conservative philosophy of government and a legislative voting record to prove it. But I was not ideologically driven, such that as Washington's landmarks hove into view I shouted, "Now at last I can promote capital formation!" I supported Reagan's economic program, of course, though with a nervousness shared by many (including my boss) that it would actually work. My motivation, plainly and simply, was to serve at the national and international levels of government I had always read and dreamed about.

This is a most politically incorrect thought among Republicans and conservatives in general. At least publicly they will assert that government service is a distasteful duty that occasionally they must undertake for the good of the Cause, mucking out the Augean stables of Washington only so long as necessary before returning to the private sector. (It should be noted that the "private sector" to many conservative activists means a Washington think tank, lobbying firm, or a policy publication, not the entrepreneurial startup elsewhere in the country that they exalt for others.) A fellow Texas Republican told me once, "I'm willing to die for my country but not to go to Washington for it."

In contrast, I freely confess to having wanted to serve in national government, and I make the further heretical admission that I enjoyed it. The more honest of my colleagues in the Reagan and two Bush administrations will admit the same. Among them was Kenneth Adelman, who was deputy ambassador to the United Nations and director of the Arms Control and Disarmament Agency during the Reagan years. Ken wrote (in *Policy Review*, Winter 1988): "I never really believed Dean Acheson's comment, 'To leave public life is to die a little.' But I do think that to be in public life is to live a lot. None of us, even the grumpiest among us, would have traded the experience. What a time it was!"

Although a "Bushie" and not a Reaganite (or "Reaganaut," as the President's most devoted cadre called themselves), I came to admire and thrill to the presence of Ronald Reagan. As this book will chart, I was fortunate to have several close, if not personal, encounters with the man. Like the Bushes, I had assumed that (in Barbara Bush's words), "Reagan was like the Reagan people" we had known in Texas, many of whom were narrow-minded, mean-spirited, suspicious, and vengeful. That Ronald and Nancy Reagan proved warm, encompassing, and tolerant should not have been a surprise, but it was—and a happy one. I salute those who saw this earlier and more clearly than I did.

This book does not pretend to be great history. At best it recreates the atmosphere of the time "when things went right," capturing some of the period's personalities and the interesting things they said and did. In this aim my model was not Edmund Morris or even, much farther down the scale, Bob Woodward, but the late Sir Henry (Chips) Channon. Born to a wealthy Chicago family, Channon was a thoroughgoing anglophile who went to Oxford and married into the Guinness brewing family. Through his in-laws he gained a seat in Parliament, serving from 1935 until his death in 1958. Though never an important figure himself, Channon knew everyone who was important and, for our great gain, wrote about them and the world they inhabited. Through Channon's diaries we have the best portrait of interwar and wartime London with all its glamor, drama, danger, and delight. They provide the color and quotations of the times, food for footnotes if not for monumental history.

Like Channon, I was able to observe and report on the Washington of Ronald Reagan and George Bush. My journal was not a project launched upon arrival in Washington but begun some twenty-five years earlier at the age of nine. Like others of the cult, I scribbled away every night less from historical duty as from habit. I was going to write down what I did in January 1981 and thereafter whether my work site was the White House or the Texas House. I strove to record my life, not national and international events. To the extent I did, it was because such events in some way intersected with my day. I could see and describe only what my jobs in the Reagan-Bush era permitted. Should detail-desiring historians wail, "Oh, why wasn't Chase Untermeyer in that meeting?" all I can say is that no president of the United States ever asked the same question.

If these pages often read like a travelogue, it is because travel was the reality of life for then–Vice President Bush and his staff (almost all of whom were single at the time). The only valuable commodity a vice president has is his time. Possessing few authorities—and those entirely in his role as president of the Senate, not as a member of the Executive Branch—Bush used his time to travel constantly. I myself made ninety-nine trips in just two years, covering some 350,000 miles (3,000 of them just by helicopter in the greater Washington area). But the frequent flying was not merely a substitution of motion for action. Bush traveled for several important reasons: To sell Reagan Administration programs, to campaign for Republican candidates, to represent the President abroad on both ceremonial and substantive occasions, and (important but never uttered) to advance himself toward the presidency.

Most of these trips were domestic missions, interesting and special in their own way but the routine business of a US vice president. The journeys abroad were considerably more glamorous, of the sort that former White House staffers regularly enchant (or bore) dinner companions in recounting. My own repertoire of stories includes a dinner at Number 10 Downing Street hosted by Margaret Thatcher, a lunch with Emperor Hirohito inside the imposing walls of the Imperial Palace in Tokyo, and a private audience with Pope John Paul II in the Vatican. But my job held little substance. As a vice presidential aide, I was (in a colleague's apt phrase) "working for someone who was working for someone." I grew especially uncomfortable with being a high-level supernumerary on the road, no matter how grand the occasion. I was and remain extremely grateful to George Bush for allowing me to see and do the things we did, but I felt as if I were a nonproductive drain on the taxpayers' dollars. I described my life as one of "living on a diet of whipped cream"—thick, rich, and delicious but nothing to chew on. I envied contemporaries who remained in Washington to run agencies and programs while we jetted off to another Republican fundraiser or foreign capital. After Bush's fascinating and important trip to Africa in November 1982—with an unscheduled dash to Moscow for Leonid Brezhnev's funeral—I began to take steps toward getting a substantive job in the place I most yearned to be: the Navy Department. I close the book with an account of eagerly giving up a niche in the West Wing of the White House and a lounge seat on Air Force 2 to venture into the Pentagon bureaucracy.

Because a journal by its nature is personal, I cannot entirely disengage myself from the entries that follow. Yet in preparing this book, I have sought as much as possible to spare the reader tiresome trivia about myself. Most of all, I have omitted whole volumes of commentary on staff squabbles and fights in committee, the stuff of the typical Washington memoir. In this I was guided by the words of the popular pianist Liberace, who said he played "classical music with the boring parts left out."

This book contains perhaps only 10 percent of what I wrote in my journal, selected as an impressionist painter might choose and apply pigments to his canvas. In the end, after all, it is the picture, not the brushstrokes or the artist, that matters. What I was or did is uninteresting; it was the *times* that were interesting. I had the luck to be living in them, and if I have captured them to even the smallest degree, I am grateful. To the extent I enter this work, I apologize. It's just that every narrative requires a narrator, and in this one it's me.

For years, people have asked, "When are you going to write your book?" I appreciated their interest in my life even knowing that literary agents and publishers would have none at all. When I finally decided to mine what I had already written—the more than 250 volumes of journals kept since 1956—agents who deigned to reply to me suggested I try an academic, not a commercial, press. In the end, it was Texas A&M University Press that proved willing to consider this book. I am grateful to Charles Backus and especially to Mary Lenn Dixon and Thom Lemmons at the Press for their interest, endorsement, and help. They deserve, in best Aggieland tradition, my heartfelt *Whoop!*

Ever since I was a state legislator, the University of Houston Library has housed my personal papers, excepting only those required to be in federal depositories. It was thus to UH that I went to collect journal volumes from 1980 to 1983 and began marking passages for inclusion in this book. I found, to my astonishment, that I had forgotten some 80–90 percent of everything there. As a consequence, reading back through journal entries from that era was an exercise in time travel. On every page were the doings of a fellow very much like myself—in fact, it *was* myself–saying all manner of intriguing things, to me if to no one else. I had the same sensation once described by the playwright S. N. Behrman upon reading his own diary:

> Characters keep appearing whose very existence I had forgotten, and yet there they are, vivid ghosts, taut in their momentary preoccupations, clamped, as I myself was, in the imperative of now. Reading through these pages, I can foresee their destinies; their futures are laid out; I know all the crisscross lines at which my life intersected theirs. It is terrible to become possessed, suddenly, of all that foresight.

Because my journal has always been a single-draft affair, written in spiral notebooks in fountain pen ink, many entries needed editing. While my edits create a variance between the original manuscript and what is published here, I assure the reader that it is all for the better. If I tell something not known at the time, such as how a matter ended up or what happened to someone in later life, this is given within the text in italics or in footnotes. Brief explanatory information that I did not include in my journal at the time but that the reader needs to know is given within brackets.

In writing nightly journal entries, I use a great deal of abbreviations and a personal shorthand to save space, time, and ink. In the present work, I have spelled out all these words. Printed diaries that are too slavishly faithful to the manuscript, saying for example "the P" instead of the president, I find irritating. I do retain the common abbreviations R and D for Republicans and Democrats, RR for Ronald Reagan, PM for prime minister, FM for foreign minister, and "the VP" for the Vice President, meaning here George Bush.

I use the abbreviation "GB" quite frequently to refer to George Bush, the name he always preferred, never the elongated handle George Herbert Walker Bush or its initials. (The late Mayor James Michael Curley of Boston always made fun of Brahmins with multiple family names. Of the baby Bush born in neighboring Milton in 1924, Curley might have said, as he said of others, "What? All four of him?") When George W. Bush came on the political scene, the press and eventually everyone began calling the father George H. W. Bush, something he accepted without protest, though surely "George Bush" without the W would have sufficed. With greater humor the forty-first president called himself "41" to distinguish himself from his son, "43." It may be fustiness on my part, but I don't like referring to presidents by number, like dishes on a long Chinese menu. So I speak formally of "the first President Bush" and informally of him as GB. Barbara Pierce Bush has always insisted that people call her by her given name, which from time to time I have done. But more often I refer to her as BPB.

Along with the fine folk at Texas A&M University Press, I am particularly grateful to Prof. Douglas Brinkley of Rice University. His enthusiasm would be greatly appreciated merely as a friend, but as a distinguished American historian—most notably as editor of *The Reagan Diaries*—Doug's encouragement has been most flattering.

Special thanks belong to my longtime friend Robert Jackson, fellow at All Souls College at Oxford University and former member of Parliament, who introduced me to the diaries of Chips Channon. Another dear friend, Lupita Arce, a life-long teacher on all matters Mexican, gave me the correct version of the Spanish proverb cited in chapter 1.

Del Wilber, a reporter at the *Washington Post*, unwittingly provided the title to this book. After telephone interviews on what Vice President Bush did on 30 March 1981, I transcribed my journal entries from that time to send him. These Del used for his authoritative account of the attempted assassination of President Reagan, *Rawhide Down* (2011). When we finally met face to face in a Wisconsin Avenue deli, I asked whether a book on the Reagan Administration might be made of more such extracts. Del encouraged me to write it, saying, "People look back on that time as when things were done right."

Mary Finch and her colleagues at the George Bush Presidential Library assisted with the photos used in this book. They have my thanks.

And for the Wordsworth quotation (*Bliss was it in that dawn . . .*) that begins this book, I thank Peggy Noonan, who included it in her *What I Saw at the Revolution* (1990), still the best-ever White House memoir.

When Things Went Right

Chapter 1

Dream Job Come True

During the climax of the 1980 presidential campaign, I was a fellow of the Institute of Politics at Harvard, teaching a seminar to aspiring politicos on how to get elected to office. My own election to a third term in the Texas House of Representatives from Houston's "silk stocking" district was unopposed, allowing me to spend autumn in Massachusetts. Election night saw me at the home of Nancy Bush Ellis, sister of the Republican candidate for vice president, in the leafy Boston suburb of Lincoln.

Tuesday, 4 November 1980

Today, Election Day 1980 and perhaps one of the most historic days in American political history, I was picked up by Sandy Ellis [Nancy's husband, Alexander] on Boylston Street opposite the Kennedy School of Government. Sandy said he had talked with son John, a political analyst at NBC, who forecast a Reagan landslide—something impossible to contemplate realistically at that hour. But John had been in touch with President Carter's pollster Pat Caddell, who not only confirmed that prospect from his own surveys but hinted that the speechwriters were already drafting the President's concession speech.

Nancy arrived at the big house [in Lincoln] shortly after we did. She was wearing a bonnet wrapped with a scarf, and her woolly sweater was studded with a variety of Reagan-Bush buttons. "Oh, Chase!" she exclaimed. "I'm so excited you're here! It makes me feel closer to them [the Houston Bushes] to have you with us!" She asked me to call the Bush house on Indian Trail; Betty Green, GB's secretary, said they were out shopping to manage the wait and the tension. I put on jeans and rain gear and went outside in the great gray dusk to stand at the edge of Sandy Pond, which is actually a good-sized lake. The only sounds were of raindrops plopping into the still water and of ducks and geese coming in for landings. This precious time of quiet contemplation was at the expense of being out of reach when GB returned Nancy's call. "Where's Untermeyer?" she said he said.

Back in a suit (and wearing the "Chase" tie GB gave me in 1976[1]), I watched the regular evening news, which melted into election coverage. The Ellises' other guests started arriving, including their son Hap, daughter-in-law Robin, and grandson Alexander IV, plus some longtime Bush troopers. These were monied, tony types, including a Mrs. Chase who is the daughter of ex-governor Robert Bradford and thus a direct *Mayflower* descendant.

NBC quickly began calling states for Reagan: Indiana, Alabama, Mississippi, and Florida. The southern states were proof enough that Carter was finished: If he lost his southern base (which, with the exception of Georgia and West Virginia, he did completely), he had no hope of building an Electoral College majority. The first champagne cork was popped by me at 7:08 EST. More returns came in: Ohio, the bedrock of every Republican presidential victory in history, went for Reagan. By now Nancy was greeting guests by saying, "It's all over!" As the big sweep for Reagan continued across the land, historian Theodore H. White compared it to Roosevelt's triumph in 1932: The "end of a political era," this time for the Democrats. At 8:15, NBC declared Reagan the victor.

Reagan's great victory was of course gratifying. But what is astounding, stupendous, and downright heroic are Republican gains in the Senate. By evening's end we were within touching distance of actually controlling a house of Congress for the first time since 1954.

Nancy was called by her mother, Mrs. Dorothy Walker Bush, in Houston. Nancy asked me to "stay near" so she could put GB on. When she thrust the phone at me with her wonderful toothy grin, I said, "Congratulations, Mr. Veep-elect!" GB sounded calm and very tired. Without being asked, he gave me some local Harris County returns: Ron Dear lost county attorney, and Ron Paul was leading Democrat Mike Andrews in the Twenty-Second Congressional District. "I knew you'd be interested in that one, because Paul's one of your favorites," George said with typical soft sarcasm.[2] Then he asked

---

1. The necktie, with the word "Chase" stitched into it hundreds of times in black, was a gift from then–CIA director Bush when I was making my first race for the Texas Legislature. "Here's what you need for the big campaign," read the cover note. "Only don't tell David Rockefeller, who gave it to me, that I gave it to you." Rockefeller was chairman of the Chase Manhattan Bank.

2. I had gotten to know Ron Paul when he first ran and lost a race for Congress in 1974. I was then the political reporter for the *Houston Chronicle* and he was an obstetrician-gynecologist

me about congressional races in Massachusetts. Before I handed the phone on to others in the study, I said, "I hope to see you all sometime soon to congratulate you in person," but this didn't prompt him to say he definitely wants to do that and talk over my role in the new administration. If there is to be such a role, I shall have to pursue it myself, hopefully with GB's blessing.

And thus ended as wonderful an election night as anyone could wish.

Although the allure of going to Washington with the new administration was strong, I hesitated to join the surging tide of Republican jobseekers. After all, I had just been returned to my seat in the Texas House, and if I had any hope of advancement in politics I needed to remain on the scene in Houston. Still, I found myself paging through the so-called plum book of federal appointments, searching for the sort of subcabinet post that had taken a couple of state legislators named Roosevelt to Washington. Then there was the vice presidential staff, not immediately appealing in itself (I worried about becoming "an assistant to an assistant") but a possible way station to an eventual appointment in one of the federal departments.

My uncertainty confounded a graduate student from Mexico who sat next to me in a Harvard lecture course I audited that autumn. Coming from a culture in which connections count for everything, especially in politics, he could not understand why I hadn't already asked the Vice President–elect for a job. He quoted a proverb his grandmother always used: "Al que no habla, Diós no escucha." (He who speaks not, God hears not.) My friend's grandmother was right.

Saturday, 15 November 1980

Today I awoke after a second night in which I dreamt I missed an Amtrak-style train because I had to deal with little-old-lady types clustered on the platform. [Texas House speaker] Billy Clayton was also in the crowd for some reason. Am I "missing the train" on which GB's staff appointments are riding?

Finally, knowing that the VP-elect was probably swamped with calls (and specifically with pleas for help in getting jobs in the Reagan Administration), I called Jeb

---

in nearby Lake Jackson. He was the Libertarian Party candidate for president against Bush in 1988 and sought the Republican presidential nomination in 2008 and 2012.

Bush, his second son, whom I had gotten to know during the primary campaign,
when we shared a desk. I also spoke with Nancy Ellis.

Wednesday, 26 November 1980

Shortly before 2:00, the network started working. Nancy called and asked,
"Has George gotten ahold of you yet?" I said no, with some surprise, given
the close attention I've been paying to my telephone for days. "He called me
to say that he's been trying and trying—wants to talk about a job or something. But you've been elusive, like the Scarlet Pimpernel!"

At 3:00 I was visited by a student in my seminar. We were talking when,
around 3:15, the phone rang. It was Betty Green, calling to connect GB with
me. The student graciously agreed to step outside. I was put on hold, cut off,
and redialed.

"Chahlie!" came a familiar voice. "I'm dying to talk to you about all
this, but I don't know what you're thinking about. There are some things on
our staff, like legislation, and maybe some stuff with me." Working for him
would be very exciting, I said, because it would "let me watch the world of
the agencies, because I'm thinking of flexing my muscles in the world of administration, as a manager of bureaucrats." George suggested we get together
early next week at the Transition Office. "Then you can ride home with me
for a pick-up supper. I'd say spend the night, but the place is so small."

Our conversation ended, and at GB's direction I called appointments
secretary (and my old chum) Jennifer Fitzgerald[3] in DC to set the date: Tuesday at 6:15.

Tuesday, 2 December 1980

On the appointed day, I arrived in the capital early enough to ensure I would be
on time to see Bush—early enough, in fact, to go see another important older man
in my life.

---

3. Jennifer Fitzgerald, who had been Bush's personal assistant while he was US envoy in
Beijing and director of the CIA, became his appointments secretary when he was elected vice
president. I had met Jennifer in 1979, in the early stages of the Bush for President campaign,
when she worked out of his office in Houston. The daughter of a British brigadier, Jennifer
was always well turned out and had a direct and humorous personality that appealed to men
of power.

Malcolm R. Wilkey was my parents' lawyer in Houston in the early 1950s before being appointed US attorney and an assistant attorney general by President Eisenhower. In 1970 President Nixon had placed him on the US Court of Appeals for the District of Columbia Circuit, considered the second most important federal bench after the Supreme Court. President Reagan would name him US ambassador to Uruguay in 1985. Over the years, Judge Wilkey had always given me some sound advice, and such was the case today.

As I left his chambers, Judge Wilkey clasped my hand and said with a fatherly waggle of his finger, "If you have the chance, young man, to come here under George Bush's patronage, you do it!" I nodded a promise that I would.

With about half an hour till my appointment, I hiked from the federal courthouse to one of several townhouses [on Jackson Place] facing Lafayette Park which the government owns and uses. The Reagan-Bush transition is currently using some of these, and the Vice President–elect's is number 734. Jennifer came downstairs to say GB was behind schedule and that we'd "have to do your talking at the house." Also waiting to have dinner with George and Barbara was FitzGerald (Gerry) Bemiss, the Virginia aristocrat I met in Maine three years ago, an old friend of GB's who is screening people who want his support for appointment to federal office.

Around 7:00, Secret Service agents and staffers began scurrying like leaves before a wind, and down the townhouse stairs came the vice president–elect of the United States, clutching a briefcase in one hand and a gym bag in the other. It was raining, so he, Gerry, and I made a dash for the waiting limousine, sandwiching ourselves into the backseat in that order. In the front were the driver and another agent, and we were tailed by one and maybe two other Secret Service cars.

"Jesus, Bemiss!" George exclaimed. "Things are so wild around here now I don't know what they'll be like after we take over." He asked about my "onerous duties" at Harvard and then quickly said, "Chahlie, let's talk about your deal. . . . Do you want to work for me or in one of the departments?"

My policy having been firmly decided since spending Thanksgiving on Cape Cod, I said it would be fantastic working for him, and I was all set to accept a bid to be the advisor on domestic affairs. This short answer was ideal, because in an almost perfect playing out of a favorite daydream of late, George said, "There'll be an office in the White House, in the West Wing. That's where I'd like you to be, as sort of an executive assistant."

In the darkness of the car as it splashed through the streets of Georgetown, I closed my eyes and gave thanks for the realization of my wildest dream. In fact, as George continued telling me what he had in mind, the blood rushing to my head and the general ambiance made it seem as if I *were* in a dream.

GB had some trouble describing what my duties will be, because they depend on what his will be, and probably Reagan himself can't answer that yet. The very impreciseness of my future responsibilities is exciting, for they will be what George Bush chooses them to be.

The limousine pulled up in front of a pleasant little house at 4429 Lowell Street NW, lent to the Bushes by friends till Inauguration Day. There was the usual great commotion of rushing Secret Service agents and doors slamming as we quick-stepped through the light rain to the house. I shall certainly enjoy playing in such scenes again and again; [in the Navy] it was thrilling enough just being with a rear admiral on a tiny naval station in the Philippines, attended by a single Marine orderly.

Barbara and C. Fred the cocker spaniel were waiting inside. I kissed her, not mentioning until later the conversation GB and I had had in the car. "How lucky for us!" she said with typical graciousness. Later, after dinner, I reminded her of a conversation we had in Kennebunkport three-plus years ago in which she quizzed me intensively about my ideas on marriage. Now is the time, I said with a smile, for BPB to "put that on your list of priority items." She responded instantly and eagerly, "That's just the sort of thing I like!"

Dinner was a shining moment, one that countless others might envy. And yet I had to remind myself that I was with Vice President–elect and Mrs. George Herbert Walker Bush and not just with old friends and second parents.

As Gerry and I waited for cabs, he said, "You've got yourself one hell of a job. You're going to love it." In the few minutes till my cab arrived, I chatted with a young Secret Service agent named Steve. I don't even know whether it's allowed for them, like the guards in front of Buckingham Palace, to speak while on duty.

To say this is the most exciting opportunity of an already-blessed lifetime is almost trite, yet what else can it be? I'll not only be working for George Bush (who may yet become the 41st president of the United States) but will make the best of contacts. Being lodged in the West Wing adds another order of magnification, for I'll be right among President Reagan's top staff and under what I hope will be the protective eye of Jim Baker. If I do well—and I am fully confident I shall—the opportunities for future government service are boundless. Tonight's ride through northwest Washington may well prove the turning point of my career.

In later years I would say of this evening, "I realized it meant the end of whatever future I had in Texas politics, so I agonized over the decision for two-tenths of a second before saying yes."

Wednesday, 3 December 1980

It had been a night of little sleep because of a head cold brought back from Cape Cod and because of busy thoughts of my imminent new life. I thus got an extra laugh out of a Herblock cartoon in this morning's *Washington Post*. Titled "Visions of Sugarplums Danced in Their Heads," it showed a row of sleeping elephants, dreaming of desk plates labeled "Director," "Administrator," and "Special Assistant."

I was right on time for my 8:30 appointment with GB's white-haired chief of staff, retired admiral Dan Murphy.[4] When we shook hands, I said we might have met briefly in January 1978 when GB and I were working on his CIA papers. No, he didn't think we had. Where our lives actually did intersect proved surprising and delightful to us as Navy men: In 1968, then-Captain Murphy commanded the carrier *Bennington* on Yankee Station in the Tonkin Gulf, and my destroyer *Benner* was her constant companion.

While GB had already spoken enthusiastically about me to Murphy, the final decision on hiring me would be the Admiral's. He asked the awkward question of what GB had said about the job and whether he had actually offered it to me. I said it was my clear impression that the job was mine, pending the Admiral's and my talk this morning. Murphy said he sees me as working more or less directly for GB, but that he (Murphy) wants to be kept fully informed. This I promised, saying I am a great believer in the chain of command. Later, he called to say he had spoken with GB "and it's all go."

On takeoff of my flight back to Boston, I gazed down on the White House and its fabled West Wing. How quickly that structure has acquired a special new meaning for me: no longer a national landmark but my future office building.

---

4. Murphy had commanded the Sixth Fleet, served four years as military assistant to Secretary of Defense Melvin Laird in the Nixon Administration, and later was Bush's deputy at CIA.

Tuesday, 9 December 1980

In midmorning I called on Prof. Richard Neustadt to discuss my job with GB. "You'll learn a hell of a lot," he predicted, adding that having been a state legislator in Texas puts me in a good position: "You're somebody from somewhere."

Considered the nation's leading authority on presidential power, Neustadt gave me a special private lecture on the problems of vice presidential staff in the West Wing of the White House. "You sit in the same house [as the presidential staff], yet one of you is observing and the other is ruling. A vice president's staff will be frustrated and will take every slight personally. Half the slights are unintentional, but they all get noticed by the VP's staff."

When I left, I asked Neustadt if I am the first product of his Government 154 class on the presidency [which I took in 1966] to go to the White House. He reflected a moment and said with a smile, yes. "You're our first West Winger!"

Wednesday, 10 December 1980

I returned to Washington for transition meetings with the staff of outgoing Vice President Walter Mondale, beginning with his press secretary, Al Eisele.

Al and I met in the Executive Office Building, or EOB, the grand Beaux Arts pile next door to the White House. He showed me the VP's ceremonial office [once the realm of the Secretary of the Navy], the best feature of which is a balcony overlooking the White House. "It doesn't look very far over there," Al said, "but it's a gulf." Mondale refers to the EOB as "Baltimore," because the psychological distance from the White House is so great "it might as well be in Baltimore."[5]

We crossed West Executive Avenue, the name of the glorified parking lot between the White House and the EOB. Then for the first time in my life I entered the West Wing. We went up to the vice presidential suite,

---

5. Vice presidents from John Adams through Richard Nixon had had their office only in the Capitol, reflecting their constitutional role as president of the Senate. Lyndon Johnson was the first VP to have an office "downtown," but it was in the EOB, not the West Wing. Mondale's West Wing office was both a physical and symbolic expression of his closeness to President Carter.

bustling with the unscheduled visit of the speaker of the Tennessee House of
Representatives, dropping in on "Fritz" to pledge his support for the 1984
Democratic nomination. In the midst of this hubbub was Jim Johnson, a tall,
handsome man of 37 with tortoiseshell glasses and flecks of gray in his hair. It
is easy to picture a political future for him beyond whatever happens to Walter Mondale; David Broder's book *Changing of the Guard* half-humorously
speculated that he will be a Cabinet officer in the administration of Bill
Bradley, now junior senator from New Jersey.[6]

Al left me with Jim, who took me into his office: a tiny place no bigger
than a squared-off walk-in closet. But what it lacks in grandeur, the room
makes up in strategic location. Jim can instantly see everyone who walks into
the VP's suite, especially if they have just come from the Oval Office. And
the floor-to-ceiling window looks down on West Executive Avenue, where
important arrivals can be monitored.

Johnson started talking immediately, and everything he said was extremely valuable, distilled from four years of guarding the time and prestige
of the most active VP in American history. I took several pages of notes. It
was a demonstration of utmost cooperation with the team that had so badly
beaten his own just a month ago. Jim said, "The single most critical issue as
to whether the VP plays a substantive role in the administration is his access
to the paper flow into the president. Someone will be in control of that flow
for Reagan. The problem for you guys is to be cut in on it."

Scarcely allowing me time even to ask a question, Johnson spoke of his
successfully steering Fritz Mondale through the political no-man's-land of the
vice presidency: "If you guys don't keep your eye on maintaining Bush's stat-
ure, no one else will. And once you've lost it, you can't get it back, provoking
the stories everyone wants to write: 'Whatever happened to George Bush?'"
The key to this protection process is astute management of the VP's time,
something Jim called "the only resource you have." He said Bush should
decide what kind of VP he wants to be—an independent player, an expert
in national security, a doer of presidential odd-jobs—and structure his time
accordingly.

At noon, Walter Mondale emerged from his office, and Jim introduced
us. The outgoing VP congratulated me on my new assignment and asked
how I liked Jim's "palatial" office. He said, "One advantage is that you can

---

6. Johnson never again served in government, though he would head the quasi-government
Federal National Mortgage Association ("Fannie Mae").

see who's coming and going. If you see the Secretary of Defense suddenly arriving, you know something is happening. Then you rush out to find out what it is."

Leaving the West Wing is almost as exciting as entering it, due to the proximity of famous facades and memories of hundreds of TV shots of VIPs standing right about *there*, telling the press what the president had just told them.

On the flight back to Boston, I read over my notes and mused on the day I had had: that corridor leading from my future office down to the Oval Office was a haunting picture in my mind. I record here names and places in the stratosphere of American politics and government, and even now I see how quickly such things can become commonplace. I hope I don't become so used to them that I lose the sense of awe and privilege I had today. I am also determined not to become so addicted to the scene that it will break my heart to leave. I must do the best I can for George Bush and for the administration. Only that way can I hope to have a good shot at returning to the West Wing many more times in my life.

The speaker at the Institute of Politics dinner tonight was Congressman Bob Carr (D-Michigan), a "Watergate baby" elected in 1974 and defeated in this year's GOP sweep. Someone asked if Ronald Reagan, at age seventy-three, could be a "viable" candidate for reelection in 1984. Carr said that, yes, he could do it if he really does become (as advertised) a "chairman of the board" manager. "If he does, he'll be tanned and fit. George Bush will look like he's eighty-four, and"—pointing a finger at me—"*you'll* look like you're fifty!"

Monday, 15 December 1980

My fellow Institute of Politics fellow Julia Chang Bloch and I went to the [Massachusetts] State House to claim seats for the 3:00 ceremony at which the Bay State's presidential electors—Republicans for the first time since 1956—would cast their votes. Seated in the gallery with us were Doro Bush [George and Barbara Bush's daughter, then a student at Boston College], Jamie Bush [their nephew], and Robin Ellis.

The top-hatted sergeant-at-arms, holding a staff that flaunted the state seal, announced "the honorable members of the Electoral College!" To applause, in marched the fourteen electors, including Nancy Bush Ellis and ex-governor John Volpe. Someone had the dull idea that the electors should be in formal dress, and so they were: the men in cutaways and ascots and the women in long gowns with sequined handbags. It was the cartoonist's idea of what Republicans normally look like. There were speeches by the state's secretary of state and by Gov. Edward King, after which came the formality of nominating and voting on candidates for president and vice president—the only election in 1980 that constitutionally matters. Volpe nominated Reagan, whereupon he and the others signed little blue cards. These were then placed in a polished wooden box with an oval hole, resembling a colonial Kleenex box.

A committee was appointed to count the ballots. It took an amazingly long time for them to do this and report back the unsurprising news that Reagan had gotten all fourteen votes. Next, Nancy was recognized for the purpose of placing in nomination a candidate for vice president. There was sustained applause when she stood to pronounce a one-sentence nomination of her brother, "of Houston, Texas."

Later, back at Harvard, I received a call from Terry O'Rourke, the Houston lawyer who's been with the Carter Administration since 1977. "I don't envy you, but I'm happy for you," Terry said. He recounted something told him by a friend who represented ex–White House aide Jeb Magruder during Watergate. This attorney asked Magruder privately how he, also a lawyer, could knowingly commit illegal acts. Magruder replied that it was as if a voice kept calling out of the Oval Office, "Come closer! Come closer!"

To reassure Terry, I said that last Wednesday, as I was leaving the West Wing for the first time, I resolved always to keep thinking of what life would be like after I left it for the last time.

Friday, 19 December 1980

At noon I joined Scott Thompson[7] for lunch at the Harvest, the fancy French restaurant he calls "my club in Cambridge." Scott is delighted with my future job, seeing it (as I do) as a tremendous learning experience, "after which you can name any job you want in the administration. But by that time, Bush will be president anyway." He wants me to meet John Lehman, the

---

7. An associate professor of international affairs at Tufts University, Scott was married to the former Nina Nitze. She was the daughter of Paul Nitze, one of the postwar "wise men" who had been, among many other things, Secretary of the Navy and Deputy Secretary of Defense. I had met Scott and Nina in the Philippines some ten years earlier.

thirty-seven-year-old strategic thinker who is in line to become SecNav [Secretary of the Navy]. Lehman is on the move, and he's someone I should know.

When the Institute of Politics fellowship ended just before Christmas, I resigned from the Legislature and returned to Houston for a frantic few days of closing down my life there before moving to Washington. Also in town was the Vice President–elect, operating out of his late national campaign headquarters at 710 North Post Oak Road. Not exactly by coincidence, my state legislative district office was in the same building. This made it easier to drop by to see him, Secret Service willing.

Friday, 26 December 1980

Right now, all the agents look alike to me: Men in their thirties with straight, blow-dried hair and droopy mustaches. For the moment I think of them as machines rather than as future fellow federal employees.

GB asked for me to come in. We would talk alone for forty-five minutes about my role on his staff, our first such conversation since the now-famous ride to dinner on 2 December. GB said he wants me to be a "generalist" and "not an aide," keeping up with the flow of important papers. For this reason, he wants me to get my security clearances quickly. I mentioned I was cleared for top secret three years ago when we were working on a book, but this is not enough. I must have "code word" clearance as well. That sounds like something risky to have.

We both recognize that we'll have to see what happens to him and how our situation in the White House develops, particularly how we relate to each other. GB says that as people in the administration realize that I have his confidence, "they'll come to you with a lot of things and relieve the burden on me." GB is proud of the staff he is assembling, stressing their/our "excellence." That's a word be began using after Iowa when "class" was purged from his lips. He is counting on his staff to impress the Reaganites and inspire both confidence and cooperation.

As our talk developed, I felt bolder about emphasizing the extreme importance of his scheduling, recalling Jim Johnson's words that the only valuable resource a VP can expend is his time. GB reassured me that Jennifer Fitzgerald won't have unique authority to make decisions on scheduling. These decisions will be made in staff meetings in which she (and I) will participate. I feel better already that politically sensitive people like [deputy chief of staff–designate] Rich Bond[8] and I shall have a voice in whether, for example, it is better for the VP to attend the Indiana State Fair or to address the B'nai B'rith on a particular day.

I mentioned another Jim Johnsonism, "the general store phenomenon," in which ranking assistants to the VP hang out around the West Wing office in order to be close to the main man. GB thought aloud that one way to prevent this is by spending more time in the EOB office. He doesn't feel constrained, as does Mondale, always to be in the West Wing. As for how the press comes to regard him, GB doesn't care whether they write "whatever-happened-to-George Bush?" stories. "They're doing it already. They did it during the campaign. But if this job [in the cleaned-up words of John Nance Garner] 'ain't worth a pitcher of warm spit,' then why do so many people want it?" He supplied the answer, uttering the unutterable: "Because with a 70-year-old president, you could become president at any time."

Saturday, 27 December 1980

The fact I am leaving Houston to settle I another city, probably for four years and maybe longer, still has yet to sink in. My mind is telling me that it's just another trip I'm making. "I now leave, not knowing when or whether ever I may return." So spoke Abraham Lincoln to his Springfield neighbors on 11 February 1861. He was never to return, and I am sure I shall, if only to accompany GB on flying trips when he gives a speech. I also very definitely intend to make Houston my home again and to pursue my "mid-career" here, be it in politics, journalism, or business. I shall miss it in the meantime, especially in cold months up East; especially when I hear the song "Galveston"; and especially when I think of good friends. Houston has been good to me: It gave me George Bush, and it gave me an independent start in politics. And now comes Washington, the place I always called "the city of my dreams." It's the only place other than Houston where I would like to live. And soon I'll learn if I was right.

I packed my 1978 Dodge Omni and left Houston the next day, visiting friends and family along the way. New Year's Eve was spent in my mother's hometown of Rus-

---

8. Rich Bond was a scrappy, hyperkinetic politico from Long Island who had brought off Bush's surprise victory in the Iowa caucuses. He liked to tell how during that campaign he had grabbed a phone and, thinking the caller was someone else, commanded Barbara Bush to "Cool your jets!" Rich survived to become Republican National Committee chairman in 1991.

sellville, Alabama. There I summed up the exciting and momentous year just past in an essay titled, "1980: Texas House to White House, via Cambridge." And I ventured a hazy look ahead:

This will be the year of GB in the West Wing of the White House and all over the world; no one could ask for more. There'll be the relatively minor discomfort and expense of settling in DC, and there may be the relatively major aggravation of dealing with the Reagan staff and the federal bureaucracy. But it will be a great year; of this I feel more confident than any prediction in the twenty-five years that I have been keeping a journal. I am on my way to carrying out the injunction placed here a year ago: that the 1980s must be a time of "takeoff" for me.

Chapter 2

Transition

Sunday, 4 January 1981

The final leg of the great semitranscontinental journey that began a week ago was rather easy. I left Roanoke and ambled north on I-81, paralleling the Shenandoah River. To my right was the ridge of mountains crowned with Skyline Drive. Near Strasburg, I turned east, straight toward DC. The road sign saying "Washington 74" was a splendid sight, and the descending numbers on each successive sign were even greater causes for joy.

I turned onto the Beltway and then I-95. Over a rise, the sudden appearance of the Washington Monument and the Capitol were evidence I was Really Here. I have made many arrivals in Washington over the years and seen the same landmarks. Yet today was powerfully different: I was arriving in my new home, probably not to spend the rest of my life but at least an indefinite number of years. And if I leave Washington to return to my abiding hometown of Houston, it will probably be with the thought of returning to live here again under different circumstances.

My temporary lodging in Washington was a grand one: the nineteenth-century Capitol Hill mansion of Stuart and Julia Chang Bloch, who were away on a winter vacation to Greece and Israel. But the house had its perils.

Monday, 5 January 1981

The low temperature (in the teens) and the Blochs' thick wool pile carpeting combined to create a low grade of terror. Static electricity crackled over me as I, in pajamas, simply walked across a room, and as I approached the shower a metal picture frame caused the hair on my arm to stand on end. I had to use my (wooden) clothes brush just to flip lights on and off. Worst of all, when I reached to turn off my clock radio, a spark erased the digital display, never to return.

I reported for duty, as pledged last month, at the VP transition office at 734 Jackson Place. Upstairs in a third-floor bullpen were Rich Bond and others. Jennifer is at the end of the hall, and Admiral Murphy is in between. During the course of the day, our small office came more and more to resemble Groucho Marx's steamer stateroom in *A Night at the Opera*. My "desk" is a circular table in the corner of the room. Rich jibed, "We don't want to spoil you before you occupy that office over in the West Wing," perhaps the tiniest that exists in Washington.

Tuesday, 6 January 1981

Bob Thompson and I got to know each other better. He's the quietly self-assured young Tulsa businessman who'll be "executive assistant for congressional relations." Susan Alvarado will have the same job but with a different title. Bobby was a traveling aide to GB during part of the primary campaign. Confused by the role GB (or for that matter any VP) has in congressional relations, Bobby thinks his own job should include general political responsibilities. He said this with some hesitancy, thinking it would intrude on my desired turf. I assured him that apart from having a voice on scheduling, I don't want to get as involved in the political end of things as will he and Rich Bond.

There is some artifice in swearing off this chore. For one thing, I know GB and I will discuss a lot of politics when we're together. And for another, the lesson to me of Watergate is that young staffers who want to succeed in government should not compete for the boss's favor by striving to get *campaign* duties. Also, it will strengthen my hand among the Reagan staff if I appear interested in—and skilled in—policy matters rather than politics.

I solved my long-term housing needs by getting a place at 2800 Woodley Road NW, a late art deco–style apartment house just off Connecticut Avenue near the old Shoreham and the newer Sheraton Washington hotels. When filling out the rental application, I came upon a block that asked "Salary." I suddenly realized that in all the excitement of being hired, I had never asked anyone what my pay would be; I just figured it had to be higher than the $7,200 a year I got as a state rep. So, rather than say "unknown," I answered $40,000.

Wednesday, 7 January 1981

The Admiral said someone from the company that owns my apartment house had called to verify the $40,000 I had put down on the lease application. "Why did you put that?" he asked sternly. I started to apologize for my presumption when the Admiral said, "We're paying you $52,000 a year." It's an absolutely astounding salary. Of course, taxes will take half or more of this pay—which is to say they'll go toward paying half my salary, requiring some poor blokes in San Angelo to come up with the rest.

A few weeks later, after the inauguration, I was with some presidential staffers bantering before a meeting. "You know the real difference between us and the Carter people?" one said. "I'll bet they never made as much money in their lives as when they worked here." As the others nodded in agreement, I smiled sheepishly.

Tuesday, 13 January 1981

Ten o'clock brought the first staff meeting, presided over by Admiral Murphy in shape-up-or-ship-out Navy style. It was also the first time I got to meet various members of the staff, among them the general counsel, Boyden Gray, a tall, bony-gaunt, and terribly aristocratic North Carolinian.

The Admiral said, "Our goal is a simple one: Make George Bush the best damn vice president in the history of the country. We're not running for president; we're running the country. Don't upstage the President's staff. That would be the quickest way to alienate George Bush from Ronald Reagan." The Admiral also demanded "no surprises and no self-aggrandizement. There's only one star on this staff, and that's George Bush."

The Mondale staff was extraordinarily helpful to me and other incoming Bush staffers. One of the most fascinating and thoughtful things Jim Johnson did was invite me to accompany Mondale on his final trip as vice president. It was back to Minnesota, his home state.

Thursday, 15 January 1981

When I got to the Bush office a little after 8:00, the excitable young Matthew Smith met me at the door with word that the snow prevented VP Mondale from taking a helo to Andrews Air Force Base and that I'd have to leave immediately in the motorcade. (In the world of the White House, the Army runs the president's motor pool and all ceremonies; the Navy runs the Mess and Camp David; the Air Force runs the VP's motor pool and of course the fixed-wing aircraft; and the Marines provide the helos and play music.) I rode with deputy press secretary Maxine (Max) Isaacs and the military assistant to the VP, an Army major who "carries the football," the super-secret codes a president or vice president may need in time of war.

We traveled to Andrews in the snow along the Suitland Parkway. The base is much bigger than I expected. Normally, the president's or VP's aircraft is waiting on the field, but in bad weather the plane is kept in a hangar. It's like entering a car in a garage or having a giant metal umbrella. Waiting for us was a white and silver [Boeing] 707 inscribed "United States of America." It was the first jet used by a president, namely Dwight Eisenhower in 1959.[1] When the VP is on board, this (and any plane) is called *Air Force 2.*

I shook hands with Mondale and thanked him for including me in the trip. "If George Bush does everything like you'll see it today," Mondale said in his highly nasal Minnesota accent, "he'll be in sorry shape!" His staff laughed instantly.

I had forgotten how far 707's must travel to build up air speed and how much noise the engines make as they rumble down the runway. Soon we were above the clouds in the sunlight. It was an odd sight to see the Air Force insignia on the wing tips. We were served an ample breakfast, and the Mondale folk came by to sit and talk with me, almost in sequence. Among them was Chuck Campion, the highly skilled trip director. He comes from the politically intense neighborhood of West Roxbury in Boston and has the accent to prove it.

Making all sorts of noises that didn't bother my hosts, the 707 landed at the snowy Minneapolis–St. Paul airport about 10:45. The motorcade took us into St. Paul, paralleling the frozen Mississippi, on which some hardy ice fishermen were standing. We headed for the beautiful state capitol, its exterior trimmed in gold and its interior in Italian marble. There Mondale spoke at noon to a joint session of the Minnesota Legislature. [This followed a choral concert by a university group. Chuck Campion, sitting alongside me, turned at one point to say, "You know what's wrong with these people? They're all so . . . so *decent!*"] The VP said people had asked him what he was going to do. "I tell them I want a job that's exciting, which pays well, which involves travel, and which has a house and a car. My staff tells me it may take up to four years to get it." Loud and prolonged applause followed.

There was no precipitation when we returned to Andrews around five. This permitted us top-level types to "chopper" back to DC. It was all so

---

1. This was SAM (for Special Air Missions) 86970, on which I would spend a considerable part of my life during the next two-plus years.

simple: When we disembarked from the plane, we walked just a few steps to a waiting "white-topped" helicopter. A shave-headed young Marine stood at stiff attention beside the steps. Fully appreciating the scene, I went right on board. Mondale indicated for me to sit in the armchair opposite his. "I wasted a year and a half of my term before I found out I could use this thing," he said as the helo taxied a little bit and then lifted into the gray sky. Mondale and his aides then helped themselves to the helo's matches and candies—typical Democrats. (Democrats also smoke more cigars than Republicans do, and *Air Force 2* was loaded with stogies. I think they think it makes them look tough.)

The helo circled over the Jefferson Memorial and came in for a landing on the Ellipse [south of the White House]. Waiting for us was a line of White House cars, including one for me. No question but that this is the way to travel.

Friday, 16 January 1981

I met for the first time Barbara Hayward, who will be GB's personal secretary in the West Wing office. She has been secretary to William Casey, Reagan's campaign manager and director-designate of the CIA. Barbara is in her fifties and like Jennifer is British, very British. With Pete Teeley[2] also a native of the UK (though raised in Canada), the Bush office may indeed seem what oddball Democratic presidential contender Lyndon LaRouche alleged last year in New Hampshire: an instrument of evil English influence, with Skull and Bones [the Yale secret society to which Bush belonged] its antecedent.

On the second floor of the West Wing I visited (at his strong request) David Rubenstein, deputy to Stuart Eizenstat as domestic affairs advisor to the President. I had been told that a conversation with David consists of his picking your brain for useful info. Tonight, however, he wanted to give his piece on how the Mondale staff made themselves and their boss so effective. There was little I hadn't heard from Jim Johnson & Co., and yet there was added weight coming from a member of Carter's staff, especially from someone with a reputation for incisive knowledge of the federal government. When I asked David what his plans are after Tuesday, he said he intends to practice law in DC. Then with a controlled smile he said, "What I really want

---

2. Teeley, Bush's press secretary during the 1979–80 campaign, continued in that role on the vice presidential staff. He served as US ambassador to Canada from 1992 to 1993.

to do is come back here in four years." Rather than rise to the (polite) bait, I said philosophically, "Oh well, if you have to wait longer you'll just be richer."

I was more correct than either I or Rubenstein imagined. David never returned to work in the White House, but as cofounder of the Carlyle Group, a private equity firm, he became very, very rich.

Monday, 19 January 1981

With 12.8 percent of the United States, [a Texas friend] is here for the great national ceremony which now is only hours away. Tomorrow, in the quadrennial American coronation, my friend and patron George Bush will become vice president of the United States—and I will join the federal payroll.

Chapter 3

Our Little Office Building

Tuesday, 20 January 1981

Today, a great one for the United States and in my life, began early. The weather was unseasonably warm (in the fifties) after weeks of severe cold for DC. My job at the transition office as sole staffer was to answer the phones. (Correct till the last, I answered with, "Ambassador Bush's Office.") The TV was on; coverage of the inauguration was punctuated with bulletins on the release of the fifty-two American hostages on the 444th day of their captivity in Iran.

Around 10:15, the Reagans' limousine passed in front of the townhouse; Mrs. Reagan was easily visible in a red coat and matching hat. A few moments later, George and Barbara arrived. I kissed her and shook hands with him, and we chatted till Sen. Howard Baker (R-Tennessee), the new majority leader, and Congressman Bob Michel (R-Illinois), the House minority leader, arrived to perform their roles as official escorts. They, like the VP-elect, were decked out in the "stroller" morning dress RR had decreed for the occasion. The principals rode across Pennsylvania Avenue to the White House, where the Carters and Mondales greeted their successors.

I then left on the good leg-stretching two-mile walk to the Capitol. (Today's was the first inauguration to be held on the West Front, which is much more dramatic.) Justice Potter Stewart swore in his friend George Herbert Walker Bush as he had done on many previous occasions, though none this grand. The Marine Band sounded "Ruffles and Flourishes," followed by an unfamiliar tune that may well be the VP's march. [*It was "Hail Columbia."*] They were all miniature figures in my sight, but against the towering majesty of the Capitol on a pretty day, the rite of inauguration was no less stirring.

The high moment came when Chief Justice Warren Burger administered the oath to Ronald Wilson Reagan as the fortieth president of the United States. A twenty-one-gun salute boomed as the band played "Hail to the

Chief." Reagan gave a masterful inaugural address, as firm and as conservative as any campaign speech he ever gave but with considerably more authority and eloquence, as when he said, "We are a nation that has a government—not the other way around." He concentrated on the plight of the nation's economy and only briefly mentioned foreign affairs—basically a warning to the USSR not to confuse our love of peace with weakness. In sum, the speech was a call for "an era of national renewal." May the people, the press, the Congress, and the bureaucracy permit it to come.

Wednesday, 21 January 1981

Today dawned drizzly and gray. If yesterday's weather was ideal for an inauguration, today's was best for beginning to govern. The scene in the VP's West Wing suite all day was one of low-level confusion, typical of any group of people moving into new offices: rustling for supplies, complaining about decor, and puzzling over telephone numbers. Dropping by were staffers for Jim Baker and Ed Meese, our bracketing neighbors. They may eventually become my closest friends, but today they struck me as thoroughly lacking in charm.

Bob Thompson and I rode with GB to the Capitol for his first session as president of the Senate. I rapped the window of the limo with my knuckles; the resulting sound was barely a squeak, so thick is the bulletproof glass. As we rounded the Senate wing, I remarked to GB, "It's taken you ten years, but you've finally made it to the Senate." Barbara Bush later corrected me: It's been over sixteen years since their first race for the Senate.

At 11:00, GB entered the chamber, rapped for order with the Senate president's cylindrical gavel, and called on the chaplain to pray. Majority Leader Baker and Minority Leader Robert Byrd (D–West Virginia) welcomed him, after which GB responded with a few gracious remarks. Senators present (including Lloyd Bentsen, to whom Bush lost in 1970) then gave him a standing ovation. This may prove the high-water mark of the Bush Senate presidency; like his modern predecessors, GB isn't likely to spend much time on the dais.

GB later paid a visit to the House Republican leadership. His remarks there were in the jovial tone appropriate for former colleagues: "I don't know Speaker O'Neill well, except that I used to see him naked in the [House gym] steam bath."

After presiding over the confirmation of Alexander Haig as Secretary of State (by a vote of 93 to 6), the VP shot off to the limo to return to the White House. "We're going to have a lot of fun," he said.

Friday, 23 January 1981

I returned a call from Anne Armstrong, down on the ranch in South Texas. She advised GB to get in touch with Dallas computer magnate Ross Perot on some item he considers hot. "He's a good friend to keep," observed Mrs. A (a veteran of the White House herself), who gave me some hints on how I should speak to Perot.

When I called Perot, he proposed that the US back out of its agreement with Iran on freeing the hostages. "There's no family that's been the victim of a kidnapping who wouldn't move to recover the ransom money once their loved ones had been returned," he said. "Millions for defense, but not one cent for tribute!" GB later told me that the new administration will honor the agreement, despite reports of brutality by the hostages' captors.[1]

Saturday, 24 January 1981

Admiral Murphy asked me to sit in for him on a White House scheduling meeting to plan the welcome for the ex-hostages ("freed Americans"). It was held in the Roosevelt Room, the grand conference salon in the middle of the West Wing. Presiding was Michael Deaver, RR's deputy chief of staff and closest personal aide. When Deaver speaks of what "the governor" likely would feel about a certain matter, he is given absolute attention. I introduced myself to Deaver when he went over to get some coffee. "Chase Untermeyer," he pondered. "Sounds like a George Bush staff name. Are you a Third or a Fourth?" One of the Reagan folk overhearing this remark reminded Deaver that it's their staff that has the numbered descendants, namely James A. Baker III and Edwin Meese III.

Tuesday, 27 January 1981

GB and BPB left for Andrews on one of the most exciting and emotional possible missions: to greet the fifty-two Americans freed a week ago by Iran. When the bus motorcade reached the vicinity of the Treasury Department, Marvin Bush [the VP's youngest son] and I went to the South Lawn. We

---

1. Was this the proverbial flap of the butterfly's wings that by 1992 became the tempest of Perot's challenge to then-President Bush, which effectively elected Bill Clinton?

ended up in a prime spot, in a roped-off area between members of the Cabinet and members of the House. Senators were farther back. (Easily visible in purple was Elizabeth Taylor Warner, wife of the senator from Virginia.) The great South Portico rose above us, the Truman balcony decorated only with a single yellow bow. The 444-day hostage episode changed the standing of the color yellow. Once it was a fighting word, an insult, denoting cowardice. But it has acquired a new and perhaps permanent meaning—that of keeping faith and remembrance—thanks to the 1973 Tony Orlando song "Tie a Yellow Ribbon ('Round the Old Oak Tree)." Members of the Army's Herald Trumpets lined the curving steps. The Army Band struck up "This Is My Country," followed by the Orlando song.

The periods of relative hush were broken by rising cheers on Pennsylvania Avenue as the bus convoy reached the White House, GB and Barbara riding in number 1. The Trumpets then announced the arrival of President Reagan, followed by the national anthem, which we all sang without cue. Reagan gave a brief speech of welcome in which he promised "swift and effective retribution" for all future acts of terrorism. A moving response came from Bruce Laingen, the American chargé in Tehran when the embassy was taken 4 November 1979. The ceremony closed with RR's asking us all to sing Irving Berlin's "God Bless America." It was all poignant without being tearjerky. Allowances being made for the pomp and circumstance, it was a simple ceremony focused on the ex-hostages and not on the President.

Friday, 30 January 1981

Installed today in the apartment on Woodley Road was my "Signal Drop," the White House telephone operated by the White House Communications Agency.[2] Simply by picking it up, a voice comes over the receiver, ready to connect me to any phone in the world. When WHCA asked what color I wanted, there was only one answer: red.

The current issue of *Newsweek* has a diagram showing the location of key offices in the White House. It's a wonderful way to show friends and family "my room," as in an old-fashioned postcard from a resort hotel. It also shows me where everyone else's office is located, something I haven't learned yet.

---

2. WHCA (pronounced "Wocka") is a child of the old Army Signal Corps. Staffers tended to rely more on the White House operators, civilian ladies famously able to locate anyone anywhere.

Tuesday, 3 February 1981

The afternoon brought a magnificent event that at least temporarily altered my glum winter mood. GB called on the Signal line to ask, "Could you please come join in this Congressional Black Caucus meeting? Mickey Leland[3] is here. We're in the Cabinet Room."

I rushed down the short corridor past the Oval Office and went right into the Cabinet Room. The eighteen members of the caucus were milling around, some chatting with GB, when I arrived. Mickey saw me and we embraced, which was rather awkward because I had tucked a notepad under my arm. "It took me to get you in here!" he said gleefully. He then introduced me to some of his colleagues, always with the notation that "we served in the Texas Legislature together." Clearly Mickey was showing me off as his contact in the White House.

All of a sudden there was a hush, and those who were sitting had risen to their feet. Through the bodies I saw Ronald Reagan enter and start shaking hands around the table; I had forgotten that this was his meeting and not GB's. As he loomed closer, I found myself saying, "It's Ronald Reagan. He's president now!" This was my first real time to see him. He was dressed in an understated blue plaid sports jacket with a handkerchief carefully wedged in the pocket. Indeed he looked like a typical ruddy-cheeked, prosperous Southern Californian male of three score and ten, which he becomes this weekend. He and I shook hands with only a pleasant nod from him and the words "Mr. President" from me.

The President and his guests made small talk about the enormous jar of Jelly Belly jellybeans, which are his favorites and this administration's equivalent of the peanut in the first smiling months of Jimmy Carter's tenure. The chairman of the caucus, DC delegate Walter Fauntroy, introduced the members before expressing concerns the group has over inflation, unemployment, proposed budget cuts, and military spending. Reagan responded at length and quite impressively. Speaking without notes in his most articulate, frank fashion, he hastened to reassure the black members of Congress that his administration won't lower the budget but seek only to reduce and eventually eliminate the widening gap between revenues and expenditures. To illustrate

---

3. Mickey and I were good friends in the Texas House, overcoming differences in party, philosophy, race, and neighborhood. Elected to Congress in 1978 to succeed the great Barbara Jordan, he would die in office in a plane crash in Ethiopia in 1989.

his point, he picked up a pad of paper and sketched a graph which he held up. Budget cuts to reduce the deficit will be across the board, he said: "No one will be spared, not even defense." He expressed his firm conviction that constitutional rights be protected "at the point of a bayonet" if necessary. But then he was inspired to launch into the sort of anecdote-filled panegyric against "welfare cheaters" that delights audiences of middle-aged white Republicans at fundraising dinners but which today failed to impress the caucus members.

As GB later said of Reagan to Mickey, "I spent sixteen years fighting the man and what he stood for. But I didn't know him." Mickey agreed, saying he saw more genuine warmth in Reagan than in Carter.

Sunday, 8 February 1981

At 1:15 I arrived at the Georgetown home of columnist Joe Kraft and his wife, Polly, an artist. Joe and I first met in October 1972, when we were both covering [Texas senator] John Tower's reelection campaign. He had his secretary invite me to brunch today. I suspected there would be a few other folks there, but I didn't begin to imagine their eminence. This I learned within moments of arriving, when Joe pointed to a gray-haired man and said, "Here's a fellow Texan I want you to meet: Bob . . ." Around turned the great and crafty Bob Strauss [former Democratic national chairman and most recently US trade representative].

From then on, the roster of fellow guests grew ever more stellar: Kay Graham, publisher of the *Washington Post*; Ben Bradlee, executive editor of the *Post*; Sally Quinn, waspish *Post* profiler and consort to Bradlee; columnist and etymologist Bill Safire of the *New York Times*; Henry Brandon of *The Times* of London [*whose wife, Muffie, would become Mrs. Reagan's social secretary*]; Sander Vanocur of PBS; columnist Joe Alsop, looking quite old and feeble; SecDef Caspar Weinberger; Marshall Brement, Soviet specialist and deputy ambassador–designate to the UN, and his wife, Pamela, a high-spirited novelist; Lane Kirkland, secretary-treasurer of the AFL-CIO; and the merry, unkempt Sir Nicholas (Nico) Henderson, Her Britannic Majesty's ambassador to the US.

When Polly announced lunch, Sir Nicholas served Pamela's and my plates. We ate together with the Strausses, and soon we were joined by the couple I was happiest to meet today: Henry and Jessica Catto. He is the debonair former chief of protocol and ambassador to El Salvador who is slated to be the next assistant secretary of defense for public affairs. She is the solid and sensible daughter of Oveta Culp Hobby and sister of [Texas] Lt. Gov. Bill Hobby. Together they publish the *Washington Journalism Review*. Henry sat on the floor next to me during lunch, and we chatted easily about Texan-Washington affairs. Afterward, Jessica and I talked about the Atlanta situation [in which black children were being mysteriously murdered]. I would like to think that the seeds of a friendship—and a potentially valuable one—were sown this afternoon with the Cattos. Jessica said she'd like me to visit them in McLean, and Henry asked if I am *un soltero* (bachelor). When I said yes, he laughed and said, "That won't last long!"

Such was my introduction, at a rather early and high level, to Washington society. Whether any further such encounters will occur is unknown and not particularly worrisome. This day might not have been like those Sundays that Theodore Roosevelt used to spend in his early Washington years, centered around lunch at Henry Adams's mansion on Lafayette Square. But it was enjoyable.

For better or for worse, I never became a fixture of the "A-list." Washington society's attitude was epitomized by what Mrs. Graham said when introduced to me by Joe Kraft: "Who are you?" But the Cattos did become dear and lifelong friends. Immediately after the brunch, I drove to the Naval Observatory to meet with GB at the Vice President's Residence. When I told him where I had just been, he said, "Let's see, who was there . . ." and proceeded to name almost every one of "the Washington Establishment crowd" who had been present.

Friday, 13 February 1981

After lunch, Jennifer took a call and said over the phone, "I'll send him right down." Then to me she said, "He wants you in the Cabinet Room." Hurrying down the hall and uncertain of my mission, I rounded the Oval Office and stopped at the closed door of the Cabinet Room. When I identified myself to the Secret Service agent and said the VP had asked for me, he acted surprised that I would say anything at all. So I went in, finding the Cabinet in full session. Along the wall in the "aidely" seats sat members of the senior White House staff. I slipped over to GB's chair (which is directly opposite the President's), and he whispered for me to take a seat: "This is interesting, and I wanted you to hear it."

The atmosphere in the meeting, as in the fledgling administration, was cheerful, confident, and corporate. There was frequent, albeit mild, humor of the sort that liberal columnists would love to lampoon. For example, Treasury Secretary Donald Regan began outlining the program of tax cuts by apologizing for not having information sheets to distribute. "I have no handouts for you, I'm sorry," he said in his growly New York businessman's voice, whereupon Murray Weidenbaum, chairman of the Council of Economic Advisors, chimed in, "But we don't believe in handouts!" Chuckles all around; so, too, the jellybeans.

The star of the administration to date is thirty-four-year-old David Stockman, director of the Office of Management and Budget. He has become a favorite of the President's, a scourge of bureaucrats, and an absolute crusader for severe budget cuts. Today the wraith-like former congressman gave the word: $42 billion in cuts from President Carter's final budget. In a nasal voice, the super-smart Stockman ticked off the figures. He warned that "we have got to hang together" to defend the proposed cuts in the face of skilled opposition by lobby groups and other entrenched forces. Otherwise, he said, "we'll be in retreat."

Ronald Reagan's eyebrows were kept constantly arched, and his eyes darted from person to person like a seventy-year-old who doesn't hear well and is afraid of missing something. But he didn't. Thoroughly briefed, the President jumped into the Regan or Stockman presentations to elucidate with figures of his own. He is obviously buoyed with the exciting mission of his administration, which conforms with the huge mandate he got last November. "If we succeed," he said enthusiastically, "we're going to make history, because no gov'mint has ever succeeded in cutting itself in size." The President thanked Stockman, saying that "while some of us have been sleeping, Dave has been up, inking in the budget." Then, with a reference to his budget director's warning, RR said, "Don't worry, Dave. We'll come to the hanging!" Later, a beaming Reagan said he is glad "we weren't the kind of people who say, 'Let's wait a year till we learn how things work.'"

My tiny office was perhaps the best people-watching perch in Washington. And during much of 1981, I looked in awe as the chain-smoking Stockman, thick budget books under his arm, hustled back and forth between the West Wing and the EOB. It is impossible now to imagine the amount of authority and respect he commanded in that time, as if he were the only human capable of understanding the federal budget. He reminded me of the little guy who yells, "Stand back! I know karate!" causing people to stand back, whether or not he actually knows karate.

Sunday, 15 February 1981

At noon I went to the VP's Residence for lunch, joining Barbara's house tour. From the circular turret room, an extension of the master bedroom, one can see the Capitol and the Washington Monument. BPB didn't like (or pretended to dislike) my exclamation about the dining room table. Formerly in John D. Rockefeller Jr.'s home on Fifty-Fourth Street [in New York], it was where little Nelson and David had breakfasted. I said, "To think that the Trilateral Commission was founded at this very table!"

Later that afternoon, the Bushes made their first trip since the inauguration, attending a testimonial dinner for New York Republican potentate George Clark Jr. Though Clark was chairman of the Kings County (Brooklyn) GOP, the event was held on Staten Island.

A little early, we arrived at Shalimar, a fancy banquet hall on Hylan Avenue built in a pseudo-arabesque style. Surveying the crowd, Saul Friedman of the *Detroit News* said, "New York is one of the few places that Republicans look like Democrats."

The instant the speeches ended, the motorcade formed up for the return to Newark. The honored guest on the return flight was Sen. Alphonse D'Amato, who last year toppled Jacob Javits in the Republican primary. D'Amato was acting like a problem student buttering up the teacher, agreeing with everything GB said, trying hard to please. I had the clear impression that, circumstances being different, George Bush would have nothing to do with the likes of Al D'Amato. But for the meantime he was playing the senator for every ounce of advantage.

Tuesday, 17 February 1981

Admiral Murphy asked me to sit in on an event listed on the President's schedule: a meeting with (ultra-)conservative leaders in the Cabinet Room. When I arrived, David Stockman was briefing the group on the cuts he was pushing. Around the table were such titans as Phyllis Schlafly, Howard Phillips, Richard Viguerie, and Terry Dolan [of the National Conservative Political Action Committee, NCPAC, or "Nick Pack"].

When Stockman left (saying "I've got to cut another billion before lunch"), attention shifted to the new Secretary of the Navy, thirty-eight-year-old John Lehman. It was my first time to see him, and he was as impressive as advertised. Lehman is not particularly striking in appearance—he has bony features and crooked teeth—but he speaks with confidence, rapidity, and perfect syntax. I sighed enviously when he began a statement by saying, "Let me tell you what I'm doing in the Navy . . ."

Reagan political director Lyn Nofziger told the group that for the administration the economic program and defense spending must come first; the "social agenda"—meaning activism on abortion, ERA [Equal Rights Amendment], and so on—must come later. This did not please some of the listeners, such as the right-to-life representative, a bearded priest. He claims the administration must fight abortion or, on that one issue, lose the confidence of Democrats who voted for Reagan last fall.

Just then the President entered, and everyone rose and applauded. Reagan, wearing a plaid suit, walked stiffly and looked closer to his age today. After shaking hands, he sat down at the Cabinet table and commanded the waves of reporters and photographers to come in. When this was over, some of the participants urged Reagan to be more forceful in cutting the budget, especially what Phillips and others called "defunding the left." Perhaps they were a bit too polite in the way people always are with a president. But I was amused with the scene of archconservatives finally having Ronald Reagan in the White House and still being outsiders.

Friday, 20 February 1981

Our 8:50 staff meeting dealt mostly with politics. GB has been invited to address a national gathering of the American Conservative Union here in DC. He'll do the event, but he impressed on us this morning he's under no illusions: "The nuts will never be for me. We might as well recognize it. I've been doing this for thirty years." The hope is only that GB can make one or more of his listeners less antagonistic. The VP thinks he can do better for himself by establishing good relations with individual conservative leaders. For example, Gerry Carmen of New Hampshire, Reagan's campaign manager there in 1980, has just been selected for GSA [General Services Administration] administrator, and GB wants to help him win confirmation. "He'd be good in that job because he beat hell outta me in New Hampshire."

Thursday, 26 February 1981

We had a good staff meeting, the mood upbeat in anticipation of the fine event to come: the official arrival ceremony for [British] Prime Minister Mar-

garet Thatcher. GB asked me to escort his houseguests, "Chuck and Lydia"—
that is, actor Charlton Heston and his wife. (All week GB has been casually
dropping their names, waiting for his listeners to ask, "Who?") The Hestons
got siphoned off by the Bushes on the South Lawn, and the rest of us followed close behind Jennifer, a master at inserting herself in such ceremonies.

The Army bandmaster raised his baton, and the Herald Trumpets (ranged
on the curving steps of the South Portico) raised their horns to sound "Ruffles
and Flourishes." A disembodied voice announced, "Ladies and gentlemen:
The President of the United States and Mrs. Reagan." To a truncated version
of "Hail to the Chief," the Reagans emerged from the Diplomatic Entrance
into the bright sunshine of a lovely pre-spring day. Then, as the trumpets
blared again, a long black Cadillac with the US and British flags fluttering
from the fender slid into view, as if from immediately offstage. It stopped on
the mark, and the new chief of protocol, Mrs. Leonore Annenberg, stepped
forward to greet the Thatchers.

The PM was in classic British attire: a black dress, a black pillbox hat
with a feather, a long-strapped handbag over her arm, high heels, and white
gloves. With her was her husband, Denis, tall and good-natured. As cannon
popped on the Mall, sending white puffs of smoke against the Jefferson Memorial, the Marine Band played the two national anthems. It was then, as
Jennifer's assistant Kim Brady said, that I felt that I was "really in the White
House," and my eyes grew misty at the splendor of the occasion.

The two leaders gave carefully written and strongly delivered remarks
hailing their countries' long friendship and their common personal commitment to free enterprise and a strong western alliance. Then the President
and Mrs. T, with their spouses, mounted the steps of the White House while
music played. They stood on the porch to wave and be photographed before
disappearing into the house for coffee and meetings. It was then back to
work for the rest of us, bringing along the little Union Jacks passed out for
the occasion.

Thursday, 5 March 1981

The West Wing office was spruced up ("titivated" in the Navy expression)
in preparation for President Reagan's visit at noon. He and GB have always
had their private lunches in the Oval Office, and today the VP returned the
hospitality. His inner office was brightened by flowers and a fire. I was in
with the VP working on a letter when I heard Jennifer say, "Welcome, Mr.
President!" GB went out to greet the chief and escort him in for a picture

with all of us in front of the fireplace. Then the President and VP sat alone for forty minutes.

The lunch over, RR emerged from the inner office and said to all of us with his head angled in our direction, "Thanks; I know we'll see each other again." Then he seemed momentarily confused over how to get back to the Oval Office, so unused is he to making the short trip down the corridor.

Sunday, 8 March 1981

At 6:45 I set out to find the secluded McLean home of Henry and Jessica Catto. Dinner there included two heavy hitters in the Washington press corps: Robert Pierpont, longtime CBS White House correspondent, now assigned to the State Department, and Rowland Evans, the excessively elegant (even snobbish) half of the Evans and Novak column. At one time, "Rowly" was considered a friend by GB. Now he and [Robert] Novak are just slashers.

We had drinks in the vast den, moved on to a delicious Turkish meal, and finished with coffee in the paneled library. Evans paid a lot of attention to me, obviously trying to milk me for usable facts. It was a good test for me in being interesting and wise without telling tales out of school. He didn't like what he claims is a Reagan plan to put GB in charge of "crisis management" in the White House instead of national security advisor Richard Allen. I let that go, not wanting to betray any info in the act of rising to Evans's challenge. I considered it a compliment when he smiled and said, "You're very cautious." It was a fine evening, once again mixing with the common folk of Washington.

Monday, 9 March 1981

When I could break from phone calls to run a personal errand in the EOB, I hurried down the narrow West Wing stairwell. "Heads up!" called a voice from below, and I saw the brush mustache and chubby sandpaper cheeks of David Fischer, the President's personal aide. [*In Washington parlance, this job is known as being the "body man."*] Knowing what (or, more properly, who) was sure to follow, I pressed myself into a corner of the landing. Up came Ronald Reagan, SecState Alexander Haig (who gave me a who-the-hell-are-you stare), and Jim Baker, who quietly said hello. Such are the traffic snarls of our little office building. It was worse last Friday for Barbara Hayward. She rounded a corner of the West Wing and rammed smack into the President. Barbara was so aghast at what she had done she could only lean, speechless, against the wall into which she had been bounced.

This evening, [deputy press secretary] Shirley Green[4] cursed the lack of information given the press office about events involving the VP. And there was a ready villain: Jennifer, who simply doesn't think in press or political terms, only in serving GB as she knows how. To Shirley, as to others, I delivered the only knowledge needed: that Jennifer always has the last word and always wins. We must all adjust to this little inescapable fact.

---

4. Shirley had been cochairman of the Bush for President effort in Texas in 1979–80. She would later become head of the large and critically important correspondence office in the White House for President Bush and serve the same function for Governor Bush back in Austin.

Chapter 4

The Rumor

In mid-March, Vice President Bush made a four-day political swing through South Florida to plump for passage of the President's economic program and, not coincidentally, to make friends in a major state with a key Republican primary.

Saturday, 14 March 1981

This evening we crossed the causeway into Palm Beach, an island devoid of neon and weighted down with mammoth mansions whose outlines we could barely make out behind tall white walls. On the sea side, the Atlantic could be detected only as a continuously swishing sound.

We pulled up at the magnificent Breakers, our home for the next three nights. It is a gigantic Italianate palace of Hollywoodish inspiration, built in the mid-1920s. My room is next door to the Bushes'. It is comforting to know that while I sleep, the Secret Service will be on guard right outside the door—not *my* door, but the door nonetheless. The glory of the room is the balcony, which looks straight out at the ocean. The green water was at its transparent best due to spotlights. As I stood there, looking out to sea and up at the deep, dark night, I said, "Thank you, taxpayers, for making this all possible."

Sunday, 15 March 1981

At a private party, I did the political routine of introducing myself and chatting with people. Soon I didn't have to do this; they came to me, pushed in my direction by GB. Typically these were people who want to serve their country in some way "that will help George," like being ambassador to Luxembourg. I did my job well enough to earn a few minutes quiet bemusement on the boat landing, looking at the forms of other mansions on the farther side of the inlet and thinking of being paid by the US government to jolly up rich widows in Palm Beach at the height of the season.

It can truly be said that Palm Beach is the one place in the country from which going to Washington is returning to reality.

Tuesday, 17 March 1981

Up the coast in Melbourne, speechwriter Vic Gold was urging GB to confront a nasty, persistent rumor that he was shot by a Secret Service agent while leaving the Georgetown home of a lady friend, namely Janet Steiger,[1] member of the Postal Rate Commission. Both GB and I think that dignifying a smear like that with a statement would be wrong. Let it die of its own foolishness.

The Brevard County GOP fundraising dinner began with a tribute to the flag composed and delivered by the former mayor of Cocoa Beach. Old Glory was wheeled in, spotlighted and ruffled by a fan. His Former Honor intoned: "Hello, there. Remember me? I am your flag." GB was introduced by ex-astronaut Wally Schirra as so "tall, handsome, and urbane that he is the first politician who may become an actor."

Wednesday, 18 March 1981

Ten in the morning brought the VP's senior staff meeting, held in the West Wing office before a fire in the fireplace. The main theme was the accelerating rumor that on a recent weekend GB left a woman's house in Georgetown at 3:00 a.m. A mugger intended to rob him, whereupon the Secret Service came to his rescue, firing a shot that grazed the VP. An alternate version has GB slashed by the assailant. Last night, while Mrs. Steiger was out, a team of reporters descended on the house to interrogate her nine-year-old son, who is GB's godson. The teenaged babysitter let them do it. Shirley Green said the press office has been inundated with inquiries, and some of the biggest news organizations in the country are working the story. Local gossip columnist Maxine Cheshire told Teeley on Friday night that her source was a Secret Service agent. The Service has firmly denied the whole episode, and Jim Baker saw their logs. GB's attitude is one of low-burning anger, but he will refrain from making a comment.

---

1. She was the widow of Bill Steiger, elected to Congress from Wisconsin in 1966, the same year as Bush. The Steigers and the Bushes became close friends. Considered a star of the greatest magnitude by Republicans and Democrats alike, Bill Steiger tragically died of a heart attack in 1978 at only forty years of age.

Rich Bond believes the story was hatched and spread by "New Right" types to take the heat off a recent story that Reps. Jack Kemp [R–New York] and Tom Evans [R-Delaware] and Sen. Dan Quayle [R-Indiana] shacked up with a winsome lobbyist named Paula Parkinson, who taped their intimate encounters with her.

Suddenly, the clues fit: late February . . . the far right . . . Mrs. Steiger. I remembered having several telephone conversations about that time with a brash NYC-DC attorney who wants to go back on the Postal Rate Commission as chairman. GB, as a favor to the man's brother-in-law (a prominent New York conservative leader), supports him for member of the commission but Janet Steiger for chairman. When the man heard this, he called me in a rage on 23 February. My notes of the conversation have him warning, "It could be extraordinarily embarrassing if [Bush's] support [of her] becomes known." When I shared this with Rich, he was instantly convinced that the man is the inventor and/or spreader of the rumor.

At the Admiral's weekly meeting for all section heads, Shirley [Green] made the outlines of the rumor known to everyone. She said that the focus of the reporters' inquiries had shifted from whether GB was shot to whom we suspect of spreading the rumor. She urged us not to speculate, for that would give a news peg for the story ("Bush Staffers Suspect Far Right of Spreading Sex Rumor").

Immediately after the meeting, Rich and I got the Admiral alone to tell him our suspicion; I had brought along my notes for this purpose. The chief of staff instructed me to tell GB, and I went back to the West Wing. GB was with Jennifer and Vic Gold discussing the rumor; hers was also a name with which the VP had been linked. I waited till they had cleared out before I announced to him that we had a suspect. "Fascinating! Fascinating!" he exclaimed as the logic of the whole thing came together.

Not long after lunch, GB called me over the intercom to come see him. There with him was Jim Baker. I was asked to read my notes from 23 February, and Baker agreed that [the man in question] is a likely candidate for rumormonger. Baker suggested that the VP immediately call "Judge Bill"— meaning FBI director William Webster. This Bush did while Jennifer and I were in the office doing a postmortem on the Florida trip. Webster had heard the rumor (a version that had GB coming out of an expensive bordello) and said he would look into the matter. GB's end of the conversation didn't sound as if he had triumphantly closed the matter. He mostly sounded like a man torn up over an insidious assault on his reputation that was now going as far as to plague his nine-year-old godson.

Thursday, 19 March 1981

At the staff meeting, the anti-GB rumor was again on everyone's mind. The VP said in passing, "They've identified the woman who started it all." She is a neighbor of Janet Steiger's who claims to have heard a shot on the night in question. Rich Bond said she had been witness to a street crime recently and "liked the publicity." GB expressed satisfaction that reporters are now looking at the DC police logs, confident these show nothing. Shirley, Boyden, the Admiral, and Ed Pollard of the Secret Service were in various meetings all day on the crisis. Aware that a half dozen major news organizations are working hard on the story, looking for the peg on which to spring it, I have a very queasy feeling. GB can't be destroyed by this, but it will be embarrassing, even if eventually seen by columnists and politicians as a smear.

Friday, 20 March 1981

GB asked me to "stand by" when, around 10:00, he was interviewed by two FBI investigators on the mugging/shooting rumors. When they left his office, the VP introduced me with the request they hear my notes from the angry call of last month. The agents seemed interested in my narrative, but later today FBI director William Webster reported to GB that it was a false lead. "So much for my career as Junior G-man," I shrugged. The good news is that the supposed witness is backing off her story, which could kill the journalist pack's interest.

Sunday, 22 March 1981

I read today's *Washington Post* treatment of the Bush rumor of recent weeks. If there had to be a story at all, this one ("Anatomy of a Rumor") was all right. It picked apart how the whole thing got started—with a policeman's telling a Capitol Hill woman one evening that "the Vice President was shot today" and the rumor spreading out from there. The *Post* shouldn't have printed anything at all but used the story as a clever means of wringing something out of all the expense of saturating the rumor with a full investigation. We handled the whole matter appropriately, grandly ignoring it and letting it die on its own. We can't forget, after all, that we're supposed to be the class act in this town. There may even be a useful by-product in that reporters who were sent out to "cover" this mutually embarrassing rumor might now feel a bit of guilt, which could lead to more favorable treatment of GB than he's already getting.

The ludicrous story did die, killed not just by truth but by monumental events just ahead. It also helped that the author of "Anatomy of a Rumor" was Janet Cooke, who only the next month would be fired by the Post for faking a series of stories for which she had received the Pulitzer Prize.

Chapter 5

"The President Has Been Hit!"

Wednesday, 25 March 1981

Today's media were full of a story how SecState Haig felt humiliated by the President's decision (announced last night) to put GB in charge of "crisis management" in foreign affairs. Some rumors today even had Haig resigning in protest. GB is grateful to have the assignment and doesn't view his getting it as the result of some great intramural battle. In fact, he thinks Haig has been childish, making this (and other things) "always such a test of manhood." The Secretary had puffed himself up as the President's "vicar" in foreign policy and literally puffed himself up for a photo on the cover of last week's *Time*. I told GB that a generous, warm statement about Haig would do much to heal this most serious public rift in the Administration to date. But Bush brought the discussion to a close, saying with mock disgust, "I've got crises to manage." This turned out to be greeting a group of gigantic high school basketball players and a bunch of student interns.

Monday, 30 March 1981

I drove the short distance from my apartment house to the VP's Residence. When GB finished his morning security briefing by the CIA, he took Jennifer and me with him in the limo to the helipad, located on the other side of the old observatory building from the residence. In light rain we boarded the Marine chopper, which lifted up over the British embassy and flew above a fascinating if drizzly panorama of Washington en route to Andrews Air Force Base. GB joked about dancing with Ginger Rogers last night at the Gridiron Show. When the helo touched down alongside the waiting 707, the rotors sent sheets of water hurtling away from us. It was then only a quick walk underneath umbrellas to *Air Force 2*.

Aboard the jet were Congressmen Eligio (Kika) de la Garza (D-Texas), chairman of the House Agriculture Committee, and Bill Archer (R-Texas), inheritor of GB's Seventh District seat. The VP greeted them but had [speech-writer] Vic Gold, Jennifer, and me join him in the stateroom for a continental breakfast while we discussed some of the issues likely to confront him today in Texas. GB prefers oral briefings to written ones.

Around 10:45 CST the jet came in over the broad North Texas plain, made green by generous early-spring rains that relieved last summer's drought. It was a warm, sunny day, the perfect welcome back to Texas. We landed at Carswell AFB near Fort Worth, a major SAC base covered with black B-52s. On the ground were a very thrilled Jack Steel and Betty Green of our Houston office, who would spend the middle leg of the day's trip with us. [The VP's Air Force aide] Lt. Col. John Matheny, [advanceman] Mike Farley, and I headed for the control car for the motorcade into Fort Worth. John grew up there and happily pointed out the sights.

Our first stop was the old Texas Hotel, which Hyatt has converted into a shimmering showplace with funds invested by Texas oilman Ray Hunt, a major Bush backer. [John F. Kennedy spent the last night of his life there.] Outside the hotel, facing a tightly compacted crowd, the VP made brief remarks and unveiled a plaque, along with Mrs. H. L. Hunt, Ray's mom. The motorcade then embarked on the short journey to the Tarrant County convention center, where the Texas and Southwestern Cattle Raisers Association were meeting. There was lunch—beef, of course—after which GB gave a strong speech in support of the President's economic program.

Back at Carswell aboard *Air Force 2,* I shook hands with Fort Worth's congressman, Jim Wright (D), the powerful majority leader of the US House. I took a seat with him and Bill Archer, and we chatted about the Legislature, in which we had all served and which the VP would address in about an hour. Also in the VIP lounge was Congressman Jim Collins (R) of Dallas. GB entertained Jack and Betty in the stateroom.

Just as the big plane was taxiing down the runway, Secret Service agent-in-charge Ed Pollard hurried up the aisle to the stateroom, saying something to Jennifer that she repeated blankly to us all: "An attempt has been made on Reagan, and two agents are down." The thunk of takeoff seemed to underscore the news. The rumor spread quickly. We were all so stunned that it wasn't for several minutes that someone thought to turn on the cabin TV. Reception was good for our altitude, though it kept cutting on and off whenever our plane would transmit signals of its own.

The networks had videotapes of the grisly episode outside the Washington Hilton Hotel only about fifteen minutes earlier (about 1:30 EST). The President was leaving the hotel, having just spoken to a building-trades group, and was walking toward his car, waving at a few spectators, when a spray of bullets was loosed by a gunman standing with reporters a short distance away. The tape showed Secret Service agents thrusting the President into his car, which sped off. There was a scramble to subdue the assailant as policed barked back the crowd. Three bodies lay on the ground: a DC policeman, a Secret Service agent, and presidential press secretary Jim Brady, who took a shot to the head. We watched the tape again and again, stricken at the sight even while glad at the report that the President was safe. GB was in the stateroom, taking calls from DC.

On the screen in the lounge, we saw ABC's Frank Reynolds and White House correspondent Sam Donaldson grab for phones and listen together a moment. "My God!" exclaimed Reynolds, pressing his fingertips to his forehead. "The President has been hit!" The horror grew.

Our plane landed in Austin, something I had done so many times before in that last, now-distant chapter of my life. The airfield was thickly bordered in bluebonnets on a radiant midafternoon. When we came to a halt next to the motorcade, I peered out the window, studying the crowd for people I know. By then, though no announcement had been made, it was clear we wouldn't go ahead with the planned events in Austin. As one of the VP's Secret Service detail said, "We have no way of knowing that there weren't gunmen sent to Washington, Fort Worth, and Austin." The ramp was pushed up, and Governor and Mrs. [Bill] Clements and [Texas secretary of state] George Strake came aboard for what would be a social visit with the VP during refueling.

Mike Farley said I could disembark if I wanted, and I did so, on the quickest trip to Austin I ever made. Various friends came up to say hello, smiling bravely and looking up at the plane, as if it were a symbol of the government in Washington, from which we all felt semi-removed. When there was extra activity around the ramp (such as George Strake speaking with reporters), I said goodbye and reboarded. The dignitaries would return to the Capitol for a brief joint session of the legislature at which the Governor would give a report and offer a prayer. And in a few minutes AF2 was streaking away from Austin, the Capitol a fond little nub on the horizon.

I was in the stateroom as GB told Ed Pollard and John Matheny that he didn't want his helo to land on the South Lawn, as they did, but back at the Naval Observatory. "At this moment I am very concerned about the symbolism of the thing," he said. "Think it through. Unless there's a compelling security reason, I'd rather land at the Observatory or on the Ellipse." What troubled GB was the notion that his landing on the South Lawn (literally right outside Mrs. Reagan's window) would seem too self-important at a time when he especially wanted to keep a low profile. Matheny said that vice presidents had used the South Lawn before. "But we have to think of other things," the VP countered. "Mrs. Reagan, for example." On the telephone with Admiral Murphy, who was in the White House Situation Room, the VP made this point very firmly.

Jennifer, Vic, and I remained in the cabin with GB. I asked about the national security risk to the country at that moment, with the President shot and the VP airborne. He said it was "no different than when the President is in the air." He told us confidentially that the President would undergo surgery to locate and remove the small-caliber bullet lodged in a corner of his lung and that as a contingency "they're preparing papers for the trans-fer of authority if that becomes necessary." I presume this meant under the presidential-disability section of the Twenty-Fifth Amendment.[1]

Mike Farley rapped on the door to say that Secretary Haig was on TV at that moment. We came out to see him saying, with all bravado, "I am in control here in the White House pending the Vice President's return to Washington." In declaring to a potential adversary the folly of trying to take advantage of the United States this afternoon, the Secretary's statement was appropriate. But as the day wore on, the networks sought to discover the legal authority under which Haig claimed to be acting. Neither presidential succession nor the national security command structure puts the SecState immediately after the VP. In the crush of today's events, probes and questions along this line were of secondary interest, but they would more shortly blos-som into a major embarrassment for Haig, already reeling from last week's self-inflicted wounds over "crisis management."

GB returned to his cabin, and I stayed with Congressmen Wright and Collins; the other congressmen had disembarked in Texas. The atmosphere was somber, and things were noisy with the jet engines and the TV cutting in and out. Around 5:10 EST there came the erroneous report that Jim Brady had died. We were relieved when this was refuted, yet we all know that a head wound of the kind Brady received can be as bad as death.

The VP asked Jennifer and me to come into the cabin for the express purpose of giving his thoughts for the record. Sitting in the armchair oppo-

---

1. The amendment would not, in fact, be invoked this day but was on two occasions later in the Administration when Reagan had surgery.

site him and writing on a legal pad, I got his stream of consciousness almost word for word.

"It's hard to describe my emotions," he said. "They're cumulative. A funny thing: the way Reagan's and my relationship has developed—not presidential–vice presidential but more like a friend. [There's] a concern for someone who's your friend. Because I see it that way—seeing him [on videotape] getting into that car, waving—I see it on a personal plane." He mused about the Polish situation and the decisions that will have to be made if the Soviets move in. "Having to be the person to determine that, [to] be the critical person to make that decision—I don't have any consternation about it at all. . . . My every inclination is to be calm, not churning around. I would have thought it would have been much more complicated about the responsibilities, but my innermost thoughts are [that] this guy is a friend. . . . I think about Nancy Reagan: Is anybody holding her hand? I have a great feeling that all will work out. The President is very strong."

Shortly after 6:00, the telephone rang, and it was presidential counselor Ed Meese. GB said, "That's wonderful—that's very good. See you at the house." GB told us that the doctors had gotten the bullet out, that the President's condition is stable, and that he's resting comfortably.

Air Force 2 banked over the Potomac and came in for a landing at Andrews. There was a bright sunset after a day of rains, and the wet streets below were orange. Security precautions dictated that the plane disembark passengers inside Hangar 7 instead of on the field. Jennifer and I went down the ramp and were directed to pass under the shiny nose of the beautiful jet and out the hangar door. Tucked in an isolated area was the Marine helo, which we boarded before GB. Lt. Col. Mike Fry [the Vice President's Army aide] took the seat opposite GB and briefed him on the items the Admiral thought he should be considering: a Cabinet meeting, an intel briefing, and so on.

The helo flew over the illuminated landmarks of Washington at dusk and put down at the Observatory. I followed the VP off the chopper. He went down the concrete walk to Barbara, who was with C. Fred [the cocker spaniel]. She and GB embraced. Then he and Ed Meese shook hands before getting into a stretched-out presidential-style limousine with hand bars on the trunk for Secret Service use. A complete motorcade, with DC police motorcycles and cars, was formed up for them to ride to the White House. Jennifer and I rode with Mrs. Bush and Fred back to the house to get our cars. "Have you ever known a day this wild?" Mrs. Bush exclaimed.

I drove straight down Massachusetts Avenue toward the White House. The guard cleared me in, and the great iron gates swung open. A small cluster of tourists peered at me, wondering who I was. (Who, indeed?) Inside, I joined other staffers to do what the rest of the country was doing: watching TV. We were bumped from the VP's inner office by a distinguished group fresh from the Situation Room: the VP, Attorney General [William French Smith], Secretary of Defense [Caspar Weinberger], White House counsel [Fred Fielding], Jim Baker, Ed Meese, and miscellaneous others. They went over the statement the VP would deliver to the press.

Deputy press secretary Larry Speakes—obviously shaken over the day's events—introduced GB, who read the statement and stepped down. He returned to our office to call the congressional leadership, and then, as becomes him, the wives of the DC policeman and Secret Service agent gunned down in defense of the President.

Rich Bond suggested we grab a quick supper in the Mess (whose hours had been specially extended tonight) so I could brief him on the Texas trip. We sat at the round table with various upper-middle-grade presidential staffers, who were making the best of a day that was ending better than it might have. Deputy press secretary Karna Small asked Dave Gergen "what our policy is now on handguns," a subject that was quickly dropped. Jim Baker and Ed Meese stopped by the table to thank everyone for their work today.

The word on the President is good. He is at George Washington Hospital and even delivered some much-quoted cracks, such as telling his doctors, "I hope you all are Republicans" and scribbling a note after surgery: "On the whole, I'd rather be in Philadelphia." GB made the decision not to visit him tonight, knowing RR needs the rest. But he did call on Mrs. Reagan in the mansion, saying afterward, "She looked tiny and afraid." Then, around 9:30, he went home.

I returned to the office to transcribe my notes of GB's midflight thoughts. And, with a look at TV to see what our plane looked like as it entered Hangar 7 (protected by Secret Service sharpshooters), I left about 11:15.

I washed up and went to bed for a nap before writing this entry. Around 1:30, I was awakened by a call from Art Wiese of the *Houston Post*. Art related the possibility that Neil Bush [the VP's son] may be acquainted with the alleged assailant, John W. Hinckley Jr. Neil and Sharon do know Hinckley's brother [in Denver] and were planning to have dinner with them tomorrow night. The Hinckleys are a prosperous family, and John Sr. may have been a Bush contributor. Art wanted to know if this connection was known by GB in flight, and I said that as late as the helo ride from Andrews to the Observatory, we weren't even sure what the gunman's name was. As Art pointed out, even a slight Bush connection in this shooting could set off the conspiracy freaks. Willing to think about this another time, I went back to bed till 2:30, when I arose to write this, finishing now at 5:00.

Tuesday, 31 March 1981

Arriving in the White House around 7:00, I had doughnuts at my desk and read the Bush coverage of the major newspapers. The *New York Times*'s subhead said, with splendid drama, "Bush Flies Back from Texas Set to Take Charge in Crisis."

Signal reported that the VP had left his residence, and down on West Executive Avenue I saw Pete Teeley and Shirley Green waiting for him. Correctly guessing what they wanted to tell him—the call each of us received last night from Art Wiese—I hurried downstairs in time to join them as the stretch limo arrived.

"What's up?" GB asked, seeing us all there.

"Did you talk to Neil last night?" Pete asked as we entered the West Basement.

"No; is it about this guy?"

"Yes."

"Jesus."

We all went into the VP's office, where Pete related the story that Wiese had been working on and which was being played big in Houston and over the wires. GB appeared only mildly concerned, so little in fact that he didn't think to call Barbara or ask any of us to do so. Pete said we should check out the entire Neil-Hinckley family connection, and I was tasked with calling Fred Bush[2] to ask elliptically whether John Hinckley Sr. had ever contributed to GB. After about an hour the report came back: no.

After all this, the rest of the day was rather dull for me. GB picked up on the ceremonial duties of the President, presiding at a Cabinet meeting and welcoming the Dutch prime minister on the South Lawn. In this and all other things he did today, he had the absolute cooperation and dedicated energies of the President's staff. The consequence for our West Wing office was that things were remarkably calm. When people called today, they would

---

2. No kin to the VP, Fred Bush was former fundraiser of the Bush for President campaign and at the time was assistant secretary–designate for tourism at the Department of Commerce.

begin apologetically: "I know things must be unbelievably hectic there . . ." But I had to tell them this was not so, that "the VP is doing one and a half jobs with two staffs."

At 3:30, Admiral Murphy convened almost the entire [vice presidential] staff to brief them on the previous twenty-six hours. Sitting at the VP's vast desk in the formal EOB office, he spoke about GB's temporary additional duties and, with a twinkle of recognition that we wouldn't be so stupid, warned us against "telling the White House staff what to do."

Wednesday, 1 April 1981

The 9:15 national security briefing usually held in the Oval Office was held this morning in the VP's West Wing office. A delicious little incident occurred. The doorknob on the door to the private office has been ailing, and this morning it ceased to work. By unfortunate coincidence, the first person to try the useless knob was SecState Alexander Haig. "Go right on in, Mr. Secretary!" Jennifer said brightly. Haig stood at the door, twirling the knob in his fingers. He then turned away with a wry smile and said, "I get the feeling it's a little inhospitable." [Barbara Hayward rushed forward to rap on the door, which Caspar Weinberger opened, to let Haig in.]

Saturday, 4 April 1981

At 9:00 I arrived at the VP's Residence to go over some routine items, mostly on presidential personnel. When our work was done, GB placed a call to George Washington Hospital to ask a presidential staffer about RR's condition. I chuckled to myself, remembering what "Mr. Dooley" [Peter Finley Dunne] once said: "What are [the vice president's] jooties, says ye? Ivry mornin' it is his business to call at the White House an' inquire afther the prisidint's health. Whin told that the prisidint was niver betther, he gives three cheers an' departs with heavy heart."

Sunday, 5 April 1981

At home I read the *Washington Post*'s account of last Monday, "The Day of the Jackal in Washington." It had several inaccuracies just in the description of VP Bush's activities. For example, it had Bob Thompson announcing to us in the VIP lounge that there had been an attempt on the President, whereas we heard it from Ed Pollard right before the VP did. The paper said the VP had been "politicking" in Texas, whereas the events in Fort Worth and Austin were wholly nonpartisan. And the *Post* said Ed Meese sent a helo to Andrews to fetch the VP, whereas it was always going to be there to take him home. If there were three sizable errors on things I knew, I wonder how correct the descriptions of Reagan in the hospital were. It also brings into question the reliability of history, which uses old newspapers in part for source material. Ah, this is where a carefully written journal can be useful.

Friday, 10 April 1981

Around 11:15 I went into GB's office to brief him on some presidential personnel matters. We didn't finish by the time (fifteen minutes later) he had to leave to visit President Reagan at the hospital, so he invited me to come along.

The limo was admitted through a barricade and stopped at a secure side entrance to the hospital. Surrounded by Secret Service agents, the VP and I went up to the third floor to the connecting corridor that has been cordoned off for presidential use. A special command post on the lobby side of the corridor was manned by the Secret Service and by lead presidential advanceman Rick Ahearn[3] and his staff.

GB immediately went in to see the President; I remained outside. As special as the command post is, the rest of the third floor is a regular hospital, with grandmotherly types shuffling about in bedroom slippers and orderlies wheeling carts of bland lunches. Names had been taped to each door [in the secured section]: Aspen, Maple, Elm, Witch Hazel, and others. I was told these relate to cabins at Camp David, and each had a special purpose: Mrs. Reagan's room, Dave Fischer's room, [presidential physician] Dr. Ruge's room, and so on.

GB left the President, closing the door behind him, and we all mounted two flights of stairs so he could visit Jim Brady. As before, I didn't go into the room but lingered outside. I did see the brave, pretty Sarah Brady. GB waved at a few patients as we walked back down the corridor, and he related the President's concern over something he had read, an attack on his budget cutbacks in special postal rates for philanthropic organizations.

We went downstairs by elevator, and outside, the VP walked over to the

---

3. Ahearn had been with the President at the Hilton on March 30 and is the husky, bespectacled young man in photos of the shooting.

press pool to answer questions. Asked how the President was doing, GB said, "He looks better each time I see him." Avoiding anything more detailed on the President's condition, the VP waved at other reporters across the street and got in the limo. Secret Service agents closed the doors for us, and we returned to the White House.

Saturday, 11 April 1981

Today was the day President Reagan returned to the White House from the hospital, twelve days after being shot. Barbara Bush came down for the occasion, and GB arrived wet-haired, fresh from running in the Secret Service marathon at Beltsville. With him, still in shorts and a T-shirt, was the secretary of agriculture, John Block, a marathoner for years. We all trooped out to the South Lawn just as rain began to pour.

The presidential motorcade came into view, passing south of the house near the fountain and swinging around to the Diplomatic Entrance. All the umbrellas and tall folk then pressed forward to join in joyful greeting. As a result, the only thing I saw of the President was one hand and a sleeve encased in a bright red sweater. In a sense, this was a special sight, for it was his left hand he was waving, the same as the moment he was shot. Today's wave was a means of saying that he's back (almost) to normal.

Chapter 6

Springtime in Washington

Sunday, 12 April 1981

Because GB was standing in for President Reagan today at Tuskegee Institute in Alabama, we got to fly in the "Presidential Aircraft." It was the two-tone blue-and-white 707 with tail number 26000 that took President Kennedy to Dallas and brought President Johnson back. Its elegant appointments make the 707 we took to Texas look like something off the back lot. It has a large stateroom and VIP lounge, both of which are enclosed by partitions. Each seat is equipped with an outlet for listening to a four-track stereophonic music system with headsets. The staff compartment has two secretarial stations, and the communications unit is so massive that it requires two men to run it, versus one for "our" 707 and none for the DC-9 we took to Florida. And here and there are special, ripe-for-snatching items such as a blue notepad with raised gold lettering, each page saying "Aboard *Air Force One*." As I remarked to Barbara Bush, "We could get used to this." "Fast," she added.

Riding with us today were Art Fletcher, a prominent black Republican, and Chris Edley, fundraiser for the United Negro College Fund. Thadd Garrett came in his ecclesiastical garb, as befits an AME [African Methodist Episcopal] preacher on Palm Sunday.

But for internal White House reasons the prime guest was Lee Atwater, a young South Carolinian with pale blue eyes and a somewhat uneasy manner. He is a minion of presidential political aide Lyn Nofziger, covering the southern states. Rich Bond and I sat on either side of Atwater during the flight and paid a lot of attention to him. With the suspicions of a confirmed Reaganite and racial prejudices that led him to oppose the Tuskegee trip for the President (and which undoubtedly made him uncomfortable traveling with blacks), Atwater is not a very *simpático* guy. But we got along well, especially when we talked about running. (We're both about the same size and build.) Later, I would hear him and Thadd in animated conversation. The subject: Lee's collection of old *Amos and Andy* shows on television. To his credit as a politician and a George Bush aide, Thadd acted as if that was just wonderful.

This was not the first time Bush and Atwater met. According to Karl Rove's memoir, Courage and Consequence (2010), both he and Atwater visited then Republican national chairman Bush in 1973 while they were leaders of the College Republicans organization. Atwater mobilized Reagan forces in the close-fought 1980 Texas Republican primary, stirring up his troops by reminding them that Bush (an "elitist") had been a member of the Council on Foreign Relations and the even more evil-sounding Trilateral Commission. Reagan won the primary narrowly. Rich Bond, a visceral opponent of Lee's, told me the day after the Tuskegee trip, "Atwater is not a good person. You will go to heaven, and I will go to heaven, but Atwater won't."

It was therefore astonishing when Bush chose Atwater to be chief campaign strategist when he ran for president in 1987–88. But it was a brilliant move, for it helped stave off a successful attack on Bush from the Republican right. Watching Atwater from a close distance during that campaign, making sure he always kept his father's interests foremost, was George W. Bush. Atwater was serving as chairman of the Republican National Committee in 1989 when stricken with a brain tumor. His death in 1991 deprived President Bush of the advisor he desperately needed the following year when he faced two crafty southerners, Bill Clinton and Ross Perot.

The hard-hustling Air Force steward served us a large breakfast, after which Lee briefed GB on the Alabama political situation and I talked with our black guests. Being good company for the VP's VIPs is probably my main role on these trips.

When *Air Force 2* landed in Montgomery, three Marine helicopters were waiting nearby. They had been ferried down ahead of us by cargo plane from DC. We took these on the twenty-five-minute trip to rural Tuskegee, flying over mobile homes, freshly plowed red-dirt fields, and forests in spring growth. We came in over the Tuskegee Institute—a collection of turn-of-the-century red-brick buildings—and landed in a baseball field. Waiting there was a Tuskegee trustee, Donald Rumsfeld, Gerald Ford's chief of staff and SecDef. I have long admired Rumsfeld, though GB is convinced Rumsfeld engineered his appointment as CIA director in order to remove him as a potential vice presidential running mate with Ford in 1976.

We staffers and guests took seats in the rear of the modernistic chapel. GB was announced and, wearing academic robes, entered to an organist's rendition of "Pomp and Circumstance." Also in gown and mortarboard was Ed Pollard, head of GB's Secret Service detail. He sat on stage throughout the convocation, conspicuous by never being introduced. Rich, Jennifer, and I called him "Dr. Pollard," and I said he would be receiving "an honorary degree in small arms."

GB gave a good speech exalting "the Tuskegee spirit" of individual effort and self-improvement, the philosophy of the school's founder, Booker T. Washington, a century ago. He said this was also the philosophy of Ronald Reagan, a rejection of "the political flimflam" of big-government proponents. Though it was a difficult message to give a black audience, the VP was interrupted five times by applause—only two of them initiated by Thadd. No claque was necessary when GB avowed the Administration's commitment to fighting racial discrimination. The speech was followed by his receiving an honorary doctorate of laws and by the lively singing of a wonderful spiritual, "Way Up in the Middle of the Air," by the Tuskegee choir.

Thursday, 16 April 1981

Secret Service agent John Flaherty gave me a sheet containing the photos and names of the six dozen agents on the VP Protective Detail. I've been studying it while on the telephone in order to learn the names of the guys I see all the time and who call me by name. They appreciate this personal touch. I confess being like a nine-year-old kid with "the Service," with a respect bordering on awe for the agents' professionalism and common decency. As late as Christmastime in Houston, I was prepared to be cool and correct with the men of the Secret Service, believing them just "machines in mustaches." This has changed as I've gotten to know many agents these past three months. And after four years with a Mondale staff that *was* cool and correct, the agents have warmed tremendously to the Bushes and Bush folk.

My personal regard for them aside, the VP detail of the early 1980s was indeed an outstanding bunch. Out of it came two directors of the Secret Service, a deputy director, several inspectors general of Cabinet departments, and chiefs of security at major corporations. The agents were taught not to get too close to staff, so that in a crisis they would not forget that the only person they had to be concerned about was the "protectee." Knowing this, I was both tickled and appreciative when an agent once solemnly told me, "I want you to know that if anything ever happens to you, I will take it personally."

Friday, 17 April 1981

At 2:00 the VP had a private briefing from Dave Stockman on the economic program in order to be prepared for the next week's run of trips. Thadd, Jennifer, and I sat in for what was indeed a remarkable display of memory, conviction, and polite condescension by the budget director. I took notes on quotes that I later put on cards so that GB can become his own Stockman on the stump.

Earlier, in a staff meeting, the Reverend Dr. Garrett had said of Stockman, "He's amazing. He never took an economics course and never even finished seminary, and yet he can just peel off those statistics." I leaned forward to say, "You mean to tell us, Thadd, that if Stockman had gone all the way through seminary he would know both numbers and Leviticus?"

Wednesday, 22 April 1981

Around 5:00, I was told that Nancy Bush Ellis was at the Northwest Gate and had no ID with her; someone would have to escort her in. At the gate I vouched for her and startled some fence-gawking tourists by embracing her. Nan was her splendid self, breezily meeting Ed Meese and Mike Deaver and kissing old friend Mac Baldrige [the secretary of commerce]. We linked up with George and Barbara and took a circuitous, crowd-avoiding route to the mansion and its attractive ground-floor library. There in a few minutes we were joined by Mrs. Reagan. She is much smaller than she photographs and far shier than her dragon lady reputation holds. GB, with a perfect combination of friendly guidance and executive command, explained what they would be doing in a few minutes.

Led by advancemen and aiguillette-wearing military aides, our little entourage passed through the oval Diplomatic Reception Room. "Ruffles and Flourishes" sounded from the porch above, and an announcer proclaimed the arrival of the "Vice President of the United States and First Lady Nancy Reagan." We walked toward the Rose Garden to the unmemorable strains of "Hail Columbia." Gathered there were members of the American Society of Newspaper Editors. GB introduced Mrs. R, who expressed the regret "my husband" couldn't be present but said he would be next year.

I took the chance to stroll off by myself and savor the atmosphere of a White House garden party, grand even on a threatening afternoon. Had I wanted, I could have nibbled canapés and wandered around the crowded state rooms looking at nametags. But my current employment affords me the freedom to be anonymous and to slip back to my niche in the West Wing, where I stayed till 8:30.

Friday, 24 April 1981

At a Republican fundraising dinner in Connecticut, Secretary Mac Baldrige told how members of the Cabinet go after the jellybean jar in meetings: Cap Weinberger is methodical; David Stockman, working on his figures, ignores it altogether; Al Haig "grabs the whole thing"; while GB searches for his favorite, licorice, but settles for chocolate, proving that "he knows what he wants, but he's willing to take second best."

Monday, 27 April 1981

Before a banquet in New York, the Bushes rested in a suite at the Waldorf Towers. [They lived there from 1971 to 1973, when GB was ambassador to the United Nations.] I was sent on a most wonderful assignment: to go to the suite of Jean (Mrs. Douglas) MacArthur and escort her downstairs to visit with her old friends the Bushes. The tiny, lively lady who escaped from Corregidor still has vast amounts of the coquettish southern charm that won and kept the man she calls "my gen'ral."

Wednesday, 29 April 1981

Just before the 8:50 senior staff meeting, I received an urgent call from Houston lawyer Charles Foster. Charles is attorney for Houston Ballet, and he had an amazing tale. A Chinese dancer, Li Cunxin, here for a year from Peking, secretly married an American member of the company and wants to remain. Last night, he, his wife, and various potentates of Houston Ballet went to the Chinese consulate general to explain the situation. There, Charles said, "the conversation deteriorated," and the consul general had Li seized. Horrified at what they saw, the young socialite ballet board members refused to leave the building till Li was released. They therefore spent all night there. Their obvious absence from a fancy party at [wealthy financial advisor] Fayez Sarofim's house (at which Li was guest of honor and to which the group was going after visiting the consulate) sparked the attention of the *Post* and *Chronicle* cultural writers. Foster called the China desk at State and then called me.

Following the chain of command, I serially notified Nancy Bearg Dyke [the VP's national security advisor], Admiral Murphy, and then Jim Lilley [in charge of East Asian affairs on the National Security Council staff], who said he would immediate tell [national security advisor] Dick Allen. Later, I told Jim Baker and GB. There was furious diplomatic activity all day, and by evening the Chinese had agreed to release Li and his bride.

This incident was the dramatic highlight of the 2010 Australian film Mao's Last Dancer, *based on Li's breathtaking autobiography of the same name. Charles Foster, who became a close friend, was portrayed in the movie, and he apologized that the writers couldn't work in an Untermeyer character. I said I couldn't imagine a duller scene than one picturing a guy in Washington making phone calls. But I was nonetheless glad to play a real-life role that led to a happy ending.*

Friday, 1 May 1981

Jennifer paused at the entrance to my enclosure and asked if I would like to take the seat of Deputy Secretary of State [Bill] Clark at this afternoon's evensong at Washington National Cathedral, the super-special occasion at which the VP, Prince Charles, and the Archbishop of Canterbury would be present. She and Barbara Hayward, both daughters of the Sceptered Isle, had been chattering all day long about possibly meeting the Prince. [*This was three months before Charles married Lady Diana Spencer.*] They had brought white leather gloves and even practiced a curtsy or two. Though I had a lot to do, it was something too good to miss.

Even with steady rain, the motorcycle escort got us to the cathedral in short order. Advancemen met us with umbrellas, leading us inside, brightly lit for cameras. The Bushes were seated on the front row, next came a row of Secret Service agents, and then came the Deavers and us Bush staffers. [Mike Deaver had once studied for the Episcopal priesthood.] This put us practically within touching distance of His Royal Highness when he, wrinklelessly clad in a gray suit, arrived with his equerry (an RAF officer) and sat beside GB. "It's not too often you see two crown princes together," I remarked to Barbara Hayward. Charles is not tall, has wavy hair, protruding ears, a scar on his left cheekbone from a recent polo accident, and a lustrous ruddy complexion. He chatted affably with the Bushes, displaying a crinkly smile.

GB later said that the Prince's offbeat sense of humor reminded him of his son George.

The evensong was the gala conclusion of the "Meeting of the Archbishop of Canterbury and the Primates of the Anglican Communion." This group [whose collective name to me connoted monkeys] included divines with such splendid titles as Metropolitan of the Province of Burma, Archbishop of the Indian Ocean, Presiding Bishop of the Nippon Seikokai, and Presidente del Consejo Anglicano Sud Americano. There was a very formal, very high-church service with Purcell voluntaries, a grand procession of the primates with banner and boys' choir, the singing of constipated hymns, and a lesson read by the young man who is (in the words of the Bishop of Washington) "one day to be Defender of the Faith." Charles was escorted to and from the lectern by a cleric holding a silver rod. The Prince walked with a measured gait that showed years of training. ("Charles, don't walk so fast," I can hear his mother scolding in the Rolls on the ride back to the palace.) He spoke with a clear, strong voice and only a few inflections. The sermon was preached by the Archbishop of Central Africa. GB had no role other than as companion in prayer.

When the evensong reached its conclusion, the Most Reverend and Right Honourable Robert A. K. Runcie, Archbishop of Canterbury, stood on the steps at the front of the cathedral, holding a staff, wearing a mitre and dazzling gold and white robes, and pronounced the prayers. He spoke with almost trancelike stolidity. When the primates filed out, His Grace paused to exchange a few words with the Prince and the Bushes.

Due to security and all that, we in the small official party left instantly. GB motioned for Jennifer and Barbara to come forward, and he introduced them to Charles as "two of your fellow countrymen." Not really expecting this, the two women were caught without their white gloves on, and they bobbed instead of curtsied. "What are you doing here?" asked a grinning prince, an old hand at quizzing people on tours. "We're taking over!" replied Jennifer. "Do you have to be Republicans?" he asked, and Barbara replied, "Yes!"

Wednesday, 6 May 1981

Rich Bond and I had a date for lunch, which was to have been in a park or lawn somewhere, but a rain changed that plan. Instead, we ate club sandwiches on the balcony outside his EOB office. We talked about the thing most on our minds: contingency planning for the time when President Reagan might die in office. Rich has already done a lot of thinking and furtive work on this subject, aware that GB would strongly discourage anything that seemed like preparing for his own presidency. Rich is searching for the transition document when Gerald Ford succeeded Richard Nixon, and he has "someone I can trust" researching the Kennedy-Johnson transition, a much closer parallel. Rich said the reason he insisted I read Robert Hartmann's bitter book[1] was to see how vice presidential aides need to take quick action to prevent being cut out by fast-moving and conniving presidential staffers. I can easily imagine David Gergen and Rich Williamson [deputy chief of staff and assistant for intergovernmental affairs, respectively] breaking down the door to get to a President Bush within minutes of the news. That is why Rich Bond and I will produce a blandly titled "Memorandum for the File," ready for the critical moment. It would include such things as how to set up a swearing-in and who would get which jobs and offices in the immediate post-event days. Before we left the porch to go back to work, I mentioned something else we should think about: "Vice presidents die, too."

Sunday, 10 May 1981

I went to the century-old Metropolitan AME Church, "the national cathedral of African Methodism," on the corner of M Street and Sixteenth Street. It was where Frederick Douglass's funeral was held, and today it was where the Rev. Thaddeus Garrett Jr. delivered his sixth annual Mother's Day sermon. Just before the service began at 11:00, the VP and Mrs. Bush arrived with Doro and Sue Bush (Jamie's wife) plus a good deal of Secret Service protection. Dr. Robert Pruitt, pastor of Metropolitan, later said from the pulpit, "We want to tell the Secret Service not to worry: We do our killin' on Friday and Saturday nights, not on Sunday mornin'!"

There was much hymn singing, and during the pastoral prayer Thadd's alto voice could heard intoning, "Yes! Yes!" The pastor welcomed the VP, asking that he notify "the councils of the mighty that we, too, are Americans. ('Amen, brother!') Don't cut too much fat." Then he invited "Brother Bush" up to the pulpit, predicting that he is destined to lead the Free World. GB

---

1. In *Palace Politics*, Hartmann (the top aide to Ford as congressman and vice president) painfully describes how he was shoved aside when the new president called Donald Rumsfeld onto the scene.

gave gracious thanks, acknowledging the preacher's plea and promising that all budget cuts "will be done in the spirit of Jesus Christ." I guess that meant they will be ordained by an ex-seminarian named Stockman.

Thadd was announced, and he began in classic black ministerial style, very low and slow. Then, with increasing intensity, he worked himself into a frenzy, moving his arms and legs as if running, and shouting such affirmations as, "If your heart needs fixing, He is a heart-fixer! If your mind needs regulating, He is a *mi-i-ind regu-la-tor!*"

Later, I was inspired to write something to spring at tomorrow's staff meeting. Titled "A Prayer the Reverend Doctor Garrett Should Have Delivered," it goes:

"O Lord, ruler of all things temporal and political, expunge from us the prophecy of thy servant, the Reverend Dr. Pruitt, that our brother, George Herbert Walker Bush, 'shall one day come to lead the nations of the Free World.' Make not our minds remember it, make not our hearts believe it, and most of all, O Lord, make not the scribes in their saloons and dwelling places in Georgetown hear it. For if they do, and if the reverend doctor's words shall then be visited upon the minions of our gracious President, then, lo, great will be their vengeance. They shall rise up with the fear of Falwells and the doubts of Dolans;[2] they shall drive us from our temple in the West Wing; they shall deprive our brother Bush of scrolls and councils to which he has been privy; and neither shall we fly in *Air Force 1* anymore. Amen."

Monday, 11 May 1981

At the staff meeting, Boyden Gray noted that word in the salons of Georgetown is that GB was right all along: the Reagan tax program is "voodoo economics." GB was quick to say that his (= Pete Teeley's) devastatingly memorable phrase applied just to the Kemp-Roth notion that "tax cuts alone will solve everything." Reagan in 1980 wasn't only talking about budget cuts but also about regulatory relief, Bush said, and the two features combined make the President's current economic program. GB recognizes that in being "right" on the economic issue he will suffer politically in the GOP, which is why he has been the Administration's biggest salesman on the hustings.

---

2. This was a reference to the Rev. Jerry Falwell of the Moral Majority and Terry Dolan of the National Conservative Political Action Committee.

Friday, 22 May 1981

At 10:00 I sat in on the hour-long talks Chancellor [Helmut] Schmidt [of West Germany] had with VP Bush, Secretary Haig, and Treasury Secretary Regan in the Roosevelt Room. The brilliant, enormously self-confident Schmidt was so much in control of the proceedings that he appeared mildly bored, as he might at a meeting of his own cabinet. He was more articulate in English than any of the Americans facing him, and he handled his listeners with a deft touch. For example, when GB concluded a forceful statement on US energy policy, Schmidt said, with a notch or two more animation, "Mr. Vice President, that is an excellent point, one which I hope you will make at the Ottawa [Economic] Summit in July. Now, on that meeting, I see three topics which must be addressed. One . . ."

Promptly at 11:00, chief of protocol Lee Annenberg—who always resembles a squat bird, looking up at the world from a short neck—entered the room to announce to Schmidt, "The President will see you now." The Chancellor frowned at the society lady playing diplomat and growled, "A few more moments!" and continued to discuss some point. Mrs. A disappeared but came back a short while later to say with a trace of scolding, "The President is *waiting.*" Schmidt reluctantly rose, finished his thought, and crossed the hallway to the Oval Office.

Tuesday, 26 May 1981

Adam Malik, vice president of Indonesia, former foreign minister, and president of the UN General Assembly during GB's time in New York, called on his old friend. Malik gave him a large carved Balinese statue of Vishnu. Later the VP read to Jennifer and me the accompanying explanation of the [Hindu] god's wondrous qualities and gave tongue-in-cheek instructions that we should refer to him henceforth as Vishnu.

We did, using "Vishnu" as our own code word for the VP, in preference to the Secret Service's "Timberwolf." To this day, Christopher Buckley still calls Bush "the Vishnu."

Wednesday, 27 May 1981

The Marine helo lifted off from the Naval Observatory and after a short ride put down in a parking lot outside Memorial Stadium in Annapolis, some distance from the grounds of the Naval Academy. The superintendent, Vice Adm. William Lawrence,[3] was there to meet us, as was a motorcade for one of the year's shortest rides, just into the stadium. The band struck up "Hail Columbia" for arrival honors for the VP. A twin battery fired a nineteen-gun salute, with flashes of orange flame against billows of white smoke. In his address to the class of 1981, the VP said, "I'm a naval person and damned proud of it. . . . I know you're sorry the President couldn't be here, but he had to be at West Point. After the beating you guys gave Army last fall, they have a little morale problem up there." The midshipmen loved both lines. More seriously, GB hailed a new sense of optimism among the American people coupled with increased respect for the military.

The VP gave diplomas to the top ninety-six grads, after which others gave diplomas to the remaining 850 or so men and women. This took about an hour and was done to the continuous, rolling, rollicking sound of cheers and friendly catcalls from the stands. The midshipmen, exhibiting a delightful youthfulness in their starched high-collar whites, leapt up, waved their diplomas toward their families, and in some cases danced or jumped right off the platform.

The oath of office to the new Marine second lieutenants was administered, from memory, by Gen. Thomas Barrow, commandant of the Marine Corps, a tall, erect deep southerner who spit out his *wudds*. Adm. Tom Hayward, the CNO [chief of naval operations], gave the same oath to the new Navy ensigns. After each oath, the middies stripped off their first-class [i.e., senior] shoulder marks and sent them flipping up in the air. Then came two traditional cheers—"To those who are leaving" and "To those we are leaving behind"—followed by the famous photogenic hurling of midshipmen's hats skyward. Diane Lawrence ran forward to grab one for herself and one for BPB, who saucily wore hers on the helo ride home.

Meanwhile, my former colleagues in the Texas Legislature were drawing up new district lines for themselves and for the state's congressional delegation. A new US House seat was created in the Houston area, and some GOP leaders sounded me out about running there.

---

3. The wise and beloved Bill Lawrence had been a POW in North Vietnam. On this day, his daughter Wendy graduated from the Naval Academy. She later became an astronaut, commanding the space shuttle. In 1984, as chief of naval personnel, Bill was to be my guide into the world of military manpower.

Thursday, 28 May 1981

It would be very hard to say no if they pled I must do my part to secure a Republican majority in the House next year. But after four months on the job here in DC, I can easily see what a step down in duties it would be to serve in Congress. Being a congressman is the great divider of sheep and goats in American politics, and it would definitely qualify me for a big federal appointment someday (assuming the party didn't need my one vote in Congress). But what member of Congress was present in the discussions Helmut Schmidt had in the White House? What member of Congress sat two seats behind the Prince of Wales at the National Cathedral? And what member of Congress regularly takes a helicopter to and from Andrews AFB for rides aboard Air Force 2? I would be highly reluctant to make a race for Congress and give up all these perks of my present job—which, after all, is also a great qualifier for a federal appointment someday under a Bush Administration. Oh well, it's something to think about during all the months the phone *doesn't* ring.

Monday, 15 June 1981

At noon I welcomed a bunch of "Bushkins": George and Laura, Doro and boyfriend, Billy LeBlond. We had an upbeat lunch in the Mess, after which I showed them around the EOB. George's business is doing all right, but I inferred he's still having troubles. Laura will have their first child in December.

Tuesday, 16 June 1981

GB and I discussed a couple of matters, in the course of which he mentioned that Vic Gold is quitting as speechwriter. The VP said "it's not a pushup item"—meaning something that made the excitable Vic so mad he flung himself on the floor to do a spate of pushups, which he does to vaporize sudden excess energy. Yet surely it's a revolt over the VP's heavy speaking schedule, which Vic recently blasted in a staff meeting as "like a goddamned campaign."

Tuesday, 23 June 1981

GB, on Pete Teeley's strong recommendation, has hired Bill Buckley's son, Chris, as Vic Gold's replacement. Chris, whom I met today, is a terribly bright, tough guy who has written a book on the Norwegian merchantman on which he served. He had "Fuck you" tattooed on the side of his right hand so that it would be visible while saluting the skipper. The tattoo has since been surgically excised. Unlike Vic, Chris will work full-time. But like Vic, I predict, he will be a temperamental soul.[4]

---

4. This first impression was wholly wrong. As I shortly came to know, Chris Buckley is one of the world's most easygoing and delightful characters, someone I have been happy to call a friend ever after.

Chapter 7

Lindbergh's Bed

In June 1981, Vice President Bush made back-to-back trips to Europe and East Asia, trekking through eighteen time zones in the space of nine days. He was careful to wait until after Secretary of State Haig had been to the same countries, so as not to spark another secretarial explosion about Bush's intruding into "his" domain.

The first stop was Paris, where the new president, socialist François Mitterrand, had just put four communists in his cabinet, to the considerable annoyance and concern of the State Department. Although a senior officer from State assured the VP a few days before our departure that no statement on the subject would be made before or during his visit to Paris, I told Pete Teeley that the treacherous Haig was not above deliberately embarrassing Bush with such a statement. This trip was special for the thirty-five-year-old me in that it was my first time in France, despite having been a French student in high school and college.

Wednesday, 24 June 1981

Under a system that combined seniority and chivalry, I was the last to get lavatory privileges in the forward cabin of *Air Force 2,* entering as we descended to land at Orly. I threw on a white shirt just as the plane drew up to a wide, thick red carpet bracketed by two long lines of sword-wielding soldiers. It was quite impressive. US ambassador Arthur Hartman (a polished professional diplomat) came aboard for a final briefing before the VP and Mrs. Bush disembarked. We in the official party all shook hands with Foreign Minister Claude Cheysson and went down the corridor of troops into the Pavillon d'Honneur. There GB delivered a formal arrival statement to a press corps restricted to a balcony off to the side. He was of course asked about yesterday's decision by President Mitterrand to take four communist ministers into his government. The VP smilingly replied that it would be inappropriate to comment on such an internal matter before speaking with French leaders.

The weather in Paris all day was overcast and humid, not the best conditions for a first visit to the great city, but I was delighted to take her as I found her. The French gave the VP "intersection control" that compared with what we get in any American city, and we streaked into the heart of Paris on brick streets past famous landmarks like Les Invalides and clusters of gawking Parisians.

The motorcade ended at the sumptuous ambassador's residence at No. 41 rue de Faubourg St.-Honoré, a townhouse of rococo splendor built in the early nineteenth century by a Franco-American family from New Orleans. The housekeeper and social secretary, a Mme. Cardonay, welcomed us and showed me to my quarters, a suite overlooking the residence's park-like gardens. It is named the Lindbergh Room because it contains a bed in which the great aviator slept after his historic flight in 1927. (He probably just barely fit.) The rest of the staff is staying at the ultra-posh Crillon Hotel, not far away on La Place de la Concorde.[1]

Alas, I fell on the junior side of the cutoff for the meeting with Mitterrand and had to see the motorcade leave for the Elysée Palace without me. Though this was regrettable, I couldn't complain, because it gave me a little free time in Paris—about forty-five minutes, in fact. I set out on a fast hike down the Champs Elysées toward the Arc du Triomphe, detouring to take side streets leading to the Seine. The Eiffel Tower, poking suddenly upward, looked flat and alien against a bright white sky. Perhaps this little disappointment is just as well, for it underscores my favorable initial impression of Paris as a city of human scale at street level. I walked along the river under a lovely arcade of tall leafy trees before finding a street heading straight back to Faubourg St.-Honoré. There I entered the grounds of the Elysée, a building of crisp classical design with a pebbled courtyard.

The Garde Républicaine, at stiff attention in their tall feathered helmets, drew swords up to the tips of their noses as Mitterrand escorted Bush out to the short front steps. Mitterrand appears a quiet, introspective man who would pass unnoticed in the streets of any French town were he not president. He made some gracious remarks that were inconsequential except to say that France's domestic affairs were its own business. Bush, reading from a prepared text, was equally pleasant but tossed in a light jab at the inclusion of communists in the government. No questions were taken; the two leaders shook hands, and our motorcade pulled away.

---

1. Ranking American officials have stayed at the Crillon since the Paris Peace Conference of 1919.

We headed for the Hôtel Matignon,[2] the official residence and office of the prime minister, located on the left bank of the Seine near Les Invalides. There GB met with the new PM, Pierre Mauroy, a big, energetic Socialist politician strongly reminiscent of Britain's [former prime minister] "Sunny Jim" Callaghan. Before becoming PM he was mayor of Lille, the Socialist capital of France. Mauroy took pains to give GB a little lesson in French leftist politics since World War I. Each time the Socialists shunned the communists, he explained, the communists became stronger. But each time the Socialists co-opted them, the Socialists gained. Therefore, in a classic demonstration of French political logic, bringing communists into his government will permit Mitterrand to achieve his long-sought object of unifying the working class under the Socialists and shriveling the communists.[3]

The motorcade recrossed the Seine and followed it downstream to the massive Hôtel de Ville, Paris's city hall, where GB paid a call on the Gaullist opposition leader, Mayor Jacques Chirac. Though destroyed during the battle of the Commune in 1871, the Hôtel de Ville has been rebuilt in imperial splendor, making it by far the finest public building we saw today. Our mob (including the press) mounted a grand marble staircase and entered Chirac's private office, a room of celestial ceilings and tapestries. Chirac is in many ways like George Bush: tall, thin, informal, and energetic. As could be expected, he expressed great doubt over the future of France under Mitterrand and said the posts given the communists (like transportation) are not minor. Waiters served champagne, fruit juices, canapés, and petits fours. Also present were two ghosts of the Gaullist past: François Kosciuszko-Morizet, ex-ambassador to the UN and the US, and Maurice Couve de Murville, de Gaulle's haughty foreign minister. Perhaps one day Chirac will be president of France, but Mauroy is likely to get there ahead of him.[4]

At 8:00 the Hartmans gave a reception and dinner for the Bushes that drew from the top ranks of the new French government: PM Mauroy, FM Cheysson, trade minister Michel Jobert, defense minister Charles Hérnu, Senate president Alain Poher (twice acting president of the Republic), and Pierre Beregovoy, described to me as Mitterrand's Ed Meese. The party also

---

2. An *hôtel* is not a lodging but a public building, usually one that had once been a fine residence.

3. This is exactly what happened.

4. I was half right: Chirac directly succeeded Mitterrand in 1995.

included celebrated Americans in Paris like actress Olivia de Havilland and ex-JFK press secretary Pierre Salinger, now an ABC correspondent. During dinner I sat next to Mme. Bernard Vernier-Palliez, the charming older wife of the director-general of Renault [and incoming ambassador to the United States]. The meal was delicious and the occasion sparkling. The VP and PM exchanged toasts, Mauroy again affirming his pro-Americanism, born of a region where American troops were twice liberators.

The political counselor of the embassy expressed amazement at my French, the product of secondary school education *seulement*. I am pleased with it myself and am certain I could become fluent if I spent any length of time in a francophone country.

Chapter 8

A Dinner at Number 10

Thursday, 25 June 1981

Air Force 2 took off at 10:00 for the hourlong fight across the Channel. GB was concerned over the release of a statement by Washington on the inclusion of communists in the French government. Not only was it tougher than what he was telling the French, it was uncharitably released during and not after his visit—just as I had predicted Haig might do. Cheysson told GB in the limo that it was "as if everything said yesterday [by the French side] had no influence on the American statement." Thus can vice presidents be humbled.

We came through broken clouds over a well-watered English countryside to land at Heathrow. GB delivered his bland arrival statement in classic fashion, outdoors, his hair blown by gusts of wind and his words lost in the roar of aircraft. Nancy [Bearg Dyke, the Vice President's national security advisor] and I rode into London with Joe Hagin,[1] who has been in London acting as local advanceman. Our destination was Winfield House, the handsome Georgian home on the edge of Regent's Park, which Woolworth heiress Barbara Hutton built [in 1937] and later gave to the US government for the residence of the US ambassador. I have a corner room upstairs overlooking a great grassy lawn hopping with rabbits. Waiting for me there was a large formal invitation from "The Prime Minister and Mr. Denis Thatcher" to tonight's dinner at Number 10 Downing Street, as grand a souvenir as one could wish.

There followed a fine luncheon at which the VP was introduced to a cross-section of British political, journalistic, and economic leadership. To my pleasure, I was sought out by the guests, my gold-on-white staff pin be-

---

1. Joe Hagin was a sunny-dispositioned young man who would serve both George Bushes in useful, behind-the-scenes roles, most prominently as the second President Bush's deputy White House chief of staff.

ing a useful conversation starter. [The lapel pins allow the Secret Service to know at a glance that the wearer is cleared for proximity to "the protectee."] Andrew Knight, the young editor of the *Economist*, introduced me to Edward Heath, Conservative prime minister from 1970 to 1974.[2] Though extremely stiff, Heath engaged me in conversation on the role of the vice president in the Congress. I introduced myself to Dr. David Owen MP, foreign secretary in the last Labour government and a leader in the new Social Democratic party, a breakaway from Labour by moderates upset at its increasing leftist control. And I had a very pleasant talk with Douglas Hurd,[3] minister of state in the Foreign and Commonwealth Office, who handles NATO and other multilateral organizations.

Following the meal, GB was most strongly addressed by Dennis Healey, the flaring-browed former Labour chancellor of the Exchequer and defense minister, whose attitude GB later humorously characterized as, "For your information, I'd like to ask you a question."

GB's motorcade left for his appointment with Lord Peter Carrington, the foreign secretary. We went past Buckingham Palace, down the Mall, and past Horse Guards to the Foreign Office, a doughty building of Victorian power and splendor. The "Widow of Windsor" herself dominates the staircase leading to Carrington's office. It has high floral-painted ceilings and portraits of Indian rajahs, which Lord Carrington installed in place of his bewhiskered predecessors. Carrington, a short, red-faced man with a prominent nose and horn-rimmed glasses, has a good-humored personality and yet is always in control. Topics were changed by his asking, "Shall we move on to something else?" in an Eton-accented tone that suggested the proper answer.

Around 7:00 the motorcade formed up for the journey toward Big Ben, Whitehall, and Downing Street. Spectators cannot stand opposite Number 10 itself, so the small but friendly cluster peered in on us from the curb as we made the turn onto the short street. PM Thatcher, in a blue gown with ruffled neck, greeted the Bushes on the step of perhaps the most famous door in the world. Inside, standing behind a pool of photographers flashing away

---

2. As Heath approached, I asked Knight how to address him. In the United States, former presidents are still called "Mr. President"; are former British PMs still called "Prime Minister"? "No," Knight answered, almost in horror. "It's Mr. Heath." This incident illustrated the British view that Americans are more title conscious than they are, despite their legions of royals, dukes, earls, knights, and various other nobles.

3. Hurd served later as secretary of state for Northern Ireland and home secretary under Margaret Thatcher and as foreign secretary under Prime Minister John Major.

at the dignitaries, I cast an eye on that open door, black with the bold but discreet numeral "10" in white. Then we ascended a tall staircase past engravings and photos of all former prime ministers.

The garrulous, blimpish Denis Thatcher greeted us at the head of the stairs and blathered on about the Trooping of the Colour [ceremony] while his wife and the VP talked privately for about fifteen minutes. Waitresses in black dresses and white aprons passed around trays of drinks. Clutching my sherry, I met some of the arriving guests: Humphrey Atkins MP, secretary of state for Northern Ireland and one of Mrs. T's top floor leaders; William Deedes, editor of the *Daily Telegraph*; and most especially Her Royal Highness the Princess Alexandra, first cousin of the Queen. Garbed in a multicolored gown that seemed to hang from her neck, the tall, bemused-looking royal did what her job requires, which is to ask questions. [Then, Prime Minister Thatcher introduced her American guests, remembering each one's name and job title.] The Princess inquired whether I had been in London before. Next she asked Nancy how she got her job, prompting Mrs. Thatcher to say, "You know, we really shouldn't be surprised anymore that women occupy such positions."

At some unheard call, the party traversed several rooms into a grand dining hall paneled in mahogany and decorated with large portraits of great prime ministers like Pitt and Wellington. I sat at the foot of an extra-long table. Nearby sat Sir Anthony Kershaw, a pleasant, highly articulate Tory MP who actually had and actually used a monocle and a golden toothpick on a chain. The menu consisted of chilled mint and cucumber consommé, salmon, Scotch beef, and wild strawberries in champagne ice. Five wines (including port) were served, followed by liqueurs.

Mrs. Thatcher rose to toast the Queen and the President and after an appropriate pause rose again to give a few warm remarks about President Reagan and VP Bush. ("Hear, hear!" various guests said.) Then she told about George Downing, an Englishman who went to America ("You were not a country yet; we had an even closer relationship then") to study at Harvard ("if one can get an education at Harvard"). Downing then returned to England to engage in speculative building, including a row of twelve houses on a street he named for himself. Only Numbers 10, 11, and 12 remain. Of the street's most celebrated survivor, Mrs. Thatcher evoked chuckles by saying, "It's not a bad pad." GB in his reply softly stated the Reagan Administration's admiration of "the Thatcher model" in restoring conservative government and free enterprise. Throughout this exchange, I rejoiced in the marvelousness of the moment, of being there.

When the dinner party rose, I met the lovely Lady Mary Fitzalan-Howard, daughter of the late duke of Norfolk and lady-in-waiting to Princess Alexandra. She had been seated on the other end of the table from me during the dinner. We talked easily about our jobs, which are similar. Her duties involve traveling with the Princess as her companion and aide-de-camp and answering a lot of letters. Lady Mary was quite down to earth and gracious. I would very much like to see her again, but when and where (and whether)?

The end of the evening at Number 10 brought something I very much wanted to do and which a word to Denis Thatcher may have prompted: a visit to the Cabinet Room on the ground floor. Mrs. Thatcher, her ministers, and the secretary of the Cabinet showed us the historic room with almost childlike pleasure, pointing out where they sit and telling what goes on. A single small painting hangs above the fireplace behind the PM's chair. It is of Robert Walpole, [considered the] first prime minister of Great Britain [1715–17].

Fond farewells were said; Lord Carrington reached out to shake my hand at the door. Then, out into the mild London night to rejoin our cars, parked under a Victorian arcade, to return to Winfield House. A long, happy day, the apotheosis of what I hoped working for the VP would be, ended soon thereafter.

Friday, 26 June 1981

Aboard AF2 at Heathrow, the Admiral said I would have to move aft, out of the forward cabin of the plane. This was to accommodate Amb. Philip Habib, who was returning to Washington after valiant efforts to stave off war between Syria and Israel over Syrian missiles in Lebanon. I said nothing, largely because it wouldn't have changed things and because I get along with the Admiral by being a good junior officer. I told John Matheny that in the five months I've been on this job, I've learned to be grateful for the things I get to do—most supremely, last night's dinner at Number 10 Downing Street—and not to get too riled over the things I don't. As Bob Hope once told the California Legislature, "Politics is like show business. One day you're drinking the wine, and the next day you're picking the grapes."

President Ronald Reagan and
Vice President George Bush
outside the Oval Office, 1981.
(White House photo)

Where it all began: the staff of freshman congressman George Bush of Texas in his office in the Longworth Building, June 1968. The author is at far left, and at far right is Don Rhodes, the Bush family's invaluable friend and helper for over forty years. Fourth from the right is Rose Zamaria, then the office manager and two decades later the director of administration in the first Bush White House. (US House photo)

The author walking with Vice President Bush from the West Wing to the White House Residence on 2 March 1981. At rear left is C. Boyden Gray, counsel to Bush as both vice president and president. At rear right is the Rev. Thaddeus Garrett, assistant to the vice president for domestic policy. (White House photo)

The Boeing 707 known as SAM (for Special Air Missions) 86970 was used by George Bush as *Air Force 2* during his vice presidency (1981–89), primarily on international trips. It was the first jet to be *Air Force 1,* having taken President Dwight D. Eisenhower on his foreign travels in 1959–60. (US Air Force photo)

The President comes to lunch, 5 March 1981: standing in the Vice President's West Wing office (under the gaze of the nation's second vice president, Thomas Jefferson) are, from left: the author; Barbara Hayward, personal secretary to the vice president; President Reagan; Jennifer Fitzgerald, scheduling assistant to the vice president; Vice President Bush; and Kim Brady, Ms. Fitzgerald's assistant. (White House photo)

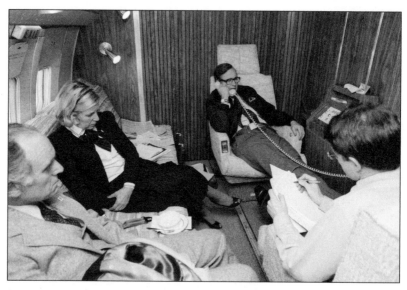

In his private cabin aboard *Air Force 2,* returning to Washington from Austin on the afternoon of 30 March 1981, Vice President Bush hears from presidential counselor Ed Meese that President Reagan had come through surgery well after being shot a few hours earlier. From left: speechwriter Vic Gold, Jennifer Fitzgerald, Vice President Bush, and the author, getting Bush's thoughts on a dramatic day. (White House photo)

The author (back to camera, second from the left) describes the model of a nineteenth-century US warship to West German chancellor Helmut Schmidt and Vice President Bush in the Vice President's West Wing office on 5 January 1982. At far left is Adm. Dan Murphy, vice presidential chief of staff. (White House photo)

Famed portrait photographer Yousuf Karsh ("of Ottawa") speaking with Vice President Bush in the Roosevelt Room in the West Wing on 6 January 1982. Through the door at the rear and across a narrow passage is the Oval Office. (White House photo)

"Just your typical palace": the Akasaka Detached Palace, where the Bushes and their party stayed in Tokyo, April 1982. The Akasaka is "detached" from the Imperial Palace, located nearby within formidable walls and moats. (Japanese government photo)

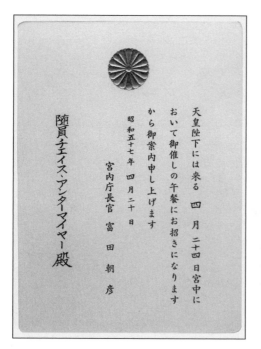

天皇陛下には来る 四 月 二十四日宮中に
おいて御催しの午餐にお招きになります
から御案内申し上げます

昭和五十七年 四月二十日

宮内庁長官 富 田 朝 彦

随員チエイス・アンターマイヤー殿

Invitation to a luncheon with the Emperor of Japan at the Imperial Palace in honor of Vice President and Mrs. Bush, 24 April 1982. The imperial seal is a golden chrysanthemum with sixteen petals; the Japanese government uses a paulownia flower on its seal. (Author's collection)

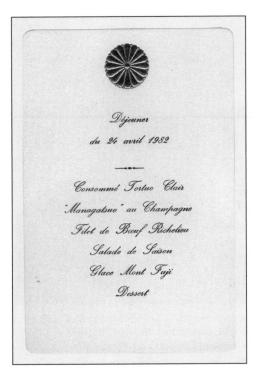

Déjeuner
du 24 avril 1982

Consommé Tortue Clair
'Managatsuo' au Champagne
Filet de Bœuf Richelieu
Salade de Saison
Glace Mont Fuji
Dessert

The menu for the Japanese emperor's luncheon (in French): clear turtle consommé, managatsuo (butterfish) in champagne sauce, filet of beef au Richelieu, green salad, ice cream in the shape of Mount Fuji, and miscellaneous sweets. (Author's collection)

Vice President and Mrs. Bush with Emperor Hirohito of Japan after a private audience in the Imperial Palace, Tokyo, on 24 April 1982. (White House photo)

Flying from Hangzhou to Beijing, China, on 7 May 1982, US officials entertain (and try to distract) Vice Foreign Minister Han Xu in the lounge aboard *Air Force 2* (SAM 86970). From left: the author; Donald Gregg, then of the National Security Council staff and soon to be Vice President Bush's national security advisor; Han; and John Holdridge, assistant secretary of state for East Asian and Pacific Affairs. The retractable partition at rear encloses the private cabin. (Author's collection)

Vice President Bush boosting the Senate campaign of Congresswoman Millicent Fenwick of New Jersey (right) at a fundraising dinner in New Brunswick, 25 October 1982. Applauding at left are Barbara Bush and Gov. Tom Kean. (White House photo)

Pope John Paul II gives the author a commemorative medallion after a private audience for Vice President and Mrs. Bush and their staff in His Holiness's private library at the Vatican, 7 February 1983. The Bushes are standing at rear. (Vatican photo)

Gov. Dave Treen (second from left) briefs Vice President Bush on a trip to Louisiana in February 1983. Listening to him in the lounge of *Air Force 2* (a C9) are, from left: Steve Rhodes, assistant to the vice president for domestic policy; the author; Ron Kaufman, Republican National Committee staff; and Lee Atwater, White House political staff. (White House photo)

Chapter 9

A Rigadón *in* Manila

After only one night back at Andrews, Air Force 2 was cranked up again. This time the destination was Manila, for the fifth—and final—inauguration of strongman Ferdinand Marcos as president. It was something of a sentimental journey for me, for I had served as an admiral's aide in the Philippines in 1969–70.

Our first stop was Beaumont, Texas, for the dedication of the school of business at Lamar University. Traveling with us was Democratic congressman Jack Brooks of Beaumont, chairman of the House Government Operations Committee. Watching the coarse, braggartly Brooks, I whispered to Jennifer, "He's so awful he's wonderful." Vice President Bush sat in "the LBJ throne chair" in the VIP lounge. With expert coaching from Jack Brooks, Bush swiveled it around and shot it forward, as Vice President Johnson used to do when making a point with one of his guests.

At the ceremony in Lamar's gym, the VP got a big appreciative laugh from the crowd when he asked, "When going from Paris to Manila, doesn't one always go through Beaumont?" The party next flew on to Point Mugu Naval Air Station, whence Bush took a helicopter to President Reagan's ranch to make a quick report on his trip to Europe.

Saturday, 27 June 1981

Air Force 2 took off about 3:45 p.m. on the final leg of today's journey. Joining us were part of our official delegation: Gov. Bob Ray (R-Iowa) and his wife, Billie, plus actor Efrem Zimbalist Jr. and his wife, Stephanie. The VIP lounge is already quite crowded, and we haven't boarded our Hawaii-based delegate yet. Pianist Van Cliburn and his mother decided not to fly aboard *AF2* but to take private aircraft; this was the day's best news. We were cramped but cheerful. On the five-and-a-half-hour flight to Honolulu, GB chatted with his guests before turning in. Others went to sleep wherever they could. Zimbalist and I talked at length. He starred in the much-repeated TV series *77*

Sunset Strip and *The FBI*. His father was a famous concert violinist [and his mother, Alma Gluck, was an opera singer]. He had some interesting stories of living in the USSR in 1935, where his father (an émigré from Czarist Russia) placed him and his sister in music conservatories.

Toward 6:15 local time, we flew along the Waikiki beachfront to land at Hickham Air Force Base near Pearl Harbor. An Air Force honor guard lined the path to the ramp, and a variety of dignitaries waited with leis for the Bushes. We are staying in the relatively remote Kahala Hilton. The plush hotel lies on the other side of Diamond Head from Waikiki. Mainlanders in the lobby applauded as the VP entered. I donned a swimsuit and went down to the beach, which I had almost to myself at dusk, an idyllic time of stroking through warm water and looking at the silhouettes of coconut palms against a pink sky. From up on his balcony, GB watched and yelled down to ask about the swim. If it's hard enough to imagine that yesterday began in London, it's amazing just to think that today began in Washington—and included Beaumont somewhere along the way.

Sunday, 28 June 1981

On board the plane at Hickham this morning was the gracious, super-sharp Clare Boothe Luce, one of the great women of America, former member of Congress from Connecticut, [ambassador to Italy], and widow of *Time* publisher Henry Luce. About eighty, she lives fulltime in Hawaii.[1] We took off and headed southwest to a 670-acre speck of mostly created land called Johnston Atoll, an Air Force missile-tracking station. From the air it looks like a huge aircraft carrier surrounded by a reef. Our refueling stop was the biggest thing to happen on Johnston since President Nixon's visit in July 1969 when the Apollo 11 astronauts returned [from the moon]. The excitement of the occasion was so intense for the locals that someone even took a picture of me.

The base commander, a lieutenant colonel, was overjoyed at the attention being given his atoll, and he and all under him hustled to satisfy the every wish of the Vice President and his party. GB came up with the popular idea of skin diving. Though I love snorkeling, I declined the chance to do it on Johnston, not wanting to risk sunburn before two frantic days in Manila.

---

1. Later in the year, Mrs. Luce would move to Washington to exult in the coming to power of her old friend and compatriot Ronald Reagan. It was my further privilege and treat to be with her there on a number of occasions until her death in October 1987.

What I did on Johnston was a fun way to remember the place: I escorted Mrs. Luce. We climbed into a gray military pickup truck and rode to the colonel's quarters, "Point House." There we had some refreshments before going to the base exchange. The most popular items there—for which I bankrolled Mrs. Luce—were Johnston Atoll T-shirts and postcards. We returned to Point House in time to welcome the Bushes back from the reef. Then it was off to the plane.

This would be a very long leg: over six hours to Guam. Somewhere en route we crossed the International Date Line, immediately terminating Sunday. It also means, longitudinally if not latitudinally, we were on the other side of the earth from London. [Vice presidential photographer] Cynthia Johnson and I broke into the Rodgers and Hart song, "I Didn't Know What Time It Was."

Monday, 29 June 1981

We landed at Guam at 2:30 local time, just before a tropical rain swept over the naval air station. We were met by the governor (a Republican) and some local lovelies who "leied" us with carnations, cowry shells, and kisses. The motorcade wound through tacky hillsides up to Government House, the gubernatorial residence overlooking Agaña Harbor. The VP's arrival was marked by "Hail Columbia" from a Navy band that later serenaded us with "The Eyes of Texas" and "The Yellow Rose of Texas." A reception followed, featuring an enormous western Pacific spread (sashimi, sushi, lumpia, and local specialties). Mostly I chatted with the elected officials present. Guamanians, like Filipinos, are natural politicians, and I enjoyed talking with the lieutenant governor and several senators, members of the unicameral legislature.

Air Force 2 was airborne again by 4:15, headed westward through two more time zones to Manila. The approach to the city allowed only about a minute's worth of viewing the green fields, tin roofs, coconut trees, and urban sprawl below us. We taxied to a special reception area where hundreds of little children in bright costumes danced and waved sun hats at us. Down a red carpet came [first lady] Imelda Marcos, escorted by the US ambassador and the eighty-two-year-old foreign minister, Carlos P. Romulo. Mrs. Marcos extended a weak handshake and a little smile to each of us. The air had that very identifiable Manila quality, the not-bad aroma of charcoal cookery in thousands of nearby homes.

As soon as the arrival remarks ended, we staffers ran for our cars, warned by our advancemen that "when Mrs. Marcos's car leaves, the whole motorcade leaves." We were driven to the Manila Hotel [the famous hostelry on Manila Bay where Gen. Douglas MacArthur lived before the outbreak of World War II]. I watched the TV news and had a much-appreciated hot shower before writing this entry. It was interrupted by the drop-in visit, somewhat to my embarrassment since I was in skivvies, by the deputy chief of mission [of the embassy] and our lead local advanceman to go over tomorrow's early, early events.

Tuesday, 30 June 1981

Today I was awakened at 4:00 a.m. by the locomotive-like rhythms of snare drums from the streets as people flooded to nearby Quirino Stadium for the inaugural ceremonies to come. I ate a couple of mangoes and dressed in the Philippine uniform of the day: Barong Tagalog [a long-sleeved, embroidered shirt] worn outside striped trousers.

The easiest way to get to the stadium was on foot. As we in the official party passed lines of smiling Filipinos, I played politician, waving at the little children. On the vast, red-carpeted inaugural platform, before an enormous Philippine flag, we found our seats. On them were special favors: a parasol, a lacy handmade fan with "Imelda" stitched on it, a commemorative medal, and a packet of reading material extolling "FM" [Marcos] and "The New Republic." It was fascinating to study the international delegates and to absorb the throbbing Asian scene: propaganda banners, multicolored uniforms and native costumes, masses of flags, and a hot sun burning its way through morning cloud cover.

When the First Family arrived, escorted by mounted soldiers (the horses recruited from the Manila Polo Club and D'Rossa Riding Academy), men in Muslim dress atop the stadium's overhanging roof sounded the traditional low tambuli horn. The peppy national anthem played, and a twenty-one-gun salute echoed off the bay. A thousand-voice male chorus sang the anthem, after which four clerics—an archbishop, an imam, a minister of the Iglesia ng Kristo, and a priest of the "independent" Catholic Church—read an ecumenical prayer in unison. As with most of the proceedings, the prayer was in English. The chief justice of the Philippine Supreme Court then administered the oath to President Marcos, whose voice resounded over the public address system, affirming the oath in Pilipino (Tagalog).

Then, during the singing of a lovely patriotic song ("Akoy Pilipino"), a middle-aged man came up the front steps carrying rolled-up plans for a housing project in Tondo [an impoverished district of Manila]. "He got all the way up—all the way!" exclaimed [White House staffer] Joe Canzeri. It was our Secret Service, not Philippine security, who gently hustled the man back down the steps. The main hero of the incident was John Baffa, Mrs. Bush's agent today. The incident clearly upset the dignitaries. [In 1972, Mrs. Marcos had been badly slashed by a man who hid a knife inside some papers.] For protocol reasons, GB's Secret Service detail was seated a considerable distance from him. Ed Pollard, in morning dress to match the Vice President's attire, was not far from Jennifer and me. He told us that he and agent John Magaw "could have gotten off clean shots against the guy, but we couldn't have given the Vice President the physical protection we like."

Marcos began and ended his inaugural address in Tagalog, but the long inner section was in English. He remains one of the world's great orators, his voice strong, assertive, and resolute. As the ceremonies ended, the massed men's choir sang Handel's "Hallelujah" chorus ("And he shall reign forever and ever!"). We Americans pushed forward as firmly as we could within the bounds of courtesy to grab our fast-arriving and fast-leaving motorcade, which moved through a tight tunnel of VIPs and ordinary onlookers, bound for Malacañang [the presidential palace] and a big inaugural breakfast. For a while we had the place to ourselves.

As soon as the breakfast concluded, I joined GB, Admiral Murphy, Nancy Bearg Dyke, and Deputy Assistant Secretary of State John Negroponte[2] for the VP's "bilaterals" with fellow visiting dignitaries. The first, in Malacañang itself, was with the gifted, direct Prime Minister Lee Kuan Yew of Singapore. As a demonstration of his catholic interest in world affairs (a small nation perforce has very big external relations), Lee's first question was about Mitterrand. His basic advice to GB and the Reagan Administration was, "Whatever your decision, stay on course."

President and Mrs. Marcos hosted the US delegation and official party at a sumptuous lunch in the state dining room. White-gloved waiters served a heavy continental meal that was more popular with the insolent flies than with me. [During the toasting, Barbara Bush was surprised when Governor Ray covered her glass of champagne with his hand before it touched her lips. She thought this was remarkably rude of such a kind man—until she saw the large fly happily swimming in the thick, sweet wine.]

---

2. Negroponte would later become ambassador to the Philippines, Honduras, Mexico, Iraq, and the United Nations as well as deputy secretary of state for the second President Bush.

TV lights burned throughout the meal, even though TV crews didn't mob the dining room till toast time. President Marcos, in long, impromptu remarks, praised the Reagan-"Boose" Administration. He called the resurgent American presence in the region "a new turn . . . which is welcomed by poor, intimidated countries like the Philippines." GB's reply [also unscripted] was shorter but probably quite welcome to Marcos's ears—and awful to those of his opponents: "We stand with the Philippines, [and] we stand with you, sir. . . . We love your adherence to democratic principles and to the democratic process. We will not leave you in isolation."

Bush's remarks caused as much of an uproar in the United States as among democracy activists in the Philippines. He later explained that the "you" and the "your" in his toast referred to the entire Association of Southeast Asian Nations (ASEAN), not solely the Philippines. But Marcos took the Vice President's words as an endorsement of his regime by the new administration in Washington. He was thus shocked and angered when the same administration refused to support him during the "People Power" uprising that followed his attempt to steal yet another term as president in 1986.

At 7:30 p.m., again dressed in a barong, I embarked in the staff van for the palace. We staffers mounted the grand staircase to the sound of trumpets. Admittedly these were for the Indonesian vice president, but the mood was the same. At the reception, I linked up with Ambassador Luce, bedecked with a fortune in sapphires. Her celebrity allowed us both to meet more people, such as the papal nuncio (an Italian cardinal) and the Philippine finance minister.

Dinner was served downstairs in the banqueting hall where we had had breakfast. The lengthy meal was wrapped around a Hollywood-style floorshow on Philippine culture that was too distant and too obscured by waiters to enjoy. There was a beautiful solo by a soprano, and I strained my unbelieving eyes to see that she was none other than Imelda Marcos, who received a huge ovation.

After dinner, we all filed back upstairs for the ball. It began when cabinet members and their wives lined up to be presented to a head table at which sat the Marcoses, Bushes, and other delegates in regal fashion. The couples bowed and curtsied before commencing a spectacular *rigadón*, straight from the Spanish colonial era, a stately but sparkling formal dance.

As we stood watching, advancemen circulated among us furtively with the report that the relentless approach of Tropical Storm Kelly ("Daling" to

the Filipinos) would force an early departure for Hawaii. We all left immediately. I escorted Ambassador Luce back to the Malacañang guesthouse. [Her
sudden need to pack was complicated by the delivery of a waist-high basket
of perfumes, fine chocolates, and other gifts from Mrs. Marcos.] The staff
van returned us to the Manila Hotel through the narrow, rain-soaked streets
of the city. As we rode, *Air Force 2* was being flown to Manila International
Airport from Clark Field. Back at the hotel, I packed for an early baggage call.

Wednesday, 1 July 1981

Today I up was a few minutes before [lead advanceman] Bob Goodwin[3]
rapped on the door to say that Tropical Storm Kelly/Daling was bearing
down on the Philippines faster than expected and that we all had to leave for
the airport right away. I shaved and hurried down to the lobby.

We got to the Manila airport about 6:00 under stable skies and boarded
AF2. A short while later, a long Mercedes limo with Philippine license "1"
came onto the tarmac. In it were the Bushes. From another car emerged
Imelda Marcos. I looked out a porthole to see Barbara leading Mrs. Marcos
up the ramp. "We're taking her back with us," BPB joked. This prompted
me to say, "We can then enjoy some more beautiful singing." As a chorus of
approbation rose, the great Imelda played coquette, blushing and tossing her
shoulders in a little giggle.

At 6:50 we took off from Manila and encountered almost no turbulence
all the way to Guam, a great relief. While *AF2* refueled at Andersen Air Force
Base, BPB went shopping, GB spoke with the governor and commanding
officers, and I sat with Clare Boothe Luce in the lounge, acting as escort and
companion. Both Bushes thanked me today for the attention I've been paying her. I said it was no trouble: "She's like a female Lowell Thomas."[4]

On the flight to Hawaii a film was shown in the VIP lounge, and the
Bushes allowed Mrs. Luce and me to take their cabin while they watched it.
Clare recalled LBJ's telling her and her late husband, "Harry," in 1960 that

---

3. Goodwin would serve as ambassador to New Zealand and Samoa under the first President Bush.

4. Lowell Thomas was the legendary traveler, author, and broadcaster whom I met on the
Bushes' China trip in 1977. Lowell became famous in 1918, when he found and later publi-
cized the exploits of the man known to history as Lawrence of Arabia. He and Clare were at the
peak of their fame in the decades just before and after World War II. I was a devoted listener
to both when they were, as Lowell liked to say, in their "anecdotage."

he "would never serve as vice president to that son of a bitch Jack Kennedy." At the inaugural ball the following year, Mrs. Luce asked Kennedy's VP to account for himself. "Clare, honey," she mimicked LBJ, "Lady Bird said I'd been workin' too hard in the Senate, and I needed a rest." Dismissing that explanation, Mrs. Luce demanded the real reason, and LBJ gave it: "Clare, honey, I'll tell you. History shows that one out of four vice presidents have become president. I'm a gamblin' man, and I'll take those odds, because it's the last chance I've got."

Clare asked me many questions and gave an incisive analysis of GB's chances to be president. She thinks his greatest weakness is that "it isn't in him to go for the jugular." On the other hand, she thinks he must constantly demonstrate the "compassion" that the GOP is supposed to lack.

What could be grander than to chat with Clare Boothe Luce at 33,000 feet above the Pacific on the plane of the vice president of the United States?

Chapter 10

Travels with the Vishnu

Sunday, 5 July 1981

Today I embarked on a ninety-minute journey into the Maryland countryside due south of Washington. The weather was murky, but the landscape provided some green relief. Outside the hamlet of Bel Alton is the 2,000-acre working (gentleman's) farm of Paul Nitze, one of the last great "cold warriors" and father-in-law of Scott Thompson. True to its name, White Hall Farm has an attractive, big clump of a white house overlooking fields of tobacco and corn. Beyond it is the Potomac, which is rather broad in that section. Down the hill from the house are a tennis court, a swimming pool, a trampoline, and a small cottage for bridge-playing. The Fourth of July weekend is a tradition in the Nitze household, with as many as 150 people showing up for the festivities, including fireworks. By this afternoon, only about a dozen hardcore celebrants were left, ranging themselves over my line of vision as if posing for a tableau of the upper class at play.

The guests gathered for cocktails and lunch back at the house, pretending to ignore swarms of flies. [Clearly a believer in taking the fight to the foe, Secretary Nitze sprayed insecticide on the flies—no matter they happened to be attacking the buffet at the time.] I chatted with the tart-tongued Mrs. Nitze and with Campbell James, a monocle-wearing former CIA officer who told of being in charge of "ship interdiction" (= piracy) during the Korean War, preventing supplies from reaching North Korea. The most interesting couple were Moorhead (Mike) and Louisa Kennedy. He had been a hostage in Iran, and she organized the hostage families and was their liaison to the Carter White House. All the while she was a Bush supporter and would have been active in the campaign had not her husband been seized. The talk at luncheon was that Secretary Haig has got to go, that he is an increasing embarrassment to the Administration.

Friday, 10 July 1981

At GB's invitation I sat in on his interview with Cal Thomas, VP for communications at Moral Majority and a mutual friend of years' standing. [He was a reporter at the Hobby-owned TV station in Houston.] Cal is very much on GB's side and, according to him, has defended the VP stoutly against many in the New Right. He asked GB fair questions about the Trilateral Commission, about his political philosophy, and about his faith.

The Moral Majority is holding back from endorsing President Reagan's choice of Judge Sandra Day O'Connor for the Supreme Court because of doubts about her record on abortion while an Arizona state senator. This dustup led to one of the best quotations in modern politics. Informed (incorrectly, Cal says) that Moral Majority head Rev. Jerry Falwell said every good Christian should object to O'Connor, Sen. Barry Goldwater lashed back in support of his constituent: "Every good Christian should kick Jerry Falwell in the ass." GB loved that so much he called Goldwater to congratulate him.

Tuesday, 14 July 1981

Deskwork kept me busy until 4:00, when GB met with Daouda Diallo, the foreign minister of Niger. Diallo was quite concerned ("scared" is not incorrect) about Libya's designs on his drought-stricken country. GB, reflecting an anti-Qaddafi attitude in the Reagan Administration, was most sympathetic. At one point, the Sterno burning under the coffee server popped its lid with a bang. "What the hell was that?" the VP interjected, turning about. "Qaddafi!"

Thursday, 16 July 1981

GB and Jennifer went to Garfinkel's [department store] to buy a necktie for the President. This was prompted by my announcing at the morning staff meeting that it was one year ago today that RR tapped GB for the vice presidential nomination. GB is so unconcerned with his own history that the reminder came as a surprise to him. He read to Jennifer and me the handwritten card accompanying the cravat: "A year ago tonight you made a phone call that changed my life and Barbara's. Thanks for making that call."

Friday, 17 July 1981

President Reagan signed a bill affecting the steel industry, and I decided to drop in to see what it was like—another of those White House events that may not be historic but are still quite grand. The ceremony was held in the Rose Garden on a fine morning: congressmen surrounding a podium and signing table, newsmen to one side, Secret Service and staffers scattered about. A voice announced the President, who emerged from the West Wing in his movie star way—arms out, head nodding and smiling, his legs carrying him down some steps in a shambling sort of dance. I'm always amazed at how broad his shoulders are and how young he looks: mid-fifties at the oldest. The President used only one pen instead of the dozens LBJ would use and hand out. Reagan seemed to hesitate before deciding to bestow it on Sen. John Heinz of Pennsylvania.

Thursday, 23 July 1981

Those of us who travel with the VP were given a special show by the Secret Service: a look at films of past assassinations and assassination attempts. These included the famous, grim Zapruder film of the death of JFK, the crippling of George Wallace in May 1972, the attempt on President Park Chung Hee of Korea (which killed his wife), and the ghastly knife attack on Imelda Marcos in 1972. The latter was especially gripping, not only because of the fury of the assassin but because there were so many parallels with the breach of security at President Marcos's inauguration a month ago. (The hero of that day, John Baffa, told me after returning from Manila that he was glad to leave, because Mrs. Marcos was lavishing too many favors on him.) The lesson for us: these incidents happen so fast that they must be prevented from taking place at all, for once they start it's too late to provide much protection. We were told to "sing out," like the agents do, if we see a weapon and to report suspicious behavior. And if something starts, hit the deck, out of self-protection and to clear the area so that the agents have an open field in which to react.

Friday, 24 July 1981

A funny but potentially tragic incident occurred on the VP's ride to the Hill: Bob Thompson [the congressional liaison] missed the motorcade from the White House and raced after it in a staff car. When the VP's limo stopped at a traffic light (Washington is the only place on earth where the VP doesn't get intersection control), Bob foolishly leapt out of his car and came running toward the limo to get in. According to Joe Hagin and Cynthia Johnson, who were in the control car, Secret Service agents in the followup car were alarmed enough to raise and cock their Uzi submachine guns till another agent sang out that it was Thompson.

Wednesday, 29 July 1981

The afternoon was dominated by news of the president's big victory on the tax bill: he needed twenty-seven Democratic votes and got forty-eight of them, probably the result of a stampede when the boys saw that the O'Neill team had lost again. There was a celebration in the Oval Office that GB attended. I observed that RR's legislative triumphs belie the chic notion of only a year ago that no modern president can govern and that the American people cannot respond en masse to a presidential appeal, as they did during World War II. GB liked this and had me send it to Chris Buckley for inclusion in his speech for the American Bar Association on 10 August.

Thursday, 30 July 1981

George Bush of Midland called for stats on Hispanic appointments for a speech he'll give to a Mexican American group soon. Incidentally, Laura is now expecting *twins*. Though delighted, the senior Bushes are worried whether Laura, a first-time mother, can carry the babies to term and a healthy delivery.

Tuesday, 4 August 1981

Something I learned today disturbed me: Mrs. Bush will be a member of the official U.S. delegation to the funeral of Gen. Omar Torrijos of Panama, who as president negotiated the treaty with the United States giving the Canal to his country. In that era, private citizen Ronald Reagan called Torrijos "a tinhorn dictator," and the man definitely flirted with Cuba and the Sandinistas of Nicaragua. For this reason it's amazing that the Reagan Administration made a big deal of Torrijos's death over the weekend (in an air crash). Worse, Barbara's presence as the only "political" person among diplomats and military men merely confirms to the Far Right that GB was for "the Canal giveaway." (Actually, he was equivocal-to-negative on the issue in 1978, though not negative enough to prevent the ultras from using the Canal to hit

George Jr. in the nineteenth congressional district that year.[1]) Why couldn't they have sent Mrs. Howard Baker, since her husband voted for the treaty?

As I pieced together the story, Admiral Murphy called the VP in Maine last weekend to report on Torrijos's death and to raise the question of GB's going to the funeral. According to Nancy Dyke, BPB said she wanted to go. Apparently no one mentioned the political consequences, although if the thought had penetrated Kennebunkport that her going would unnecessarily rile the Right, GB probably dismissed it contemptuously as akin to attacks on him for having belonged to the Trilateral Commission. As much as Rich Bond and I might sigh, no one is going to be GB's political advisor but GB.

Wednesday, 5 August 1981

At 9:30, I welcomed Judge and Mrs. Malcolm Wilkey in the West Wing basement to attend the arrival ceremony for President Anwar Sadat of Egypt. It was one of the largest crowds ever to gather on the South Lawn, reflecting Sadat's deep and genuine popularity as the man who dared to go to Jerusalem in 1977 and to conclude the Camp David agreements of 1978 and 1979. Ours was a good but distant prospect of the proceedings, standing right behind the color guard holding the flags of the states and territories. In their statements, the two presidents conveyed sincerity and respect for each other, to which the crowd reacted warmly. Sadat looks on Jimmy Carter as "a brother," and he will visit the ex-president in Plains. So, part of Reagan's job this week is to charm old Anwar.

President Reagan fired all the striking air traffic controllers today, a bold move likely to be popular, though no one knows how long the airlines can operate with reduced flights—or how safely.

Sunday, 9 August 1981

We staffers had SAM 86970, the plane we took to Manila, all to ourselves on the hour-long flight to Pease AFB. The air traffic controllers are still on strike and still fired. In any case, our (and others') route was monitored by military personnel. I went aft to chat with Joe Masonis, the sole Secret Service agent on board. Joe's family is from Sicily, and he's the Service's Italian specialist. He

---

1. George W. Bush won the nomination in the big West Texas district against a Reagan supporter but lost to conservative Democrat Kent Hance in the fall.

was reading *Corriere della Serra* when I sat down to talk. Joe told me about working with Henry Kissinger. The former SecState liked the macho agents. An amateur psychologist, Joe speculates that in his youth Kissinger learned to seek the friendship and protection of bigger companions. He liked to point to the men in his detail and say, "Dese are my animals." He would call individual agents "Animal" as a term of affection. Joe earned that sobriquet when once he stopped a would-be assailant, but he told the Secretary he didn't like it. Henry was crushed.

When we landed at Pease (on the New Hampshire–Maine border), I deplaned to breathe the cool, salty air and meet Carl Yastrzemski, the veteran Boston Red Sox hitter who was GB's guest today for the All-Star Game. In about twenty minutes the Bushes arrived from Kennebunkport, bringing retired Oklahoma coach Bud Wilkinson and his young wife, Donna. (In 1964, Wilkinson and Bush were both losing GOP Senate candidates.) On the 100-minute flight to Cleveland we staffers chatted with the likeable "Yaz" till the Bushes came into the lounge.

Around 6:30 we landed at Cleveland and were met by Mayor George Voinovich, a Republican.[2] In the control car my companion for the first time was Lt. Col. Bill Eckert USAF, a tall, quiet guy who is John Matheny's relief. Our driver was Steve Mason, perhaps my favorite member of the VP's Secret Service detail for his nonstop affability and humor. As we drove through a seedy section to Cleveland Stadium, which fronts on Lake Erie, Steve called Cleveland "the mistake on the lake." The VP was met by commissioner of baseball Bowie Kuhn and led up to a lavish reception for owners and local potentates. I did the standby routine, and GB called me over to meet Tom Vail, publisher of the *Cleveland Plain Dealer*.

After the reception, GB gave a press conference before a small group of friendly young sports reporters in an office of the Cleveland Indians. He reminisced about his days as a first baseman for Yale. Then a circuitous route took us down a long, narrow, wooden-planked corridor that ended at the American League dugout. Emerging onto the field after hours of being in close confinement, in the air and on the ground, I was awed by the vastness of the stadium and the size of the crowd, which cheered loudly when GB was announced. He shook hands with players from both squads before taking his seat in Kuhn's box. My seat was between homeplate and third base.

---

2. Voinovich would be governor of Ohio from 1991 to 1999 and U.S. senator from 1999 to 2011.

It was the first game of the 1981 season since a two-month strike ended a week ago. Everything was done with dash and dazzle. A veritable regiment of Armed Forces personnel held (and waved) an enormous U.S. flag as the national anthem was sung by a full-voiced Cleveland baritone named Rocco Scotti. He got one of the biggest hands of the evening and was later seen greeting fans. When Rocco got to the part about "the bombs bursting in air," fireworks shot off above us. Also above us was a Goodyear blimp. GB threw out the first ball to a thirteen-year-old kid chosen at random. The game was slow for most of the six innings we watched and got lively just as we left. (The National League eventually won, 5–4.)

With a big police escort, we streaked to the airport and were wheels-up for New Orleans at 11:15 p.m., arriving after midnight local time. Another grand motorcycle escort took us to the New Orleans Hilton.

Monday, 10 August 1981

At 10:30, GB was announced before the general convention of the American Bar Association. His speech was a reminder how supposedly learned people a year ago were declaiming that no president could govern anymore because our national institutions were decayed and had been rejected by the American people. Ronald Reagan, by force of personality and old-fashioned leadership, has shown all these obits to be ridiculous. The speech was well received, and when it ended we returned briefly to the top-floor suite, with its sweeping view of the great crescent of the Mississippi.

When time came to go, we staffers left for the elevators slightly ahead of the Bushes. An agent asked us to take the second elevator, which we dutifully did. Unfortunately, this elevator didn't move when the VP's did; in fact, it didn't move at all. We were forced to take one of the slow regular elevators. When we all finally got downstairs, the motorcade had left, to our horror. Fortunately, a car in the motorcade peeled off and returned for Jennifer, Chris, and Thadd. An intern in the advance office and I jumped in a New Orleans police car, which led our two-car motorcade on an exciting, even terrifying, chase after the VP. With the siren whooping, a Gulf Coast monsoon rain descending, and the young officer careening through traffic, we had a fantastic ride. We managed to catch up to the motorcade just as it was pulling alongside *AF2*. To reach the ramp I had to slosh through an inch and a half of water on the tarmac, leading to the scariest moment of all: a bolt of lightning struck somewhere nearby, causing my left leg to tingle. Soggy, we all got on board the 707 in a good mood. On the short flight to Mississippi, I let my shoes and socks dry in the very low humidity of a pressurized cabin.

We landed at Meridian, to be met by the local congressman, Gillespie V. (Sonny) Montgomery, GB's congressional classmate and close friend. The motorcade took us the short distance to the enormous National Guard armory and flight facility being dedicated today. Montgomery's name was on the side of the building in huge letters. The mayor of Meridian joked that to save taxpayers' dollars it should have been called the G. V. Montgomery *Memorial* Armory so it won't have to be repainted in the future.

In a holding room we met eighty-year-old Sen. John Stennis (D-Mississippi) and Rep. Charles Stenholm (D-Texas), a member of the southern Democrat "boll weevils" in the House. Montgomery was a leader of the weevils, who supported the president's tax and spending legislation this year. One would have thought we were in deep Republican territory today, due to the lavish praise heaped on the Reagan-Bush Administration by these top Democrats. As Lt. Gov. Brad Dye said to great applause, the new administration "has made us proud to be Americans again." We Washingtonians feel that, but the folks in that hangar today really believe it. Thadd and I sat together, which led to an amusing moment when we joined in the standing ovation for Stennis, grand prince of old-time racist senators. "I can't believe I'm doing this!" Thadd exclaimed in a stage whisper.

Later, in Biloxi, there was a big $50-a-plate fundraiser for the state and county parties plus Trent Lott, the local congressman.[3] He gave a rousing if overlong introduction of the VP that once again marked how far George Bush has come in the hearts of Reaganites in a year. And GB responded with a hard-hitting, campaign-style speech that closed with both a tender tribute to RR and a defiant blast at the USSR.

Tuesday, 11 August 1981

When we landed at a big military airfield near Pomona, New Jersey, we were met by Republican gubernatorial candidate Tom Kean (an instructor of Boyden's at St. Mark's) and by eight of the twenty-one county GOP chairmen. I rode in the creamy supermobile of one of these sachems, Phil Matalucci, Cape May County chairman and county treasurer. A classic of the breed, Matalucci was

---

3. When Stennis retired in 1988, Lott was elected to succeed him, rising to majority leader.

fat, wore a white suit, had a jangly bracelet of gold nuggets, wore an enormous matching ring of gold and diamonds, and mopped his brow. We of course had a nonstop political gab all the way to Atlantic City and back. Matalucci is confident that Kean (pronounced "Cane") can win in the swell of pro-Republican feeling created by the success to date of the Reagan-Bush Administration and with visits by both leaders. But the race is tough because the Democratic nominee, James Florio, is congressman from Camden and thus has a base in "South Jersey." When added to the traditional Democratic strongholds of the north, Florio has a huge vote advantage. Cape May, carefully tended by Phil Matalucci, will deliver its votes to the Republican column, but it's only a small county. Matalucci with great emotion predicted that GB will be president someday, and I responded with a now-standard line: "He already *is* president—of the Senate."

Wednesday, 12 August 1981

In the West Wing office late this morning, GB affixed his name as president of the Senate to the historic budget and tax reduction bills. Two Capitol Hill clerks brought a cardboard box containing the legislation, printed on parchment for the National Archives. The budget (or "reconciliation") bill weighed between 15 and 20 pounds and was about 18 inches high. There was no public ceremony; just Cynthia Johnson taking pictures. The bills travel by courier to California, where President Reagan will sign them tomorrow [on his ranch].

Monday, 17 August 1981

Air Force 2 (the DC-9) landed in Philadelphia, and as soon as the Bushes disembarked, our motorcade sped off to the municipal auditorium, where the VP gave the keynote address to the eighty-second annual convention of the Veterans of Foreign Wars. I am glad GB located his VFW cap, for when he strode into the hall wearing it, there were approving *ah*'s over the applause of the 7,000 members and wives. On the stage with him was a living legend: Gen. Jimmy Doolittle. The text was a strong Buckleyan creation, with slams on the Soviets, which landed on the evening network news. The best part was when GB, after reciting Soviet criticism of President Reagan's decision to stockpile the neutron weapon, quoted General McAuliffe: "Nuts!"

As the VFW rose in ovation and the band played "Anchors Aweigh," we quickly left the hall and returned to the airport for a flight across the Delaware. On board was Ron Kaufman, who covers New England for the RNC [Republican National Committee] but is working the governor's race in New Jersey. We landed at Lakehurst Naval Air Station, where the *Hindenburg* exploded in May 1937, and proceeded to [a high-dollar fundraiser for Tom Kean]. In the cocktail reception, Rich had me meet Mrs. Webster Todd, grande dame of the New Jersey GOP. She wants a position on a part-time board or commission for her attractive daughter, Christie Whitman.[4]

A lavish lunch was served under tents on a perfect afternoon. When Kean got up to speak, one of his weaknesses became immediately apparent. "What's a guy with a Back Bay accent doing, running for governor of New Jersey?" I asked Ron, who has a suburban Boston accent himself. Ron agreed: "He can't say 'New Joisey' right."

Sunday, 23 August 1981

Working in my West Wing office, I listened to Secretary Haig on ABC's *Issues and Answers*. He never misses a chance to exalt himself. Referring to last Wednesday's episode in which two American jets shot down two Libyan aircraft, Haig noted that although "two principals were out of town"—meaning RR and GB—"the crisis was successfully managed." This was a slam on the absent GB, aka the crisis manager.

President Reagan was not only in California but also asleep at the time, and Ed Meese chose not to wake him with the news. Afterward, Reagan said with mock displeasure, "I've given strict orders to my staff to wake me if this sort of thing happens again, even if I'm in a Cabinet meeting."

Thursday, 27 August 1981

Chris Buckley and I were scheduled to have breakfast with the foreign minister of Paraguay today. This was arranged by a former Florida congressman who represents Asunción but only on commercial matters. When the Paraguayans discovered that their foreign minister had sidled into the political sphere by setting up a breakfast with "people from the White House," they became both outraged and embarrassed. So at the suggestion of the Paraguay desk at State, they cancelled. Chris and I got a big laugh out of this, noting that we had to be pretty low-grade officials to be stood up by the Paraguayans.

---

4. Whitman would serve as governor of New Jersey from 1994 to 2001, when she became administrator of the Environmental Protection Agency for President George W. Bush.

GB is being given the rare honor for a foreigner of accompanying President José López Portillo of Mexico at the Grito ceremony next month. Mexican presidents give the *grito* (the "cry" of independence) in Dolores Hidalgo in the fifth year of their six-year terms. Unfortunately, overnight accommodations are so limited that not all the official party can stay there or even attend the proceedings. Bowing to the inevitable, the Admiral put Jennifer on the list but not me. I'm concerned that the Mexicans will simply assume she's GB's mistress. After all, they might say, why would the Vice President need or want his appointments secretary with him—to plan some future events, *eh*?

Saturday, 29 August 1981

I turned on the noon news, and the top item directly affected me. Lowell Thomas died this morning of a heart attack at his home in Pawling, New York. Through the kindness of GB, I got to know that remarkable man four years ago and since then became one of his many friends. My initial reaction was: "Lowell dead! He was only eighty-nine!" So vigorous and durable was "LT" that one could easily imagine his living another decade at least.

Because I was on leave in Houston at the time, I was not able to attend Lowell's funeral in New York with the Bushes. But when I returned to Washington and checked my mail, there was a letter from Lowell written only two days before he died. "It was chatty and full of wonder about a recent gold mine discovery in [his native] Colorado—in other words, typical LT," I wrote that night. "How blessed was I to have known him!"

Thursday, 10 September 1981

Tonight brought the big "Jazz Salute to Lionel Hampton" at the Kennedy Center. This was something Jennifer and I helped arrange, but the idea sprang from Lionel[5] as a means of raising funds for his foundation's scholarships for young musicians. GB endorsed it early as a nongovernment way to support

---

5. The great vibraphonist was one of very few prominent blacks who were Republicans, and he was a great pal of GB's. Like other distinguished seniors Leon Jaworski and Henry Cabot Lodge, Lionel called me frequently to pass messages to the VP. One Saturday at the office, Barbara Hayward and I were listening to a "big band" radio station as we worked. The announcer introduced a selection by saying, "We haven't heard from Lionel Hampton in a while . . . ," whereupon she and I burst out laughing.

the arts. Muffie Brandon of Mrs. Reagan's office made the South Lawn of the White House available for an elite, invitation-only concert this afternoon as a means of luring big-name jazz talent to tonight's function for free.

Lionel, thrilled at seeing his big festival come to life, gave us ten free tickets to the sold-out concert. From start to finish, he looked on it as his private party. Dressed in a red silk vest and tux, he smiled his trademark smile—tongue sticking out, eyes popping—and danced his hands over the vibes as expertly as he must have done forty years ago. And out came the great talent, young and old, to deliver their musical tributes: Pearl Bailey, Tony Bennett, Charley Pride, and Stephanie Mills. There was a lengthy jam session with Lionel on vibes, Dave Brubeck on piano, Illinois Jacquet and Zoot Sims on sax, Louie Bellson (Pearl's husband) on drums, and Clark Terry on trumpet.

As exciting an evening as it was for jazz buffs, I was quite tired and actually dozed off during the show. Sue Cockrell and Barbara Hayward laughed at how I jumped when suddenly Lionel brought down his mallets on the vibes.

GB and BPB came on stage to hug Lionel. The honoree was so overwhelmed that he gave what amounted to a political plug for the Reagan-Bush Administration. As the audience grew edgy at this commercial, Lionel caught himself: "We really got to support our leaders, ladies and gentlemen, because . . . because . . . if we don't . . . the bears and kangaroos and elephants will come over and get us!"

By 12:30 a.m., we were all anxious to go, and after Lionel played his signature piece, "Flyin' Home," I did just that.

Friday, 11 September 1981

Lionel Hampton was on the helo to Andrews. We all praised last night's concert, and Lionel said its success was owed to the support he got from the VP, Jennifer, and me. He said this so many times this morning that I cheerfully gave up, taking credit where credit wasn't due. Waiting for us on the C-9 were Mr. and Mrs. Clarence Mitchell, fifty-year stalwarts of the civil rights movement and the NAACP in particular. They joined us for the trip to New York and the Roy Wilkins's funeral.[6] When we landed at LaGuardia we were given a police escort to the nondenominational Community Church of New

---

6. Wilkins was cofounder of the Leadership Conference on Civil Rights and executive director of the NAACP from 1964 to 1977.

York on West Thirty-Fifth Street, just around the corner from the Empire State Building.

We staffers sat in the last pew, enabling us to see the parade of dignitaries filing in: former vice president Mondale, Sen. Ted Kennedy, Gov. Hugh Carey, Mayor Koch, ex-mayor Lindsay, and a panoply of civil rights leaders. There was a surprisingly pat eulogy from the usually pyrotechnic Benjamin Hooks, Wilkins's successor at NAACP. This was followed by a stirring spiritual, "Precious Lord," sung a cappella by soprano Leotyne Price. Next came a personal tribute from Arnold Aronson, Wilkins's compatriot and friend, after which Ms. Price sang the "Battle Hymn of the Republic," all of us joining in the chorus. Finally, Clarence Mitchell spoke, making sure to mention every ranking dignitary present, even including Thadd.

Crowds lined the street, soon to be led by Ms. Price in choruses of "We Shall Overcome" as Wilkins's casket was carried down the steps and put into the hearse.

Saturday, 12 September 1981

At a function in Bridgeport, advanceman Dan Sullivan beckoned me outside, where Pres Bush [Prescott Bush Jr.] waited with his new toy: a thick report from Decision Making International, the outfit of presidential pollster Dick Wirthlin, on his prospects to become U.S. senator from Connecticut. The poll shows that even with relatively low name ID, Pres can beat incumbent Sen. Lowell Weicker in a GOP primary. He gave me the book to read and show GB. In the motorcade I jotted down an index of key findings for the VP and gave the book to GB. He looked it over with great interest, impressed that his brother is so strong at this early stage. BPB worries that Pres's enthusiasm, absent-mindedness, and "lack of guile" will cause him to stumble badly before the Senate race even begins. GB stands to be embarrassed one way or another by his brother's interest in going to the Senate.[7]

---

7. Their father, Prescott Bush Sr., represented Connecticut in the Senate from 1952 to 1963. It was Nutmeg State political lore that bad blood existed between the Bushes and Weicker, who entered the Senate in 1971.

Chapter 11

Goose-stepping Nurses, Soapless in Grand Rapids, and the President of Puerto Rico

Vice President Bush arrived in Mexico City to great fanfare on 15 September, afterward proceeding to the town of Dolores Hidalgo for the Grito ceremony. I did not make it there, but my suitcase did. With only the clothes I had worn on the trip down from DC, I remained in the capital and watched President José López Portillo give the cry "Viva Hidalgo! Viva Morelos! Viva Guerrero! Viva México!" on television. This he did while ringing a bell with one hand and waving a flag with the other, a display of physical coordination akin to patting your head and rubbing your tummy at the same time.

Wednesday, 16 September 1981

Today was *El Dieciséis*, Mexican Independence Day. Our group arrived at the presidential hangar for some breakfast prior to the 9:30 arrival of President López Portillo's 727, *Quetzalcoátal 1*. The Bushes were on board with him. The President was rendered brief military honors, after which a police escort took us all at high speed into El Centro. We went down a narrow street empty of people except for a double line of soldiers every few feet as a cordon of honor. Emerging into the enormous Zócalo, the motorcade swept majestically around the square and halted to cheers at the Palacio Nacional. The VP received a quick tour of the spectacular building, the former residence of Spanish viceroys. First we saw the awesome, if Marxist, murals of Mexican history painted by Diego Rivera in the 1920s. Then we looked into baroque rooms and corridors with gilded ceilings and intricate parquet floors. Our route ended at a balcony facing the Zócalo where the Vice President, Congressmen de la Garza and Lujan [of Texas and New Mexico, respectively], and the rest of our delegation stood to watch the proceedings unfold below.

They began promptly at 11:00 with the arrival of President López Portillo, riding an open jeep and wearing the embroidered red, green, and white sash of office. Two fixed army bands rendered honors in the curious fashion by which one plays the *himno nacional* and the other plays a tinny trumpet arrangement that may be the Mexican equivalent of "Ruffles and Flourishes." "JLP" entered the palace and came out onto a red-draped balcony adjoining ours. Then it started, a seemingly endless procession of military hardware and personnel (35,000 in all) that lasted the next hour and a half.

It was a sight unlike anything ever staged in the US but common in so many other countries. There were armored personnel carriers, rocket launchers, goose-stepping soldiers and goose-stepping nurses, sailors with boats, patrol dogs, cadets, fire trucks, police cruisers with flashing lights, and even tow trucks. There were two especially arresting sights. One was the periodic flyover by the fleet of presidential aircraft, half a dozen 727s flying wingtip to wingtip. The other was the arrival on the plaza of several large horse trailers, out of which charged cavalry units. Horses and riders lined up in perfect formation before the palace, and their commander lifted his sword to shout, *"Viva el Presidente de la República! Viva la Caballería! Viva México!"* At this, the horsemen headed back into the trailers in opposing curves.

That evening at his residence, Amb. John Gavin[1] gave an informal but high-powered dinner in honor of President López Portillo. The elite of Mexican government were there[2] but not Señora de López Portillo: Doña Carmen was invited, but she has a reputation for failing to do her duties as first lady, supposedly out of pique over her husband's liaisons. I was seated at what Jeb Bush called "the kiddie table" with him, Columba, and younger members of the López Portillo family. Next to me was Paulina, the slim, beautiful daughter of the president, who stands in for her absentee mother on state occasions and foreign trips. She also writes *informes* (reports) for her father, working out of Los Pinos [the Mexican "White House"]. We spoke throughout the dinner *en español* until she was called to the head table by her father. She returned to our table with word that he wanted her to sing a composition she had written for the guitar, a song in English called "Just." Paulina dashed down the lyrics on the back of a menu, which she later signed and gave to me. Fond toasts were delivered by GB and JLP, after which the president,

---

1. An actor who was in *Spartacus* and *Thoroughly Modern Millie*, Gavin was an able and effective citizen-diplomat who spoke excellent Spanish.

2. Dinner guests included Miguel de la Madrid, who would shortly be declared López Portillo's successor.

admitting to being a proud father, introduced his daughter. Paulina's song was a great hit; indeed, if sung by a well-known artist in the US it could become a real hit.

Air Force 2 next made the nonstop flight from Mexico City to Grand Rapids, Michigan, for the dedication of the presidential museum of hometown boy Gerald Ford.

Thursday, 17 September 1981

We landed at Grand Rapids minutes after a heavy shower. The President's plane (SAM 27000) was on the field, as was a poncho-covered high school band bidding all VIPs welcome. We pulled up to the Amway Grand Plaza Hotel, a doughty old hostelry renovated and made plush by the Amway Corporation, sellers of household products door to door. My bathroom has only one slim bar of soap, as if an Amway representative is meant to come by later and make some easy sales. Also staying in the hotel is President Reagan and what appears to be the entire West Wing staff, including receptionist Nell Yates.

After dinner, we all filed into the auditorium named for Richard DeVos of Amway for the "gala." There was great excitement and applause as the dignitaries took their seats in the boxes above us: Ronald and Nancy Reagan, George and Barbara Bush, Gerald and Betty Ford, President López Portillo, PM Trudeau of Canada, FM Sonoda of Japan (which gave $1 million to the museum), and former French president Valéry Giscard d'Estaing. The quick-stepping University of Michigan band formed on stage to blare their famous fight song—which was also the fight song of Nancy Dyke's high school in Idaho and mine in Texas. Then out came Bob Hope, prompting me to say to Nancy, "This really *is* a state occasion."

Hope is around eighty, and unfortunately he now is showing his age, slurring over the lines of his mostly funny monologue. But when he and fellow stars Danny Thomas, Glen Campbell, and Sammy Davis Jr. flubbed a song, the worst occurred: the NBC producer made them do it three times till they got it right. It was a monstrous imposition on the President of the United States and the other potentates, and it showed the power of television in America, making them mere props in a *Bob Hope Special*. This was underscored in a scene in which Betty Ford [a former professional dancer] appeared on stage to dance a soft-shoe with Hope. It was charming, but he never even said good evening to her; the former first lady was strictly an extra.

Skipping the champagne reception, Nancy and I returned to the hotel. My main aim was to get another bar of soap. Soon I had some from several sources, the last and most surprising being the ambassador of the United States to Mexico. Jack Gavin came by with both soap and questions about tomorrow's schedule. [I now had enough bars to become an Amway distributor!]

The next vice presidential trip was to Puerto Rico, a place that held a special history for George Bush. When he was seeking the 1980 Republican presidential nomination, campaign manager Jim Baker decided Bush should enter every primary. This included the brand-new Puerto Rican primary, which islanders staged not so much to influence the midwinter nominating process as to promote tourism. They wanted TV pictures of candidates seeking votes under sunny skies and palm trees, in contrast to their tramping through snow banks in Iowa and New Hampshire. With Jeb Bush living full-time on the island for months, GB won the primary by a huge margin. This had absolutely no effect on the race against Reagan, but 1980 was to make George Bush vice president of the United States and president of Puerto Rico. Islanders, especially those favoring statehood (which Bush had championed during the campaign), saw him as a powerful, simpático friend in Washington. Therefore, his visit to the island as VP to address the Southern Governors' Conference was practically a triumphal occasion.

Sunday, 27 September 1981

I left for the Naval Observatory on a fine Indian summer's morning. The Bushes and Admiral Murphy arrived on foot. Aboard the helo, Mrs. B gave details on a remarkable report that appeared in yesterday's *Washington Post*: the family of a lower-ranking member of the Cameroonian embassy moved into Silver Spring, Maryland, where the simple house they occupy had a cross burned before it. The Cameroonians knew the neighborhood was unfriendly, but they thought the burning was a sign of welcome! Seeing the story, the Bushes decided on the spur of the moment to pay a visit. The Cameroonian family was tipped off by the Secret Service, so they weren't surprised, but they certainly were overwhelmed. Perhaps most revealingly about the Bushes, no press was told about the event, but it's a dynamite story.

Flying with us to San Juan are Gov. and Mrs. John Dalton (R-Virginia), Mr. and Mrs. Delio Rojo (major GOP contributors), deputy VP counsel Rafael (Keko) Capó, and the usual traveling crew. Toward 2:00, AF2 flew along the north coast of Puerto Rico. Soon the beautiful narrow peninsula of

Old San Juan came into view on the port side of the plane, followed by the skyscrapers of the modern city. We landed at the international airport and taxied over to the Air National Guard's section of the field. Waiting there was an honor guard of troops, Gov. Carlos Romero Barceló, Mayor Hernán Padilla of San Juan, ex-governor Luís Ferré, and most every cabinet chief in the Commonwealth government. Symptomatic of Puerto Rico's strange political status, the VP's arrival was very much like one abroad, complete with reviewing the troops, receiving a nineteen-gun salute, and the playing of two anthems. (Puerto Rico's non-national anthem has a fine *danza* rhythm.) Yet Puerto Rico is part of the United States—very proudly so, something a stateside visitor must always keep in mind. And yet the flavor of this visit is that of a sovereign to a crown colony, only it's not a colony but since 1952 a "self-governing commonwealth." The UN this year or next may declare Puerto Rico once again to be a colony. Governor Romero hasn't helped matters by establishing a "Decolonization Commission," which he insists does not imply that the island is colonized to start with. I may run out of paper if I try to explain all the "and yets" of Puerto Rican politics.

Puerto Rico's status is partway between that of a state and an independent country. The people have been US citizens since 1917 and can vote in local elections but not for Congress or president. The great political divide on the island is not between Democrats and Republicans but between those who favor making Puerto Rico the fifty-first state and those who want to maintain its "commonwealth" status indefinitely. Politics can be confusingly crosscut between island and mainland; while Romero, Padilla, and Ferré were all "statehooders" (or estadistas), Romero was a Democrat, and Padilla and Ferré were Republicans.

After the governor and the VP had made their statements, we staffers rushed to our cars for the heavily armed motorcade to the municipal gym. Our route was marked by lightpole signs and overpass banners saying, "*Bienvenido á Tu Casa, George Bush*" ("Welcome home, George Bush"). Doña Julita Rivera de Vincenti, GB's organizer in 1980 and now Farmers Home administrator, had predictably packed the gym with 2,000–3,000 ordinary folk from all over the island. It was a real Latin American political rally, with all the enthusiasm, massed bodies, banners, bands, and boiling heat of that art form. A leather-lunged crowd warmer brought on the (statehood) stars—Romero, Ferré, Padilla, and then the Bushes—with tumultuous rounds of applause for each. Somewhat to our surprise, Carlos [the governor] received the biggest and most sustained hand. Originally, he was not invited to this "picnic," but he couldn't be denied. Perhaps he also decided to pack the place with his own supporters in order to outshine Padilla, his prospective rival in 1984.[3] If so, he succeeded. Educated at Exeter and Yale, Romero is a commanding orator of the sort I yearn to be—only that women's Republican clubs do not provide much opportunity to practice.

The star nevertheless was GB. Introduced by Doña Julita, he sprang to the podium and immediately started stripping off his coat and tie and rolling up his sleeves. The crowd loved it, just as they did his game efforts at pronouncing a short statement written in Spanish for him by Keko and Chris Buckley. He said he had promised during the 1980 campaign to return to Puerto Rico, "*y estoy aquí*" (and I am here). Then he dropped the phrase made famous during that quirky primary: "*Estadidad ahora!*" (Statehood now!)

As soon as the VP finished, we all hurried out to the motorcade, which went exactly one block to an empty baseball stadium, in the middle of which stood several Huey helicopters. To avoid the danger a motorcade being ambushed on the forty-minute drive to our remote hotel, the Secret Service insisted on the helo airlift.[4] The vice presidential chopper took off, after which helo number 1 (mine) rose in the air, giving the odd sensation of floating while seated. Then the pilot gunned the engine, and we moved forward, fast, while gaining altitude. The ride along the Atlantic was beautiful, but I'm still edgy about entrusting my life to the maintenance standards of the Puerto Rican Air National Guard.

---

3. Because politics is so intense and so passionate on the island and because the stakes are so high—government jobs and contracts—Puerto Ricans discipline themselves by voting only once every four years. Held at the same time as mainlanders are choosing a president, these elections are for everything from governor down to school board trustees and city councilmen.

4. This precaution resulted from a December 1979 terrorist attack on a bus carrying U.S. Navy sailors at Sabana Seca, not far from San Juan, killing two and wounding seventeen.

Chapter 12

The Air Force 2 *Coup*

Thursday, 1 October 1981

We landed at San Francisco International Airport at 11:00 and were driven into the heart of the city to the elegant old St. Francis Hotel on Union Square. At noon, GB addressed the Commonwealth Club, perhaps the most prestigious forum in the state. I sat next to Ron Smith, a political consultant handling the reelection campaign of Sen. S. I. (Sam) Hayakawa.[1] (The Admiral kept calling him "Hiawatha.") GB gave perhaps the best speech of the year, a highly informative, reasoned, and hard-hitting appeal for Congress not to block the sale of AWACS [airborne warning and control system] radar planes to Saudi Arabia. He made a direct plea for his audience to contact their members of Congress, which is quite unusual for him.

But the prime target, uncommitted on AWACS, was snoozing away on the dais. Alarmed at the devastating "visual," Ron rose and went to the head table, pretending to give Hayakawa a message. The senator stirred, accepted Ron's business card, and went right back to sleep. Meanwhile, the larger audience was all in GB's corner. Asked, "Will there be any Bushes in the Rose Garden?" GB laughed and stepped up to the microphone. "I have always believed in hitting a tough question straight on: thank you, ladies and gentlemen!"

Thursday, 6 October 1981

While GB met in the West Wing office with former Nixon press aide Herb Klein, now publisher of the *San Diego Union*, Barbara Hayward arrived and

---

1. Hayakawa was a recognized semanticist who gained national fame as the tough president of San Francisco State College in a time of student protest. This propelled him into the Senate as a Republican in 1976. Then in his seventies, Hayakawa became known as "Sleepy Sam," notorious for nodding off during Senate hearings and public events. He retired rather than run again in 1982.

asked me if I had heard anything about an assassination attempt on President Sadat of Egypt. We turned on the radio to hear the first sketchy reports of a bizarre scene in Cairo in which Sadat and others were shot by commando units in a big military parade they were reviewing. Nancy Bearg Dyke and the [regular] CIA briefer came in with the same small information. I knocked on the door and interrupted the VP with the news. As the story grew and worsened during the day, I wondered why the VP wasn't notified much earlier by the Situation Room or CIA or whoever does such things.

At 10:30, Bob Thompson and I left with the VP in the limo for Capitol Hill and his regular Tuesday visitation there. It was raining—"crisis weather," I used to call it. Tipped off that reporters were waiting for him in the Capitol, GB phoned the Sit Room for confirmation of network reports that Sadat had died; they couldn't give it. Later, Admiral Murphy phoned the VP with word from the Sit Room confirming the news, and GB gave Senate majority leader Baker the go-ahead to announce it on the Senate floor. But the Admiral's information was faulty; the death still hadn't been officially confirmed by the Egyptian government, and Jennifer reported that unnamed White House officials were "furious" that the VP would in effect make an announcement before the President did.

GB returned to the White House for a previously scheduled luncheon with Henry Kissinger. Jennifer and I chatted with a depressed VP as the TV droned mournfully on. The CIA finally called to confirm the news that had been known for hours. Kissinger arrived, and GB introduced us. I mentioned that I had been his student in Government 180 in 1967. ("Oh, vere you?") I went to the Mess for a meal with [presidential speechwriter] Tony Dolan, but he was in and out working on the statement the President would soon deliver.

When I got back to the VP's office, I beheld a poignant scene: Bush sitting with Kissinger and Haig, all mutely staring at a TV giving the Egyptian government's official announcement of President Sadat's demise. Their silence and drawn looks spoke pages of newsprint about the possible unraveling of US policy toward and position in the Middle East, going back to Kissinger's days of shuttling between Cairo and Jerusalem. No one knows yet how stable the regime of VP [Hosni] Mubarak will be. A strong air force commander who visited with GB at the VP's Residence only the day before yesterday—and who miraculously survived today's fusillade—Mubarak may prove less of a factor in Egypt's festering internal problems.[2] Bush and Haig left the suite for a meeting, and I removed the Mess steward so that Kissinger could speak with his old boss, Richard Nixon, on the VP's phone.

Wednesday, 7 October 1981

I expressed my concern to Admiral Murphy that the VP learned of yesterday's shooting some forty minutes after the fact and from Barbara Hayward (via me), not the Sit Room. The Admiral said it is highly important that GB head the delegation sent to Cairo for Sadat's funeral. It would demonstrate his importance in the government and allow him to conduct sensitive talks with the new Egyptian leaders. Ralph Basham[3] of the VP's Secret Service detail left last night for Cairo to scope out the place.

But it was all not to be. I was sitting peacefully in my cubby while GB (I thought) was lobbying a couple more senators on the AWACS vote. Suddenly, he and Jim Baker charged into the tiny space. "Chahlie, excuse us!" GB said, and I dutifully squeezed out. Behind me I heard Baker say, "That was his decision," and GB reply, "I understand completely." The President's decision was to send his three predecessors—Nixon, Ford, and Carter—in a delegation headed by Haig. Dave Gergen fortunately told the press that security considerations eliminated sending either the President or VP, so Haig's selection won't seem like a slap. GB, good soldier he, did accept the President's decision, though late today he said that Amb. [Roy] Atherton in Cairo felt that the American delegation was still, *incredibile dictu*, "too low-level."

Thursday, 8 October 1981

Secretary of the Interior James Watt, now a hero of the Far Right, brought conservative organizer Paul Weyrich on a sort of peace probe, or at least a get-to-know-you mission. Weyrich and his spawn fiercely opposed GB's selection for VP. Both Rich Bond and Pete Teeley were banned from attending the session because, as supposed liberals on the VP's staff, their mere presence might be inflammatory. We were all curious to know what happened, but as

---

2. In fact, Mubarak would be in firm control for the next thirty years, making him one of the most durable leaders in 5,000 years of Egyptian history.

3. Basham was director of the Secret Service from 2003 to 2006.

usual GB didn't have much memory of the meeting, saying only "it was like some dogs sniffing around."

As evening approached, excitement built in the West Wing due to the sensational albeit simple send-off to Cairo that RR was going to give his three predecessors. Only three times before in the twentieth century have as many as four presidents been alive at the same time,[4] and they never got together. (The fact that four men have served as president just since 1974 bespeaks the political instability of the US during this epoch.)

Around 7:00, a Marine helo beat its way down through the early darkness to land near where I stood, and out of it came Jimmy and Rosalyn Carter, followed by Gerald Ford and then Richard Nixon. The applause rose to its height when RMN appeared; it was only his second time back at the White House since he boarded a similar helicopter on the same spot on 9 August 1974. (He attended a dinner Carter gave for Deng Xiaoping in 1979.) The group went inside for cocktails with the Reagans and Bushes.

Then, around 7:30, they emerged, escorted by President Reagan, who stepped up to a microphone and reminded us all that this was not a festive occasion. Vowing defiance of those in the world who rejoiced at the assassination of Sadat, Reagan bade his guests farewell with the Irish prayer: "May God hold you in the hollow of His hand." Looking through a mass of swaying shoulders, I was able to see the historical gathering of four presidents before they boarded the helo. Carter was closest; the blondish head of Ford farthest; Reagan at the left; and a sleek, hunched Richard Nixon at the right. As the chopper's rotors gained sufficient velocity to lift it back into the night, we all waved.

Ah, to be an invisible observer on that plane to Cairo! Three former presidents trying to make small talk in the crowded lounge, Nixon and Ford silently cursing the presence of their former assistant, Haig, in the forward cabin!

Friday, 9 October 1981

At 4:30 there was a big meeting in the Admiral's office in which [advance chief] Mike Farley walked us through the itinerary of the South America trip. The plans in Rio seem spectacular, but literally living till then will be

---

4. In 1961–63: Hoover, Truman, Eisenhower, and Kennedy; in 1963–64: Hoover, Truman, Eisenhower, and Johnson; and in early 1969: Truman, Eisenhower, Johnson, and Nixon.

a challenge. Three-quarters of the advance party came down with intestinal problems in the Dominican Republic, where students have been staging big demonstrations around the embassy for the past several days, building up to the VP's arrival Sunday. Secret Service agent Gene Thompson said rocks, bottles, and Molotov cocktails are "likely," and agent Wayne Welch said we should stay in our hotel rather than go outside. This is as much for rampant street crime as for protestors.

With this chilling assessment settling into our minds, Mike continued by saying, "Bogotá makes Santo Domingo look like a piece of cake." The M-19 guerrilla group will probably try a bombing somewhere in connection with our visit, and (as in the Dominican Republic) the kidnapping of one of us could be staged to embarrass the US. (Last year M-19 held a houseful of ambassadors hostage in the Dominican embassy for two months.)

Pete Teeley said that in both Santo Domingo and Bogotá we could find ourselves in "a Richard Nixon–type situation" (a reference to the riots against the then-VP in Caracas and Lima in 1958), which would be disastrous for GB even if no one were harmed. "I mean, what the hell are we doing there?" Everyone, the Admiral included, grunted agreement, but of course the trip will proceed. Joe Hagin summed up the mood as we left the meeting: "I couldn't believe it: a roomful of adults told they would be going into a dangerous situation, and they're still going ahead with it."

Saturday, 10 October 1981

On the eve of the VP's thirty-sixth trip of the year, his fifth abroad, my mood is one of excitement and unease. I have no way of knowing how much real danger awaits us in Santo Domingo and Bogotá or whether all the scare talk is like the warnings given people against walking alone at night in Washington, DC, which I've done since arriving here without incident. I don't mind a *little* adventure, however. *Vaya con Diós.*

Sunday, 11 October 1981

AF2 came over the rugged mountains of Hispaniola and made a wide circle over the Caribbean off Santo Domingo. When we landed, we saw the first of what would be saturating security: troops, rifles at the ready, their backs to us, keeping a watch into the underbrush. The sun was searing when we in the official party (including Deputy Assistant Secretary of State Ted Briggs and Roger Fontaine of the National Security Council) came down the ramp and walked along a red carpet. A radio-like announcer called us all off by name, including Don Moorphy, Zhenifair Fitzgeróld, and of course Zhorj Hairbairt Walkair Boosh. (My own name was completely unrecognizable.) There were military honors, including a sporadically fired nineteen-gun salute before an exchange of remarks by GB and his opposite number, Dominican VP Jácobo Antonio Guzmán, candidate of the ruling party for president in next year's elections.

The route into town goes right along the Caribbean, a rich blue, fringed by palm trees. There was scattered graffiti which the government hadn't yet removed, saying *"Fuera Bush!"* (Bush out!) and *"Agente de la CIA."* Chris Buckley claims to have seen *"Sadista y Criminál,"* which is of course much better. Any concern we had about being caught in a violent demonstration— at least today—evaporated upon seeing the large number of uniformed personnel mustered for our benefit, soldiers standing before any appreciable group of people with weapons drawn. Once I saw a *soldado* watching an old couple on their porch. If anything, the reaction of bystanders was friendly, with nary a bottle tossed.

Due to hurricanes and uninspired modern Latin architecture executed on a low budget, very little of Santo Domingo has any appeal. The best part by far is the Zona Colonial, where a careful effort has succeeded in making the buildings look as they must have in the sixteenth through eighteenth centuries. Our last stop was the cathedral, oldest in the Americas, begun in 1521. Its columns and vaulted ceilings are made of pink coral, and in its narthex is the Spanish-Victorian tomb of Columbus. There is a debate whether the great navigator's remains are really here or in Seville, but it's the thought that counts.

After a violence-free official visit to the Dominican Republic, the vice presidential party proceeded to Colombia.

Tuesday, 13 October 1981

We flew through a long valley between the Cordilleras and landed at Bogotá at 10:45 a.m. The placid green farms and distant mountains on our approach seemed German. So were the spiked helmets on the Presidential Guard mustered at the military airport to greet us, looking like real toy soldiers. To discourage any ambush by M-19, we boarded zippy Colombian helicopters for the fifteen-minute ride into the city. Whatever anxiety I had over riding in such things was suppressed by paying attention to the scenery and the approach of Bogotá proper. Unlike Caracas,[5] which is hemmed in by two mountain ranges, Bogotá sits in a broad valley, backed by a magnificent green range. High-rises are therefore less common, and the city maintains a scale in which old architecture can both survive and be appreciated. We got a superb view of central Bogotá as the helos circled El Nariño, the presidential palace. The smaller buildings have red tile roofs, and many of the larger ones are built in the solid handsome style of eighteenth- and nineteenth-century Europe. I felt very much as if I were at last truly in South America.

When our helo touched down, we jumped out and were startled to see a 50-caliber machine gun emplacement, fully manned, right nearby. The roofs of neighboring buildings had soldiers on them, and troops had apparently cleared all the streets in the vicinity of the palace. We were led down gold-hued corridors to a drawing room, which would be the staff hangout while the VP conferred with President Julio César Turbay.

Later, in black tie, we returned to El Nariño for President Turbay's dinner in honor of his American guest. The broad-flagstoned grounds were rainswept and floodlit. The scene both outside and inside was one of grand but simple elegance. The Colombians present were poised, attractive, and friendly, especially when I spoke *en español*. The only odd element about the evening—and it was jarring—was the constant, loud, and bouncy playing of popular tunes on an organ. It was the same music one would have heard at a ballpark or roller rink. (Why not a piano?) The organist kept at it even during the toasts, carried on live TV.

Wednesday, 14 October 1981

The motorcade took us to the playing field of the Cavalry School, where waited a squadron of helicopters. Security in the two toughest places on this trip, Santo Domingo and Bogotá, proved to be superb, making me wonder if the Secret Service was crying wolf last Friday when we staffers were briefed. Jennifer suspects it was all a trick by the Service to have maximum control over the trip, "because they know they've got a real creampuff" [meaning

---

5. VP Bush and party had visited the very modern Venezuelan capital on 2–3 October to attend the funeral of Rómulo Betancourt, the man who restored democracy in Venezuela in 1958.

GB]. Then came the hop to the airport, the spike-helmeted honor guard, the twirling batons of the two bandmasters, farewells from President and Señora Turbay, and a 9:30 takeoff from Bogotá. BPB, looking quite peaked (the effect of a lifelong aversion to altitude), went immediately to bed, sleeping through the entire four-and-a-half-hour journey to Brasilia.

The Secret Service does plan for the worst and expect not much better. In the case of this particular trip, their concern was validated a few days later when 22 pounds of dynamite were found at the end of the Bogotá airfield. It was unclear at the time whether M-19 truly intended to blow up Air Force 2 on takeoff and was foiled by our using another runway or whether they planted the dynamite after we left to show what they could have done. Agent Ralph Basham later told me that their investigation pointed to the latter, a mere PR stunt.

AF2 flew over thick clouds that parted just in time to catch sight of a broad, pale Amazon 33,000 feet below. Toward 4:00, AF2 came in over the bright red clay hills of Brazil's Planalto (high plains) to land at the twenty-year-old capital city of Brasilia. I suppose only foreign government officials see Brazil first through Brasilia; everyone else goes through Rio and São Paulo. During the flight, the old samba "Brazil" was constantly playing on the tape recorder of my mind. Brasilia on first exposure doesn't quite seem Brazilian, at least in the Copacabana sense. And yet its mere existence is a powerful statement of this nation's idea of itself.

The brand-new US ambassador, Langhorne (Tony) Motley,[6] came aboard to greet us. There were airport honors, rushed through before an angry rain-cloud reached us. We quickly boarded cars for the ride to the ambassador's remote residence. The rain struck, a furious "whitewater" inundation that a shaken Ted Briggs called "a biblical storm." I playfully reminded him of what I said was an old Brazilian song:

Though October showers may come your way,
They bring the flowers that bloom in November.

---

6. Motley was born in Rio of an American father and Brazilian mother. After serving in the US Air Force, he forged a successful career in Alaska real estate. A fluent Portuguese speaker, he exemplified the best of "noncareer" ambassadors. The State Department, usually scornful (or at best tolerant) of "political appointees," paid him and his wife, Judy, the supreme compliment of having them instruct new ambassadors, including career officers. From 1983 to 1985, Motley served as assistant secretary of state for Inter-American Affairs.

After a briefing at the Motleys' dining room table, we drove to the center of governmental Brasilia, that compote of ultramodern architecture that is this city's fame. Brasilia's plan is in the shape of a swept-wing airplane, the "nose" being the Praça dos Tres Poderes, or Plaza of the Three Powers (executive, legislative, and judicial). We went to the Planalto Palace, the White House of Brazil (though the president lives in the graceful Palace of the Dawn), supported by the patented Brasilia arches. The VP entered through a line of soldiers in white uniforms and tall plumed helmets. Inside, he met with acting president Aureliano Chaves, ordinarily the VP of Brazil. When President João Figueiredo (a general) recently suffered a heart attack—one so bad he will leave in a few days for surgery in Cleveland—the behind-the-scenes military rulers of Brazil decided to let Chaves become in effect the first civilian president since 1964.[7]

We returned to the residence to change into black tie for dinner at Itamaraty Palace, perhaps the loveliest of Brasilia's ministerial halls and the one occupied by the Foreign Ministry (Relaçoés Exteriores, the first word pronounced "ray-lah-*soinj*" in the curious, wonderful Portuguese way). The name comes from the nineteenth-century building which used to house the Foreign Ministry in Rio. Roger Fontaine told me that the highly professional Brazilian foreign service insisted on getting a beautiful building in Brasilia before they relocated to the interior.

On a terrace we all had drinks, the most popular being cachaça, the Brazilian firewater, made of coconut water and sugarcane brandy. We dined on pheasant and quindim, a rich coconut dessert. The acting VP of Brazil, Nelson Marchezan, president of the Chamber of Deputies, gave a friendly speech in which he expressed hope that the Reagan Administration would demonstrate a "spirit of renewal" in Brazilian-American relations. This fit with GB's great unstated mission on this part of his trip, which is to assure the Brazilians that the US looks on them as an equal in world affairs, not as a little sister from the days of the Good Neighbor Policy. The dinner ended early by Brazilian standards (about 11:00), and after cafezinho (the wonderful, rich, strong "Arabian" coffee served in demitasses with lots of sugar and no cream) we mounted the motorcade. Despite the coffee, I dozed all the way back to the residence.

Lt. Col. Mike Fry and I closed the evening having a very relaxed and enjoyable chat with Tony and Judy Motley. Clearly one of the best benefits

---

7. Brazil did not become a full-fledged democracy until 1989.

of staying in the residence is getting to know them personally. After some cheerful words with the solid, stolid men of the Secret Service on their lonely watch, I went to sleep.

Thursday, 15 October 1981

The strain of the trip and the crush of crowds in today's official events in Brasilia is showing on the VP. BPB gave me the first tip that he is thinking of leaving Rio tomorrow early, flying through the night to get back to DC rather than go directly to Williamsburg [for meetings with the French]. Ostensibly this is so that staff not needed in Williamsburg can spend the weekend at home. But everyone would rather have a full night in Rio, where a dinner and a gala floorshow have been laid on for the traveling party. Our votes don't count, however, and by evening GB had given the order to leave early. This may prove his most unpopular decision of the year.

Friday, 16 October 1981

As soon as the VP's press conference [in Brasilia] ended, I hurried onto SAM 86972 singing, "My Rio / Rio by the sea-o / flying down to Rio where there's rhythm and rhyme."[8] The 707 flew along the Atlantic coast before making a turn toward the great landmarks of Rio de Janeiro, most notably Sugarloaf (Pão de Açucar). It was a hazy, mostly cloudy day, yet the excitement of finally reaching one of the world's most ideally situated cities was strong. (The others I place in this category are San Francisco, Sydney, and Capetown.) We landed at Galeão Airport, remembered from a 1960s bossa nova song and located on an island in Guanabara Bay. A small corps of syncopated-stepping Brazilian airmen approached the ramp, and a bugler blew honors for the VP. We staffers rode in a fancy Italian bus, our enthusiasm rising as we came deeper and deeper into a city of splendidly jumbled architecture, nineteenth-century baroque interspersed among glassy skyscrapers, and greenery of all sorts (including very tall palms) everywhere.

The motorcade drew up alongside the posh Rio Palace Hotel on storied Copacabana Beach, which had its requisite number of tanned, lean bodies in the thick white sand. After GB addressed the annual meeting of the Inter-

---

8. "Flying Down to Rio" by Vincent Youmans, introduced by Fred Astaire in the 1933 movie of the same name.

American Press Association, a group of us, with limited time, went to the most spectacular sight of all: the Christ the Redeemer statue atop Corcovado (Hunchback) Mountain, which opened exactly fifty years ago this week. There, all Rio lay 2,000 feet below us.

GB spoke to employees at the US consulate general, after which we went to the Brazilian naval academy, located at the old Santos Dumont Airport on an island connected to the mainland by a small arched bridge. Tied up at the pier was the 50-foot *Tamarind*, a sleek yacht owned by a Rio publisher and TV magnate. We embarked on a sunset cruise around Guanabara Bay. Rio behaved just as she ought: Sugarloaf looming, Corcovado's statue glowing, and all the buildings sparkling.

Tamarind docked and discharged a staff delighted with the cruise to the point of forgetting the nightclub dinner and floorshow that had to be cancelled by the VP's decision to leave tonight for DC. Well, not completely forgetting.

Once *AF2* had taken off from Galeão, we in the forward cabin were startled by rising voices aft. Chris Buckley was on the PA system, pretending to be spokesman for a junta deposing "the Vishnu" (GB), ordering the execution of Admiral Murphy and me as "enemies of the people," and calling for *vivas* for the new Vishnu, Pedro Te-ley. Up came Pete wearing a leather jacket, a Secret Service holster, Mike Fry's Army hat, Joe Hagin's sunshades, orange *AF2* napkins tied to form a sash, and a penciled mustache. At his side was Ed Pollard, who had defected to the new Vishnu. Chris read off the names of the junta and cried for "More beds! Less speeches!" When a laughing VP looked, a single piece of bread and a glass of ice water had been placed before him. Mugshot pictures were taken by Joe, and a good laugh had by everyone. But as dinner and bedtime came, we were still flying up from Rio.

Chapter 13

Shutdown!

October 1981 marked the bicentennial of George Washington's victory over Lord Cornwallis at the Battle of Yorktown, winning the Revolutionary War and securing American independence. The victory was made possible by the bottling up of the British fleet in Chesapeake Bay by units of the French navy under the Comte de Grasse, thus preventing Cornwallis's escape. To celebrate this early apogee of Franco-American relations, François Mitterrand came to Williamsburg, Virginia, near Yorktown. It was another opportunity for him to get to know the two men whose presidencies of the United States would be overlapped by his presidency of France.

Saturday, 17 October 1981

The Bushes arrived, followed by President Mitterrand. A fife and drum corps in colonial garb announced the two men and gave tinny renditions of the national anthems.

Toward 8:00, refreshed and spruced up, Jennifer and I were driven to Providence Hall, the handsome wooden colonial building where the Bushes are staying, for their dinner in honor of President and Mrs. Mitterrand. It was elegant but relaxed in the Bush fashion. There was candlelight, a husky-voiced female singer and guitarist, waiters in knee britches, and a menu that featured pumpkin soup and baby pheasant. The singer was charming, the food ample, and the bonhomie real. To my right was Adm. Philippe de Gaulle, a hauntingly perfect copy of his late father. Also on hand was Jean-Bernard Manceron, an old man with a wild white beard, a polio victim in a wheelchair who is official historian of the Mitterrand government. GB read a graceful toast, to which Mitterrand responded ad lib and warmly. But, as GB noted, it was 3:00 a.m. in Paris, and the French were ready for bed.

Sunday, 18 October 1981

USS *Comte de Grasse* was at anchor in Chesapeake Bay off Yorktown in a special squadron of US, French, and even British ships mustered for the battle commemoration. Visiting the ship was a marvelous excursion, the sort of thing that fits the fun-loving world of George Bush but which was a rare privilege, especially for us retired lieutenants (junior grade).

Marine 2 lifted straight over the Williamsburg Inn golf course and crossed to Yorktown above a splendid multicolored canopy of tall trees. The helo circled "the Count" and landed on its flight deck with not much surface to spare. As soon as the vice presidential foot hit the deck, his white flag was "broken" on the forward mast. Sideboys and a bo's'n piper awaited him inside the hangar. The VP was welcomed by the destroyer's commanding officer, Cdr. Philip Dur, who had worked at the Pentagon with Admiral Murphy and Nancy Bearg Dyke.[1] Already on board were SecNav John Lehman and Vice Adm. James (Ace) Lyons, commander of the Second Fleet.

GB was presented with the standard plaque, flight jacket, and "baseball-type" cap. Then we began a tour of the DD (destroyer). During the Vietnam War, a DD was something like [my ship] *Benner*, a World War II relic. *Comte de Grasse* (launched in 1976) has this designation, yet she also has missiles and an onboard manned helo. On the mess decks, the VP thanked the crew for their sacrifices and assured them that the Reagan Administration wants to strengthen US defenses. Secretary Lehman, clever lad, told the men that the VP, working behind the scenes, was responsible for their recent pay raise.

We staffers boarded the helo ahead of the VP, who was boyishly excited and expansive as he climbed aboard and we lifted off. How lucky I am: Rio de Janeiro on Friday, dinner with the president of France on Saturday, and a drop-in on a destroyer on Sunday. I must enjoy these "ruffles and flourishes" while I may; when GB is either president of the United States or a private citizen, we (= I) won't be doing so many grand things at such a pace.

---

1. Six years later, then-Captain Dur anchored his command, the cruiser *Yorktown*, off Kennebunkport, Maine, to the delight of the townsfolk and their most distinguished summer residents.

Monday, 19 October 1981

At 10:00 the VP was visited by Helmut Kohl, the probable CDU-CSU [Christian Democratic Union–Christian Social Union] candidate for chancellor in the next West German elections. Speaking in German, Kohl proved expansive but professorial, giving long answers to simple questions. When, for example, GB asked about rising anti-Americanism and neutralism in Europe, he received a fifteen-minute lecture on German history from the time of Frederick the Great. Germany has had alternate periods of looking east and west, Kohl said, but the German people today are deeply committed to NATO. So is François Mitterrand: "He may have communists in his government, but he doesn't want East German troops on the banks of the River Rhine opposite Strasbourg." The young people of Europe don't have fresh memories of the Red Army or of the hunger that gripped Europe after the war, Kohl said. He applauded the Reagan Administration's determination to "restore America to its proper strength" and said that if the Left's anti-US sentiment reaches great proportions, his party will confront the issue and prompt a national debate. If Germans are forced to choose, Kohl said, they will stay with the West. The Bush-Kohl meeting ran a half hour overtime with another lecture, this one on East Germany.

This was the first meeting between two men who would become close working partners during their time in power and close friends ever after. Kohl's personality proved far more appealing to Reagan and Bush than that of the arrogant Helmut Schmidt. He would become chancellor in 1982, and (as will be seen) VP Bush made a veritable campaign appearance for him in Germany in January–February 1983, a month before national elections swept by the CDU-CSU coalition. Kohl became chancellor of a united Germany in 1990 and served until 1998.

Tuesday, 20 October 1981

A half hour after the VP left for home, the Admiral convened a meeting in his office, with the bar open. It was perhaps the most valuable staff conversation of the year to date. He said neither he nor GB wants to upset the White House and State Department (meaning Secretary Haig) by appearing to do more than spread smiles and goodwill abroad. Still, the Admiral feels GB must travel overseas to interpret Reagan Administration policy in a way that's not being done. I doubt the White House will be mad if GB takes a more vigorous stance, so long as he doesn't embarrass the Administration. Yet he has a tunnel-vision idea that he will succeed in this government by not "blowing on," by doing his job, and by cultivating his personal relationship with Reagan.

In what was the most interesting insight of the day, Admiral Murphy said that RR has a good personal relationship with the whole wide world: "He's as warm to me as he is with the Vice President, and he doesn't treat Meese or Deaver any better than he does some guy off the street." The Admiral's point is that GB may be deluding himself in thinking he has close ties with RR. A corollary is that the VP can do a whole lot more, becoming bolder in his efforts to help the Administration, and RR would benignly bless it.

Pete Teeley worries about a personality trait in GB that manifested itself in the disastrous debate with Reagan at Nashua, New Hampshire, in February 1981[2]—the dogged determination to stick to his commitments and plow straight ahead. Technically and morally he may be right, but politically he may be heading for the reef. We all recognize that our biggest task is to convince GB he must be more assertive.

Wednesday, 28 October 1981

Today, for the first time in several days, the weather was fresh and sunny as I walked to work. Less so was a Lynn Rossellini profile on GB in the *New York Times*, which said he had "dropped from sight" in the Administration. David Gergen unhelpfully said the VP concentrates on just a few topics at a time, and an anonymous aide said he is "not included in the paper loop" of documents going to the President. Another nameless neighbor [in the White House] said GB hasn't worked hard for the President's programs. (I wonder what Mr. X thinks we've been doing on those dozens of trips around the country?) A better piece, by Lars-Erik Nelson in the *New York Post*, lamented that GB hadn't been involved more in AWACS and other foreign policy issues.

Inasmuch as we'll be gone the next few weekends, I tended to deskwork

---

2. The *Nashua Telegraph* sponsored a debate between Reagan and Bush, the top contenders in the presidential primary to be held a few days later. When the other candidates showed up, Reagan was willing to let them participate, but Bush was not, insisting that the newspaper's invitation be honored. This made Reagan appear open and confident and Bush appear crabby and old-school.

and declined a chance to sit in the gallery when the Senate voted this afternoon on the sale of $8.5 billion worth of arms, especially the controversial AWACS radar planes, to Saudi Arabia. The number of bodies scurrying through the halls of the West Wing increased. SecState Haig arrived, hailing me and assistant presidential press secretary David Prosperi with a hearty "Hello, lads!" as he passed. The radio brought the wondrous word that the Senate voted 52–48 to disapprove a resolution blocking the sale, a narrow but stellar victory for the President. The vote bolsters our reputation for reliability in the world.

Thursday, 29 October 1981

This afternoon GB received Prince Bandar of Saudi Arabia.[3] He was the royal family's personal lobbyist on AWACS. Possessed of an Americanized sense of humor, he said with mock horror that a terrible mistake had been made: "Five AWACS? What we wanted were five Big Macs!"

My main project was to draft the remarks GB will give Sunday at the big rally for [GOP gubernatorial candidate] Tom Kean in Paramus, New Jersey. This is the only real speech I've done (to give a hand to Chris Buckley during a busy week), and it is a doozy: a hard-hitting attack on the Democrats and their candidate, Congressman Jim Florio, for being tied to old ideas and programs. It was written to be spoken, so I concentrated on rhythm, applause lines, and alliterations like calling Florio "a parrot of the past." The Admiral and Chris liked it; we'll see if GB will go through with it. I think the partisans in Paramus will love it.

Sunday, 31 October 1981

On the ride to Paramus, Ron Kaufman predicted that Kean will beat Florio by four points. Today Kean picked up the endorsement of the *Camden Courier* in Florio's hometown. We went to something called the Imperial Manor Catering Hall, where a Kaufman-whipped-up crowd was waiting both inside and out. A uniformed high school band was performing as the motorcade pulled in, and a kiddie corps of fifers and drummers played as the Bushes entered the hall. GB delivered the speech I wrote, shortened and toned down

---

3. Prince Bandar would serve as Saudi ambassador to the US from 1983 to 2005, during four American presidencies.

by Teeley, to about a thousand pure Republican and Kean loyalists. It wasn't the excision of my finger-waving phrases but GB's lack of preparation that made his performance flat. He's just got to practice more than fifteen minutes before landing.

Either because of or despite the VP's oratory, Kean was elected governor of New Jersey two days later in the closest gubernatorial election in the state's history to that time.

Monday, 2 November 1981

I walked over to the East Room for a special treat the White House social office offered to us staffers. Along with just a few others, I sat on a golden chair and heard Benny Goodman, seventy-two, rehearsing with a small combo for tonight's state dinner for King Hussein of Jordan. The jazz great smoothly delivered two signature numbers: "Don't Be That Way" and "Stompin' at the Savoy."

Saturday, 7 November 1981

The Nebraska-Oklahoma game was by far the biggest thing happening in the Cornhusker State today, and a vice presidential visit to Lincoln had to be structured accordingly. At Pershing Auditorium, several hundred Nebraska Republicans were gathered at a fundraising lunch, eating in semi-darkness as the game was shown on several big TV screens around the hall. The first half ended with "Big Red" leading 17–0, so the crowd was in a good mood. Out for the halftime entertainment came George Herbert Walker Bush. In his flat twang, Gov. Charles Thone asked for "a rising, rousing N'braska welcome" for the VP, who proceeded to give an ad lib performance that played well to conservative hearts. How great to have a state with fewer people than Harris County [Texas]!

Then there was that odd thing, three hours of pure "down time" back at the hotel till the next event. Taking advantage of Lincoln's long straight streets, I walked a mile or so to Nebraska's striking skyscraper capitol, the "Tower on the Plains," built between 1922 and 1932. I copied down an unattributed motto carved in stone above the entrance to the building: "The salvation of the state is watchfulness in the citizen." This sums up something I've long felt about the area of the country between the Great Lakes and the Pacific Northwest: it is better governed because it has better citizens.

Later, in Minneapolis, we went to the Carleton Hotel for the big dinner for Sen. Dave Durenberger (R-Minnesota). The show featured not just politicians but also musical comedy great Carol Channing. Obviously on hand for pay rather than politics, Channing let slip "my friends the Kennedys, the Carters, and of course dear, late President Johnson."[4] Wearing a ludicrously feathered hat, she sang "Hello, Dolly!" and her original trademark number, "Diamonds Are a Girl's Best Friend," tossing rhinestones out into the crowd. Later she brought out a birthday cake for Durenberger's junior colleague, the irrepressible Sen. Rudy Boschwitz. With that, our hectic Midwest trip ended. (Minnesota was the thirty-first state the VP has been in this year.)

Monday, 9 November 1981

From my window at noon I had a perfect view of the happy/sad return of press secretary Jim Brady to the White House for ceremonies marking the opening of the remodeled press room [named in his honor]. Severely wounded with the President on 30 March, Brady was brought to West Executive Avenue in a van configured to carry a wheelchair. Jim's left side is still paralyzed, and Pete Teeley said he hasn't fully regained control of his emotions. But Brady appeared happy to be back in the White House. Waiting for him as the special ramp door lowered the wheelchair were Larry Speakes and Karna Small, Jim's former colleagues in the press office. It was an emotional moment for everyone, magnified when Brady entered the press room and the Reagans joined him. Clearly it will be a very long time, maybe never, till Brady can function as press secretary.

Wednesday, 11 November 1981

My main chore was reading the fascinating and now extremely controversial article "The Education of David Stockman" in the just-released issue of the *Atlantic Monthly*. It was written by William Greider, an associate editor of the *Washington Post*, based on breakfast conversations with the budget director that were supposedly off the record. The brutally honest, direct quotations chart Stockman's speedy passage from convinced "supply-sider" to despondent, worldly-wise government official who saw craven vote-buying on the tax bill kill any chance for a balanced budget in our time. The quotations

---

4. In 1964, Channing happily sang "Hello, Lyndon" to boost his election over Barry Goldwater.

have Stockman saying he really didn't know what effect his policies would have on the economy when they were spun out at the start of the year; that "the numbers" used were meaningless; and that the tax bill was "a Trojan horse," selling cuts for the rich by cutting rates for everyone. The Democrats have jumped with glee on these confessions, and the prime topic now is whether Stockman is out. I wonder why anyone as politically astute as he would allow himself to babble on to a reporter for the Administration's chief news critic. Maybe Stockman *wants* to be fired or to resign to atone for his confessed sins.

Thursday, 12 November 1981

GB called me in to go over the *Atlantic* story. He wanted a sound command of the article for a meeting in the Oval Office with the President on the Stockman crisis. "Very serious" was all he could say. I don't know what role GB played today other than he was very active. Perhaps he could see in a threat to Stockman a threat to others—such as the popularizer of the phrase "voodoo economics"[5]—who share his doubts over the efficacy of the Reagan economic program.

At 4:30, Stockman held a press conference which Barbara Hayward, Jennifer, and I watched. With a quavering voice, the OMB director announced that at a searing lunch with the President he offered his resignation—which RR, after delivering a suitable dressing-down, refused to accept. What was both painful and remarkable was Stockman's saying he had been "careless" and witless in having those extensive breakfast meetings with Greider of the *Post*. If he gains a little humility of this, Stockman will be a better man. But the furor continues, heated up by Democrats asking whether Stockman's utility on the Hill is dead. The word everyone was using today was "credibility."

At 5:00, I sat in on GB's meeting in the Roosevelt Room with Norwegian foreign minister Sven Stray. He has only recently taken his portfolio, after the election of a conservative government. Stray is tall, bald, and of radiantly sunny disposition. The VP commenced talking about anti-NATO demonstrations in Europe, and after five to ten minutes [national security advisor] Richard Allen burst through the door, saying, "The President!" We all rose, and Ronald Reagan glided into the room. There was much hand-

---

5. Namely himself, in his victorious Pennsylvania primary campaign against Reagan in April 1980. The deathless phrase was the creation of Pete Teeley.

shaking, bowing, and beaming. RR praised the new prime minister's "speech of November 3rd," a nugget that Dick no doubt prepped the President to drop. The President also spoke of "a great American hero." Stray, thinking this a reference to the [space shuttle] *Columbia* astronauts successfully launched today, offered his congratulations. "I was thinking of someone earlier," Reagan said. "A man named Knute Rockne." This got an instant laugh from everyone, remembering that Reagan starred in the football flick *Knute Rockne—All American* in 1940. The President's little drop-in was brief and unearth-shattering, and yet it was undeniably thrilling, further proof of the magical aura of the presidency.

Friday, 13 November 1981

GB invited Jennifer and me to ride in the limo, where topic A was the David Stockman affair. To the VP, Stockman's foolish revelations to William Greider underscore his (Bush's) yearlong dismay with White House officials who conduct interviews on "background." Later, aboard the plane, GB invited me to sit in the seat opposite his to continue the discussion. He asked me whether I thought Stockman would survive, and I said yes, though if the sentiment on the Hill grows that the OMB director lacks "credibility," he might then have to quit.

GB told more of his personal involvement in *l'affaire* Stockman. On Wednesday, on his own initiative, he called Stockman to get his side of the story. Next he called Baker and Meese and was surprised that neither had phoned their embattled cohort; indeed, they made fun of the incident. That's why GB then acted as volunteer grand intermediary. Yesterday, after our joint review of the Greider piece, he saw the President and arranged for Stockman to do the same. The VP told Stockman he had a lunch date with RR and took the opportunity to counsel him to resign. The budget director did a double take, and GB continued that he didn't know how the President would react; Reagan was reportedly furious. But Stockman was given the second chance that was due. GB said he also asked Stockman if there might be more damaging material on any of Greider's tapes, such as unkind references to individuals, and he said yes. It was a fascinating glimpse into how GB tries to make himself useful in the Reagan White House, drawing on his experience in past governments.

Although Stockman remained until the end of Reagan's first term, he was much diminished from the days of his veritable godhood in early 1981. At the time, I shared the view that Stockman's genius was irreplaceable and thought the President's decision to keep him was wise. But on reflection I now believe that Reagan should have fired Stockman as an assertion of his leadership, as a demonstration that no man is indispensable, and as a warning to potential leakers. As Voltaire wrote in Candide, *noting the execution in 1757 of a British admiral who lost a battle to the French, "It is a good thing to kill an admiral from time to time to encourage the others."*

Around 11:45 we came in over the brown, treeless plains of West Texas, pockmarked with drill sites. Rising in the middle of them is a nodule of skyscrapers that is Midland, the Bushes' home from 1948 to 1959. Waiting on the ground for us was the VP's son George, Jack Steel, and Betty Green of our Houston office. After a barbecue lunch in the Permian Basin Petroleum Museum, the VP proceeded outside for the dedication ceremony. There was a surprisingly small crowd, half of which was a high school band. This made it easier for GB to give the remarks I had written, a warm testimony to his and Barbara's days in West Texas, followed by the statement that the Reagan Administration, unlike its predecessor, "doesn't look upon the oil industry as an enemy of the people."

When the ceremony ended, we went to George's house. Laura is in Baylor Hospital in Dallas with complications (possibly severe) in her advanced pregnancy with twins. BPB was with her today, missing the Midland events but later joining us in Lubbock. The VP, George, some Secret Service agents, and I suited up for a run, which we did on the track of a junior high school. George and I immediately ran ahead of his dad, but after a while George, being a daily long-distance runner, cut out ahead of me. Though I did thirteen laps, longer than either Bush did, it was not an easy run because of the barbecue and the sun.

The forty-minute flight to Lubbock was a party in best Texas tradition. On board were George, the Bushes' Midland friends the Holts and Alldays, and Congressman and Mrs. Kent Hance, the Democrat who beat "Little George" in 1978.[6] We landed at Reese AFB outside Lubbock, where I immediately went to the holding room to pass a message to the White House staff. The person who answered was Jim Baker, which was useful, because GB

---

6. One of the most skillful and delightful characters in modern Texas politics, Hance later became a Republican state officeholder and chancellor of his alma mater, Texas Tech University, in Lubbock.

entered just then and was able to speak with him. They discussed the newest White House staff flap: a revelation by a Japanese newspaper that Dick Allen accepted and kept a $1,000 "honorarium" for an interview he had arranged with Nancy Reagan. It seems innocent, Allen simply forgetting about the money and locking it away in a safe. But it's especially unhelpful now.

Before going to bed [in Houston,] I watched *Bedtime for Bonzo*, the classic flick starring Ronald Reagan and a trained chimp, which I saw as a boy when it came out in 1950. It was astounding to see the man who is now president of the United States, even a thirty-year-old version thereof, in a film comedy. The man I see nowadays around the office is slower and more dignified, but the mannerisms of both are exactly the same. The film closed with the cast of players, and "Ronald Reagan" looked ridiculously out of place.

Wednesday, 18 November 1981

AF2 landed in Detroit at 4:15. Secret Service intelligence of Libyan assassins loose somewhere in the US, with a hit list that includes the President and VP, meant that for the first time on a domestic trip we had a CAT (counterassault team) car right behind the control car [in which I ride]. These are the rough-and-ready gang of the Secret Service, who wear flak jackets and baseball-style caps. Their job is to stay and fight the bad guys while the limo is hustled to safety. Not Libyans but a bad wreck forced us to take an alternative route to the "Ren Cen" (Renaissance Center) for tonight's series of events for Gov. Bill Milliken.

I sat in on a rarefied meeting the VP had in his elegant aerie with Secretary of Commerce Mac Baldrige and Phillip Caldwell, chairman of Ford Motor Company. I took notes for Boyden Gray's benefit on their discussion on revising the Clean Air Act. The only quotable line was Caldwell's, describing local economic conditions: "Life is pretty tough in the cookie factory."

When we landed at Andrews at a little after 11:00, Baldrige came aboard the helo. "Bush, you sure know how to travel," commented the Nebraska-Connecticut cowboy. He is one of the best members of a strong Cabinet.

Friday, 20 November 1981

After I reported on a few items to GB, he asked me to close the door and then asked if I'd like to go up to Camp David tomorrow. Though I'll have to cancel some plans, it was an irresistible invitation; who knows whether the chance will come again?

Saturday, 21 November 1981

Dressed in jeans and a sweater, I arrived at the Naval Observatory simultaneously with *Marine 2*. Already there, also in warm casual clothes, were Jennifer, Lt. Col. Mike Fry, and Lt. Eric Louie, a Navy doc. Soon we were joined by the VP, his college friend (and fellow Bonesman) Tom Moseley of Cleveland, Doro Bush, her friend and my secretary Liz Grundy, Don Rhodes,[7] and C. Fred the cocker spaniel. Barbara Bush is visiting Ghana with Loret Ruppe, director of the Peace Corps, marking its twentieth anniversary in the first country to take volunteers. We were all in a holiday mood about our special outing.

The helo lifted off and flew up over the District [of Columbia] and the placid, reddish-brown farmland of Maryland. About a half hour later, we landed in the thickly forested preserve in the Catoctin Mountains that is formally and sonorously called the Presidential Retreat. In 1942, Franklin Roosevelt selected one of three camps built in the 1930s by the CCC [Civilian Conservation Corps] and WPA [Works Progress Administration] for his weekend getaway spot. He nicknamed it Shangri-La after James Hilton's mythical Himalayan kingdom. President Eisenhower changed it to Camp David in honor of his grandson (now the husband of the former Julie Nixon). The Navy runs Camp David, with Marines providing security. A commander met us at the helipad with a small motorcade of golf carts driven by sailors. After we drove off, aviation crews moved our chopper into a fully equipped hangar.

The carts took us over perfectly maintained asphalt byways through stands of trees shorn of their leaves. The VP was delivered to Cottonwood Lodge, across from Aspen, which is for the President's sole use. We all regrouped right away for the short hike to the skeet shooting range behind the helipad. The range is a Marine Corps activity, and its telephone rang repeatedly, summoning the VP [to discuss the brewing showdown with Congress over the budget]. Both GB and Tom are excellent shots who had a close-fought battle that the boss eventually won. Doro and I vied to see who could miss the most clay pigeons; we tied at zero-all.

---

7. Don was a Texas Aggie who in decades of loyal, anonymous service was the Bush family comptroller, paymaster, odd-jobber, and even archivist. Until the US government assumed charge of George Bush's personal papers, they were stashed in boxes in Don's house on the north side of Houston. One Bush friend had a test whenever name-droppers bragged about being close to "George and Barbara." She would ask if they also knew Don Rhodes. If they responded feebly, she knew for a fact they were lying.

I surged back, however, in the next event, which was jogging. The VP and I ran along the perimeter of the camp, its boundary unmistakable: there are two lengths of chain-link fencing topped with bladed coils of ugly but effective concertina wire. In between these fences is an electrified wire. Marines in fatigues, shouldering rifles, patrolled it on foot, halting to render the VP a smart salute and bark "Good morning, sir!" as we ran past.

After a change of clothes, we all gathered in Laurel Lodge, the ten-year-old dining and conference facility, where a big fire was going. With no objections from any of us, GB asked if we'd be willing to spend the night. None of us had come prepared for an overnight, but the joy of added hours at Camp David erased this concern. [The Navy provided necessary toiletries.] We lunched on crab salad and quiche, served by Filipino stewards, and watched the latest James Bond flick, *For Your Eyes Only*. It was silly in the usual gizmo-filled, derring-do way, but the former director of Central Intelligence loved it all. Afterward, we staffers took bicycles on the perimeter road, which has some steep inclines. The day was gray, but having Camp David all to ourselves made everything perfect.

I am alone in Red Oak Lodge, a relatively new and attractive "cabin" with a sloping roof, picture windows, a deck, a fireplace, two bedrooms, two baths, and a small kitchen stocked with canned drinks and snacks. (SecState Haig stayed in Red Oak earlier this year.) The only sound came from the rustle of leafless trees etched against the last light of day.

At 7:30 we came together at Laurel for drinks and dinner (steak and baked potato), followed by another movie. This was *The Fan*, about a psychotic young man infatuated with Lauren Bacall. To some extent the horror of the scenes (featuring slashes with a barber's razor) spoiled the glowing good atmosphere of the evening. But I could walk back to Red Oak knowing I was in the safest possible place.

Sunday, 22 November 1981

The sun broke through morning clouds to give us a good farewell to Camp David. Stewards delivered newspapers and a thermos of coffee to my cabin, which I enjoyed while sitting in the comfortable living room, listening to Haydn and Vivaldi. I had breakfast in Laurel Lodge with Mike, Eric, and Tom. The stewards wrote down my name, which I'm sure means that charges will show up on my monthly White House Mess bill. That's fine; the prices are rock bottom, and who minds paying for a weekend available to few of earth's souls?

There's something about a slow walk to a waiting Marine helicopter that sums up the glory of our current way of life. We landed at the Observatory at 9:15, after which came goodbyes to everyone and thanks to GB. At 1:00 at the White House, I found a lot of activity around Jim Baker's office, the war room for the Administration's battle to get a smaller "continuing resolution" than Congress wants. By evening it was clear that Reagan will veto the bill, literally shutting down the federal government. But isn't that what a lot of people thought RR would do if elected?

Monday, 23 November 1981

Today was the day of the great budgetary showdown between the President and Congress. The Cabinet met at 8:00, and a few minutes later the President went on nationwide TV to announce he was vetoing a continuing resolution that would have kept the government going at existing spending levels until appropriation bills could all be passed. These levels are higher than what the Administration wants, and RR was willing to take a risk none of his predecessors ever attempted—to allow the federal government to come to a halt when its legal authorization to spend money expired. RR said that as of noon, all "nonessential" functions would cease. The Democrats called this "theatrics." RR doesn't mind a conflict with "the budget-busting Congress" and cancelled his Thanksgiving trip home to the ranch.

This had an immediate impact on GB, for he soon cancelled our trip today to New York. For one thing, the Air Force had no money to fly us. Admiral Murphy declared that only the national security and congressional staffs were to remain on duty after noon—not us West Wingers, even though Barbara and I are Senate employees.[8] We could not even volunteer our time, for we would be occupying federal property. At noon, the Admiral said, "Lock the doors and go home. Don't call us; we'll call you."

Back in the office, I had an hour left. I wrote some letters and took a call from a lady in Midland pleading that her husband's federal court sentencing be delayed. Giving the line, I said we couldn't help, because "the federal government is closing due to the inaction of Congress." In truth we probably wouldn't intervene in such a matter, but to her and hundreds of thousands of others, the federal government of Ronald Reagan had become even more

---

8. By being on the payroll of the president of the Senate, I had more political freedom of action than as a White House staffer.

callous. As I was on the phone, the Admiral, conducting a sweep of all offices, jerked his thumb and said, "Chase, get your butt out." The call done, I dutifully got my coat and briefcase and walked out of the White House into the bright cool of a November noon in Washington.

I felt uneasy, as if I had just been laid off, was a striker or a deserter; certainly I felt no thrill in helping prove some great ideological point. But the undeniable benefit of this half-day off was being able to do all kinds of personal chores I never have time to do.

Tonight, the radio said that the Congress has passed a stopgap continuing resolution lasting till mid-December [that the President will sign]. This means we bureaucrats can all return to work tomorrow, but it doesn't necessarily end the budget battle. I'm afraid RR looked sillier than he did Churchillian today.

Chapter 14

A Czar Is Born

Wednesday, 25 November 1981

On this Thanksgiving Eve, Pete Teeley and I made a field trip to the Pentagon. That enormous office building for the Department of Defense is someplace we both need to know, and today we saw its guts: the National Military Command Center (NMCC). We were met at the River Entrance by an Army lieutenant colonel and taken to NMCC. A soldier in full dress uniform stood at ease outside the entrance but came to heel-clicking attention as we approached. We entered a large conference room that resembled a theater, with many big screens and rows of chairs. There is an alternate NMCC (aka Fort Ritchie) inside a mountain near Camp David. Even more survivable in a nuclear attack is NEACP ("Kneecap"), the National Emergency Airborne Command Post, the specially configured Boeing 747 we always see parked at one end of the runway at Andrews.

Eventually we entered the small space containing the Washington-Moscow Direct Communications Link, known to the military as Molink and to the public as the Hotline. It is for direct and immediate contact between only two people: the president of the United States and his opposite number in the Kremlin. The public perceives Molink as two red phones, but it really is a battery of instantaneous teletype machines. An on-duty "presidential translator" said that once an hour each side transmits a test message in its own language. These are nonpolitical and nonoffensive, though each side tries to throw obscure or slang expressions at the other. Ready to roll during our stop was a text on the handling of gerbils, and the translator said the Soviets send such things as treatises on mushrooms.

Back in the White House, Barbara Hayward related the good news that Laura Bush gave birth to twin girls today. They were delivered by Caesarean section due to continued concern over Laura's own health, and both babies (weighing about 5 pounds each) are fine. They were named for their grandmothers: Barbara Pierce and Jenna Welch. The Western White House called for details so Nancy Reagan could call Laura. *NBC News* tonight showed GB, emerging from his Senate office shortly before leaving for Maine, announcing the arrivals and calling them a Thanksgiving blessing "that makes all else, continuing resolutions or whatever, irrelevant." It was a wonderful scene that probably won a nationwide coo.

Monday, 30 November 1981

Lane Kirkland, head of the AFL-CIO, visited GB in the West Wing office this afternoon, and this evening the Bushes had a collection of labor leaders to the Residence, an effort to show there is literally an open door to the unions. I think this is wasted effort, but GB believes it won't hurt.

Tuesday, 1 December 1981

In the senior VP staff meeting, Thadd reported that the President would announce that GB would be labor's high-level contact in the Administration. The VP said this would not be on "an hour-by-hour, bitch-by-bitch basis"; that is what the secretary of labor is for. While the VP clearly welcomes this new role, he doesn't want to earn Sec. Ray Donovan's enmity. (Donovan, who's from New Jersey, may feel surrounded by Bush. The new governor of the Garden State, Tom Kean, is a staunch Bush ally who is using Bush's close friend Nick Brady as his personnel chief during the transition.) Thadd said that Donovan is indeed miffed over the President's action.

Wednesday, 2 December 1981

The day closed with a surprise birthday party for Ed Meese in the Roosevelt Room, attended by the Reagans. Nancy monopolized GB's time, expressing her anguish over all the catty publicity she receives about her clothes and interest in redecorating the White House. GB vowed to help with *Newsweek*, but the problem is within Mrs. Reagan. Her shyness makes her unusually sensitive to criticism, and to compensate for her shyness she wears expensive clothes and does flamboyant things with the White House.

Monday, 7 December 1981

At noon I welcomed my predecessor, Jim Johnson, for a thank-you lunch on the anniversary of his helping me learn the ropes. Because we are both clever, charming chaps, we enjoyed a full hour together filled with spirited conversation without once mentioning policies of either the Carter or Reagan administrations or the 1984 elections. Jim said he is enjoying private life, in which he is officially a government consultant (with twenty clients, no longer just one), but of course he is Walter Mondale's full-time political advisor. He made an interesting observation, like the other many acute observations of a year ago, that "four years are about the right amount of time to be vice president, and four years is more than the right amount of time to be a vice presidential aide." The highlight of the visit was showing Jim the West Wing and EOB offices with their new glamor. "This looks like the White House!" he declared.

Tuesday, 8 December 1981

In the context of describing some potential clash over a deregulation bill with Sen. Paul Laxalt (R-Nevada), one of the President's closest friends, Boyden Gray quoted [presidential aide] Rich Williamson: "There are four rules about this place: Don't spit into the wind; don't step on Superman's cape; don't cross Paul Laxalt; and don't let Mrs. Reagan know who you are."

In the afternoon, I returned to the White House for GB's meeting with Vice Premier Zbigniew Zadej of Poland. Zadej started talking immediately about increased US agricultural and financial aid to Poland. GB didn't say what the US will do, but he asked the question a lot of Americans ask: why doesn't the USSR bail out its satellite? Zadej described the Solidarity free labor movement as "negative" and "immature." GB said that Solidarity (which in Polish sounds like "Zolidarinosh") has captured the imagination of Americans.

Four days later, Poland's communist regime declared martial law to quash (only for a time) the rising tide of Solidarity's support among ordinary Poles. Defecting to the US in protest was the Polish ambassador in Washington, Romuald Spasowski, who had accompanied Vice Premier Zadej to the meeting with Bush. In his holiday message, President Reagan asked the nation to fulfill Spasowski's request that they burn candles in their windows on Christmas Eve in support of the Polish people.

Thursday, 10 December 1981

The day's biggest political news was announced by Pete Teeley at the VP's senior staff meeting at 10:00. In half an hour, he said, the RNC would reveal its selection of [our deputy chief of staff] Rich Bond as the new deputy chairman for political affairs. It is great news for Rich and for GB. Later, when I was able to congratulate Rich, he said he's excited about having "the most powerful job in American politics in 1982" but is fully aware that he will amass enemies by the battalion next year. He starts 15 January. There is no hint what will happen to Rich's political portfolio on our staff. Yes, I would like it, and my qualifications don't need any advertising. If I am to be chosen, I will be chosen. But neither the Admiral nor the VP has discussed the matter with me.

GB asked me to research what [ex–deputy RNC chairman] Mary Crisp said in a letter to pro-choice supporters, namely that on 30 July 1968, then-Congressman George Bush made a statement on the floor of the House in support of family planning. The White House library sent it to me, and I read over it to underline the pertinent parts. It seemed familiar, and I quickly remembered that I was the author! As I confessed in a note to the VP, the statement (an extension of remarks in the *Congressional Record*) was the last thing I did for him before entering the Navy.[1] He is no less committed to family planning (and opposed to abortion) today, despite the risk this poses with pro-lifers. "We don't want a bunch of ignoramuses running around getting people pregnant," he explained in a vivid image.

Friday, 11 December 1981

The *New York Times* today quoted [conservative] direct-mail whiz Richard Viguerie as saying, "Bush and his people clearly are in control of the government, and I see their influence growing in the Party, too. . . . Bush lost the [1980] nomination but won the election." More open-minded was Paul Weyrich, who mused that perhaps Rich Bond "will get into office and sell out to us." All this would be funny if Rich's own skin weren't in jeopardy. GB later called him to discuss this matter and urge him to be calm.

At the Waldorf Towers [in New York], I rendezvoused with Nancy Bearg Dyke for the ascent to the residence of the US ambassador to the UN, Jeane Kirkpatrick. She gave a tea for GB and invited various members of the UN

---

1. Congressman Bush became interested in "population control" as an appropriate objective of US foreign aid. This became my policy specialty, earning me the nickname "Pop" from Bush's longtime personal secretary, Aleene Smith.

community, including Secretary General Kurt Waldheim, General Assembly president Ismat Kittani of Iraq, Prince Sadruddin Aga Khan,[2] and several ambassadors. By great coincidence, this occasion immediately followed the surprise break in the Security Council's balloting for a new secretary general. Waldheim withdrew as a candidate for a third term when time after time China vetoed him and the US vetoed his chief rival, FM Salim Salim of Tanzania. Today the Council chose Javier Perez de Cuellar of Peru, and one of my assignments was to raise him by phone for a congratulatory call. This proved impossible because all international circuits into Peru were jammed with people with the same idea. Prince Sadruddin finished second to Perez de Cuellar and would have been elected if the USSR hadn't vetoed him.

Thursday, 17 December 1981

Heading to Andrews en route to New Mexico, Jennifer and I rode in the limo, which is always more like going to camp than to the ball, because the deck is covered with bags and briefcases. In the three-way dialogue to follow, Jennifer would be my advocate. She weighed in to urge that only one person should handle politics [on staff] and that it should be me. Bush was receptive to the discussion but didn't commit himself. He asked if I would like to do that, and I gave a calm yes, suppressing a more earnest "I do! I do!" Separating myself from the matter temporarily, I said it does make more sense to have one person as the "day-to-day point of contact" for and by the political community and to work with Jennifer on scheduling, the big political chore of 1982.

We all know that GB is his own political advisor. Yet undoubtedly there would be fascinating things to do, such as sitting in on more meetings. I sensed that GB liked the idea of making me political man, even though he didn't say anything like, "You'd be great!" If this comes to pass, it will be justification of the policy that [then–Air Force aide] John Matheny urged on me last summer, when I expressed frustration at how hollow being GB's executive assistant is. Be patient, John said, and my personal relations with the VP would bring me more responsibility.

---

2. For many years UN high commissioner for refugees, "Sadri" was the uncle of Prince Karim the Aga Khan and half-brother of the celebrated postwar playboy Aly Khan. He and Bush became close friends during Bush's tenure as ambassador to the UN.

Returning 2 January 1982 from Christmas leave in Houston, I penned a traditional New Year's summary of the year just past.

1981—More and Less

The job as executive assistant to Vice President George Bush was both more and less than what I anticipated a year ago at this time. It was the richest fulfillment of my daydreams: the atmosphere of the West Wing of the White House, the foreign travel, the planes, helicopters, limousines, motorcades, famous people, and very special events and places (like Camp David). But it was also less—a less than meant more than the more.

I arrived in DC in clear but bitter cold weather on 4 January for the final two weeks of the Carter-Reagan transition. In those weeks it looked as though I would be very much involved in policy issues. The VP-elect had me meet with representatives of the Jamaican government to hear what they wanted in the way of American assistance; I composed a memo on the White House Conference on Children and Youth that the President's staff later used; and the VP's chief of staff and I outlined a procedure for handling the "paper" going to the boss that would keep the Admiral clued in on what was happening in the far-off West Wing.

But Jennifer Fitzgerald asserted her old role as paper handler for George Bush, to the Admiral's consternation, and I was left to swim against a flood-tide of letters, telephone calls, and presidential personnel cases. I dealt with policy only in fleeting, tangential forms. Trapped in a prestigious but tiny office, I felt imprisoned in many ways. During this period I called myself "the highest-paid secretary in Washington." About the same time, Jennifer and I arrived at a tacit alliance, perhaps because she realized I was a fixture just like she. This pleasant if not intimate relationship was to bear little dividends during the rest of the year.

Because my job is more defined on the road, the increase of trips in the spring contributed to my improved sense of worth. As Air Force 2 took us to Europe, the Philippines, and Latin America, I resolved to enjoy things while I could and to depress a constant level of guilt and uneasiness about being overpaid and underemployed. I regularly described my life as "living on a diet of whipped cream." The year's end brought the prospect of having a larger role on the staff in 1982, gaining some if not all of Rich Bond's political duties. As of this writing, though, I have no idea whether these things will actually fall my way or what form they will take. It can't make life any *less* vital, I tell myself.

Yet I won't be surprised if in the new year my emotions take another downturn and I start to pay attention to possible openings for assistant secretaryships in the various departments. Taking one of these would give my Washington experience some real responsibility, even at the sacrifice of the supposed glamor of my present life.

Sunday, 3 January 1982

Around 3:00, I called Barbara Bush at the Residence to ask if I could drop by to leave something off. Through the drizzle I proceeded up Massachusetts Avenue from the White House and found the Second Couple watching a film. GB put the flick on "pause" during my fifteen-minute visit. I gave BPB a box of shelled pecans that a former colleague in the Texas House sent me. It belongs in their kitchen and not within reach of my snack-drawn fingers. I also showed them my scrapbook,[3] which won appreciative comments. But the comment I most appreciated was one GB made just as I was about to leave: "Are you set for your new duties as political czar?" It was the first official word that I would assume Rich Bond's political responsibilities. Fred Bush may become the new deputy chief of staff, except GB said rather firmly today that "Fred [a professional political fundraiser] will have to be told that you're in charge of politics." I left the house in fine spirits.

Tuesday, 5 January 1982

The highlight of the day was the 10:15 arrival of Chancellor Schmidt of West Germany. The teutonically handsome Schmidt walked in holding his trademark blue Hamburg sailor's hat. GB introduced him to our staff, a typical Bushian gesture, and I greeted him with "Herr Kanzler!" Schmidt was seized not with my German but by the size of my office. "Such a small office!" he exclaimed, placing the palm of his hand flat up against his nose. (Did the Chancellor mean to suggest I need more *Lebensraum?*) A few minutes later I was called by GB to explain the [old US Navy] ship models [in his office] to Schmidt, while a horde of cameras clicked away.

After lunch with the President and Chancellor Schmidt, GB said the

---

3. In 1981 I began keeping scrapbooks to preserve and organize the growing mass of unique paper items acquired in a White House life: invitations, photographs, menus, helicopter and airplane seating cards, event programs, and more. They are the "illustrations" for my journals.

talks went well, though there's confusion as to how much (or how little) West Germany supports US sanctions against Poland and the USSR. To Jennifer and me he hinted, "I wouldn't be surprised if we made a trip to China sometime soon," presumably so that GB's special ties to the Chinese could ease China's current testiness over the Reagan rapprochement with Taiwan. The VP said that Secretary Haig informally dropped such a suggestion in a recent meeting.

Wednesday, 6 January 1982

Slightly before noon I was called by Admiral Murphy, who gave me the final official word that (1) he has hired Fred Bush as deputy chief of staff, and (2) "You're the top political guy." Fred will handle the nettlesome [political] mailing list and budgetary responsibilities (the latter being the aggravating business of telling party folk how much they must pay the US government to have VP Bush attend an event). Every week, Jennifer and I will meet with Ed Rollins [successor to Lyn Nofziger as head of the White House political shop] to go over political scheduling. GB later stressed that he will have final say on such matters, but the hope is Ed will act as bogeyman for all events we decline. I am pleased that my proclamation as "political czar" has been made, even if I'm more of a grand duke than a czar.

I was ecstatic over what I next got to witness: A forty-five-minute session GB had in the Roosevelt Room with Yousuf Karsh, perhaps the twentieth century's greatest portrait photographer. Karsh is a small, dapper Middle Easterner [an Armenian by birth] who lives in Ottawa. His are the classic photos of such folk as Winston Churchill (whose scowl of defiance isn't directed at Hitler but at Karsh, who had just snatched away his cigar) and Pablo Casals (whom he was inspired to shoot from the back). All these glittering personages allow Karsh to enchant his subject of the moment with anecdotes; clearly he is the greatest name-dropper, short of Lowell Thomas, I have ever met. Working with GB [and measuring distance from his lens to Bush's nose with a simple string], Karsh used body English and specific instructions, such as "Quizzical, but with a sense of humor!" I stood with [VP staff photographer] Cynthia Johnson, Torie Clarke (Cynthia's assistant), and Secret Service agent Dave Mowrey to watch in fascination and admiration. To our astonishment, though, GB later confessed he had never heard of Karsh!

Chapter 15

In Recession America

Thursday, 7 January 1982

For today's trip to South Carolina, we had the cream of the state's Republican leadership aboard SAM 86970 at one time or another: Energy Secretary (and ex-governor) Jim Edwards, young congressmen John Napier of Bennettsville and Carroll Campbell[1] of Greenville, plus Lee Atwater, the White House political specialist on the South. Lee may not be a true friend, but today he was especially friendly, congratulating me on my new political duties and introducing me to Campbell as "one of the best politicians Texas ever produced." I think he also aims to exert an influence over me apart from whatever his new boss, Ed Rollins, says and does. "Ed and Admiral Murphy will do the big picture," Lee said, "and you and I will do the photography." (Rich Bond advised me to deal only with Rollins.)

We landed at Myrtle Beach about 10:15 and went to the convention center for the induction of Sen. Strom Thurmond into the South Carolina Hall of Fame. Thurmond is a near-legendary figure: a troglodytic segregationist who ran for president on the States' Rights ticket in 1948, won a seat in the Senate on write-in votes in 1954, switched to the GOP ten years later, and began fathering children with his beautiful second wife while in his seventies. In his remarks, GB recalled that Thurmond holds the Senate filibuster record of over twenty-four hours, "battling for principle, I might add." Thadd Garrett would be upset to hear that, for Thurmond was in particular battling the Civil Rights Act of 1957.[2]

Thurmond rode with us on the half-hour flight to Charleston—a place,

---

1. Campbell was congressman from 1979 to 1987 and governor of South Carolina from 1987 to 1995.

2. Trent Lott of Mississippi would give up becoming majority leader of the Senate in 2003 for having praised Thurmond's past.

locals like to say, where two small rivers meet to form the Atlantic Ocean. The senator reportedly called to Alixe Reed, an assistant press secretary, "Little girl, come wash these grapes for me!"

There was a press conference that delighted Lee Atwater. "If we can get your man into about forty congressional districts [and talk] like he did today," Lee said with the enthusiasm of new discovery, "we can *pick up* seats this fall!" On the flight back to DC, Lee sat opposite me to talk political strategy for '82. He again pressed his idea of sending GB into marginal congressional districts, believing that the typical falloff from a presidential to an off-year election is 2 percent. "If we can close the gap that much [through a vice presidential appearance], we can then buy the election," Lee said, inelegantly using that phrase to mean turn the GOP's plentiful resources loose on media. Lee said the Administration should drop talk of wanting to win the House, because history is against us. We need twenty-six seats for that, and the only president to gain House seats in an off-year was FDR in 1934 with a grand total of eight. Instead, we (meaning GB) should say we want to "keep control of the Senate and minimize losses in the House," both of which we can realistically do this year. Lee, incidentally, is doing a doctoral dissertation on off-year elections.

Friday, 8 January 1982

The Admiral wants to learn more about politics since that subject will dominate 1982 in the world of the VP. This became clearer when at 10:00 Rich Bond, Jennifer, and I met in his office along with Ed Rollins. The Admiral announced that I shall be the guy for Ed to contact on political matters on a daily basis. Ed is not much taller than I but considerably huskier; Rich says he was a Golden Gloves boxer who won 148 consecutive fights. He offsets a premature pate with a multicolored (mostly reddish) beard of Mormonic style. He is quiet and plain-dealing; I expect him to be a good working partner and am glad my tenure didn't coincide with the trickier Lyn Nofziger.

Monday, 11 January 1982

An NBC crew set up for the finale on the "magazine" piece they are doing on GB: the scene of his leaving the office for the night. Barbara Hayward was either so petrified or blasé that when the VP asked her what a particular book was, she blurted on camera, "It's from David Stockman. It's not important."

The producer afterward told a horrorstruck Barbara that *of course* they will use that segment in the film. With his arms filled with briefcases and envelopes stuffed with letters and photos to sign, the VP called over his shoulder at the door, "Good night, Chase. See you *mañana!*" Not only does this mean my name will be mentioned on the air, it will prove that my duties do not include carrying his briefcase!

Wednesday, 13 January 1982

After the senior staff meeting, Pete kept the VP, Jennifer, the Admiral, Thadd, Boyden, and me behind to brief us on the forthcoming exposé on Jennifer by Ann Devroy of Gannett. The VP stressed anew that if Jennifer gets the rap for various scheduling decisions "it's because she's doing what *I* want her to do."

Jim Baker was interviewed by Garrick Utley of NBC on the piece about the VP. He came into my tiny office beforehand to ask what spin to take on it. "Don't say it's a Bush administration," I said in reference to a cover story *Conservative Digest* is supposed to be developing. "Just say it's the same old Baker administration it's always been."

Thursday, 14 January 1982

GB had a private lunch scheduled with presidential pollster Dick Wirthlin, but he opened it to all senior staffers. Wirthlin didn't get to eat much, but he certainly gave the rest of us a lot to chew on. The President's popularity is strong, he said, but it's fallen considerably since the glory weeks of summer. The people support what he's doing, but it's still mostly on philosophy and faith. Results would be far more convincing, but the economic aspects of the Reagan program won't bear fruit till the second half of the year. If, Wirthlin warned, there's 10 percent unemployment in the fall (it's 9 percent now), and the President's popularity is down in the midforties, the GOP could lose dozens of seats—making 1983 and 1984 very difficult indeed. Unemployment has replaced interest rates and inflation as the public's chief concern.

Wirthlin said RR is viewed as anti-black, anti–blue collar, and anti-women. The latter is not so much on the grounds of feminist issues as on the fear RR will get us into war. He said we are in danger of losing the blue collar, ethnic, Northeast-Midwest coalition that elected Reagan-Bush. GB asked Wirthlin to advise him on where his and the President's personal unpopularity would be greatest so as to avoid tarring candidates in those places.

He recalled the negative impact of then-VP Agnew's visit to East Texas during his [GB's] 1970 Senate campaign. Translated, that means GB wants regional readouts on his popularity.

After GB left for home, I stoked up the fire [in his office] and read parts of a biography of Herbert Hoover. Today, during Dick Wirthlin's presentation, I was haunted by the notion that we are a new Hoover Administration—one of competence and beneficent purpose but doomed by economic disaster. Oh, well: I've always longed for the nostalgia of the 1930s.

Tuesday, 19 January 1982

Gannett reporter Ann Devroy had a two-hour interview with the Admiral this afternoon in pursuit of her wacky Jennifer-the-All-Powerful story. The mere knowledge of this sent Jennifer into streams of tears, the only time I have ever seen her so distraught. She feels persecuted by Devroy and unable to strike back.

Wednesday, 20 January 1982

I joined the motorcade heading to the Departmental Auditorium, a grand, monumental, early twentieth-century structure with soaring ceilings, enormous interior columns, and gilt trim. Going on was the "Reagan Administration Executive Forum," a gathering of 2,200 political appointees to hear top officials praise the record of the past 365 days.[3] When we arrived, Secretary Haig was speaking in his extemporaneous, hush-voiced, Douglas MacArthur fashion. Though overlong, it was well done. GB came on next, to the sound of "Hail Columbia" played by the Marine Band. His talk on regulatory relief seemed feeble after Haig's sweeping review of foreign policy, but he was given a long and fond hand afterward.

Then "Hail to the Chief" and cheers for the fortieth president of the United States. Reagan looked radiant, shaking hands with all on the dais and waving to the audience with his familiar choppy, head-tucking gestures that mark him as so modest and affable. The President praised his listeners for their hard work, slammed the Democrats for criticizing his programs when it

---

3. These unabashed Administration pep rallies, held every year on the anniversary of Reagan's inauguration, were excellent morale boosters, especially among appointees far from the White House swirl. It was an exciting opportunity to see and hear the President and be reinvigorated in the fight to implement his policies in the departments and agencies.

was their failed policies he had to correct, and closed with a classic anecdote about a man with two sons. One son was a pessimist, the other an optimist. To cure these eccentric tendencies, the father gave the first boy a roomful of toys and the second a roomful of horse manure. The first lad wailed in fear that someone would come and take away all his toys. But the second dug happily into the mess, saying enthusiastically, "There's got to be a pony in here somewhere!"

It was an apt story to tell on 20 January 1982, after a year of great achievement but with a virulent recession in force that threatens to undermine us politically this November and three Novembers hence.

Thursday, 21 January 1982

Ed Rollins and I spent a few minutes with GB and his guest, Gov. Frank White (R-Arkansas). White is a popeyed, expansive, good ole boy whom GB befriended [in his campaign for president] and casually suggested that he run for governor in 1980. His victory over boy governor Bill Clinton was one of the biggest upsets of an upsetting year for the Democrats. White is bursting with confidence, claiming he's raised over $500,000 and saying that his two putative opponents, Clinton and ex-congressman Jim Guy Tucker, can't raise much money. The ACLU [American Civil Liberties Union] may try to block the removal of Cuban refugees from Fort Chafee in Arkansas, the issue that elected White and now threatens him. The White House has promised White that all Cubans will be gone by about 1 March.

By all means the big event of the late afternoon was the arrival over the wires of Ann Devroy's profile on Jennifer. Pete said I should come to his office to read it, which I promptly did. The long piece was just the gut job that Jennifer feared, claiming that she has enormous power over GB that affects his politics and policy impact, infuriating present and former Bush aides, and scheduling the VP into tony events that serve only to reinforce his "preppie" image. The article ignores certain facts. For example, it suggests that Jennifer drove Rich Bond out of his job, totally failing to mention he left to run the RNC.

Friday, 22 January 1982

Topic A on today's flight to Kansas City was Ann Devroy's article on Jennifer Fitzgerald. GB acted amused by the whole thing at first, but BPB felt strongly opposite: "It hurts Jennifer, of course, but she's just a tool. It really hurts George and Dan Murphy." After a while, GB showed how much the piece did rile him, criticizing Rich Bond for his prepared statement on how difficult it had been for him to work with Jennifer. The VP allowed that he'll have to be more careful about the slang expressions he likes to use; his joking description of Jennifer as "the czar" was picked up by Devroy. GB reiterated that Jennifer doesn't do anything he doesn't want, that he likes the way they work together and isn't going to change. But he conceded that Jennifer has severe PR problems on staff.

For all of us in the traveling party, especially the Bushes, our main interest was focused not on the evening Missouri GOP fundraiser but on *NBC Magazine* at 7:30. It was favorable, with some friendly interviews and fine footage, except that Garrick Utley pitched everything as its title suggested: that GB is the "President in Waiting." Utley said GB is doing all his traveling in order to earn IOUs for a race for president in 1984. Of course, there's that possible advantage to what we do, but in the first and only instance that matters to him, it's part of doing his job. And if he does well—as he did tonight in St. Louis—then he helps himself as well as the GOP.

Sunday, 24 January 1982

Crunching along in the snow, I got to the helipad on foot in about twenty minutes. The chopper was already on the ground. GB was like a kid: he was off to Super Bowl XVI between the San Francisco Forty-Niners and the Cincinnati Bengals. When we arrived at Andrews, party time began. The plane was filled with VIPs for our non-government-paid flight to Michigan on "Super Sunday." The celebrities included presidential counselor Ed Meese, Secretary of Transportation Drew Lewis, Federal Maritime Commission chairman Alan (Punch) Green, Penn State coach Joe Paterno, RNC chairman Dick Richards, and ex-footballers Larry Brown of the Washington Redskins and Darryl Stingley of the New England Patriots. In the after cabin were Bush aides and some nonworking press.

We landed at Detroit about 12:30 p.m. and first went to a GOP fundraiser in suburban Oakland County. With full police escort—no doubt making many fans unhappy—we proceeded to Pontiac and its Silverdome sports stadium, the roof held up by air currents. The Bushes spent the whole game in Box Number 1, owned by William Clay (Bill) Ford, son of Edsel and grandson of the great Henry. The Secret Service had installed bulletproof glass for the box, which also included a large lounge and bar.

We staffers had a specially constructed section right beneath the box and behind the rows of permanent seats. My seat was on the forty-eight-yard line right next to Bob Teeter (GB's former pollster) and his wife. There were some distractions, such as the shrimp and crab claws at the owners' reception and the general elite atmosphere in Ford's box, to which all of us were invited in groups.

Back in the stands with the common folk—remarkably young and unrich—I watched the game, which the Bengals won after we left the stadium, 26–21.

Monday, 25 January 1982

Karl Rove[4] was my guest for lunch. His direct-mail company, with [Texas governor] Bill Clements as prime client, seems to be doing quite well. We talked Texas politics during the meal, after which he had a few private words with his old boss, GB.

Wednesday, 27 January 1982

At the staff meeting, the sensitive subject of GB's trip to Florida next month to meet with the AFL-CIO executive council came up. It's sensitive because organized labor prefers dealing with the VP and not with Secretary of Labor Ray Donovan, whom they strongly dislike. GB rather likes the role of special emissary to the goons, to the point of not really caring how much Donovan is undercut. The poor man is under federal investigation for possible racketeering operations in New Jersey anyway, and he's the weakest member of the Cabinet. Things are so bad that Donovan, trying to get invited to the Florida meeting, called White House labor liaison Bob Bonitati, asking Bob to call Thadd Garrett to get the VP to call Lane Kirkland to call Donovan. GB doesn't dislike Donovan and doesn't want any embarrassment for the President, but he doesn't want to fight the Secretary's battles with labor for him.

While GB saw the outgoing and incoming French ambassadors, I was warming up a French Canadian from New Hampshire, State Sen. Bob Monier (pronounced "Moanier"). He is a candidate for the GOP gubernatorial nomination, and the Birch Society's *Review of the News* recently said his

---

4. Rove would later be the "architect" of George W. Bush's elections as governor of Texas and president, as well as a major political and policy advisor to him in the White House. We had first met early in 1977, when I was a freshman state legislator and Karl was aide to a veteran Republican member.

election is necessary to prevent "liberal" elements (= GB) from winning the 1984 primary.[5] This afternoon, though, Monier's mission was to convey his compliments to the VP and to say how much he and other doubters have been impressed by the way GB has served RR. The VP replied humbly, saying, "This man [Reagan] is such a joy to work for, and that's something you had the pleasure of knowing before I did."

Saturday, 30 January 1982

I slipped into the rear of the hotel ballroom in Monterey, California, to hear Barbara Bush's speech to the State Republican Central Committee's luncheon, substituting for Sen. Jeremiah Denton of Alabama. She told "what I do all day" in a warm, elegant way. It was filled with anecdotes, following the Broadway requirement of one laugh every thirty seconds. For example, she reeled off the stats on GB's travel, ending with " . . . and he's visited nine foreign countries. *I've* been to eleven. Vice presidents don't go to funerals; vice presidents' *wives* go to funerals." At the close she told of being "a convert—a convert to Ronald and Nancy Reagan. (Applause.) And as you know, a convert is much harder-core than you regulars." She got a long, fond ovation, undoubtedly helping implant the Bushes in the affections of party loyalists.

Monday, 1 February 1982

Noon brought a special treat: I had Clare Boothe Luce to lunch in the Mess. She is a member of the President's Foreign Intelligence Advisory Board (PFIAB, pronounced "Piffy-ab") and is currently doing a one-month stint as special advisor to the new national security advisor, Bill Clark.[6] I consider myself lucky to dine with the most remarkable living American woman, now seventy-eight. In addition to giving grave assessments of the US intelligence community's ability to meet the Soviet challenge, Clare was full of other observations. Recently she was in the hospital, where she concluded that the 1969 film *M.A.S.H.* and its long-running successor TV series caused a certain

---

5. The nomination and the election were won by John Sununu, who would figure massively in Bush's favor in the Granite State in 1988 and later serve as Bush's White House chief of staff.

6. Clark succeeded Richard Allen in December 1981. A stolid, much-admired California rancher and judge, Clark was an insider's insider during the Reagan Administration. He began as deputy secretary of state, keeping an eye on Alexander Haig, and after service as national security advisor, he replaced the controversial James Watt as secretary of the interior in 1983.

impertinence and unprofessionalism among younger interns and nurses. She decried the way they dress ("with the hair showing"), look, and talk. "Of course they immediately start calling you by your first name," Mrs. Luce said with disgust in a Connecticut clubwomanly voice that was not lowered for the occasion.

Afterward, I took her on a walking tour of the West Wing, where we concentrated on the paintings and other artwork. As we stood examining a [George] Catlin print in the narrow corridor connecting Ed Meese's office with the VP's, a Secret Service agent suddenly appeared and asked if we were pass holders. In a flashing, I saw the reason why: Ronald Reagan was rolling toward us, accompanied by Jim Baker and Judge Clark. RR embraced Clare, who teased him about removing the original Catlin oils from the corridor, a bit of knowledge just acquired from me. Surprised, the President reacted by pointing to the print of an Indian chief in full war dress and saying, "This is a picture of me before going into legislative battle." It was a fine little moment that certainly made Mrs. Luce's day (and mine). She seemed most appreciative of my attention, and she turned on her special ultrafeminine charm, whose power still is irresistible. How she must have made men melt in the 1920s and 1930s![7]

Tuesday, 2 February 1982

I was having a desktop breakfast and reading the *White House News Summary* when I lazily noticed the VP's limo pull into the EOB arcade around 7:20. A few minutes later, the White House press office called to ask where the VP was, saying that CNN had a report that "a motorcade was shot at" in the streets of Washington this morning. When NBC's *Today* show identified the car as GB's, I called the Secret Service. Assistant special agent-in-charge Dick Hankinson said that "a projectile did hit the car. We heard a noise and don't know what it was." The object struck the left rear corner of the roof, that is, the side opposite the one on which the VP sits. No one was hurt, and the motorcade proceeded to the EOB, whence the limo was hauled off to the lab for examination of the dent in the vinyl roof.

---

7. And the 1980s. I had Clare to lunch at the Pentagon when I was an assistant secretary of the Navy. I also invited Jim Webb, the Vietnam War hero and novelist. Then an assistant secretary of defense, later secretary of the Navy and US senator from Virginia, Jim was as smitten as I. Speaking of Mrs. Luce, Jim told his wife, "You should be grateful there's a forty-year difference in our ages."

Lots of calls came in from the press, not to mention dozens all day from Bushkin, friends, and admirers. The VP himself said there was nothing either scary or "heroic" about the incident—just a "thump!" I joked with the Secret Service detail, "We're putting out the story that when the incident occurred, the VP threw himself on the bodies of his agents, grabbed an Uzi, and took out five Libyans and three secretaries who work for GSA." Meanwhile, DC police, Secret Service, and the FBI cordoned off a four-block area around the site (Twenty-Second and L), conducting a room-to-room search in every building. They wore flak jackets and carried weapons. A helo patrolled overhead, and FBI agents slowly walked over the route, looking for a bullet. And the Secret Service made the VP go by car from the EOB to the West Wing!

By midafternoon, the Secret Service and FBI concluded, by lab tests on dust particles in the roof indentation, that the car had been hit by a brick or rock, similar to construction materials in the area. Perhaps it was thrown in anger, but that's the most it was. End of scare—except GB was met by a mob of reporters when he went to the Hill this noontime. Smiling broadly and boyishly, he said, "I'm not used to such attention in my job." The whole affair points out how gun-shy we all are after last year's assassination of Sadat and the attempts on the President and the Pope.

A sad personal event of the day was the start of work on the all-weather canopy that will protect persons arriving in the rain at the basement entrance to the West Wing. No question this is needed, but it will deprive my window of its status as the best in Washington for people-watching.

I had dinner tonight with Bob Wurmstedt, *Time* correspondent in Cairo (formerly in Houston), who is in town for the visit of President Hosni Mubarak. We had a good talk about the Middle East, but Bob also inquired about Jennifer Fitzgerald. This reminded me that Chris [Buckley] said *Time* had put out an advisory to its correspondents about the Ann Devroy piece in the Gannett papers. I told Bob the things I would have told Devroy: that GB makes scheduling decisions, with Jennifer the fall guy; that she has no interest in policy and almost never sits in on the meetings she schedules; and that, after all, there is nothing either new about an unpopular appointments secretary or noteworthy about a *vice* presidential scheduling operation.

Wednesday, 3 February 1982

I showed Jennifer the memo I had just written the Admiral and Pete Teeley on last night's probe by Bob Wurmstedt. I knew she would be concerned, but

I sure didn't expect her to become furious with me—and for the reason she did. The memo reported how I dutifully tried to depress *Time*'s interest by pooh-poohing Devroy's characterization of Jennifer as a "Rasputin" who controls GB's life through her own whims. "Don't you say anything *nice* about me?" she demanded. "How I work hard and am a good person? Not all this [in the memo] how I don't do this and don't do that? Really! This staff is so negative!" She went on down this line, getting angrier and angrier. I tried to calm her down by reading once again my words detailing the truth that she's a much-abused conveyor of GB's own scheduling decisions rather than the manipulator, but this only made her madder. That's when I realized that, for all the anguish over Devroy's piece, Jennifer *liked* being described as omnipotent! And my effort to protect her and the VP from a similar story by *Time* was therefore to her a gross insult.

Jennifer stormed off to the EOB, and a short while later I was called by Pete, to whom she had gone. Though he had to be cautious since Jennifer was in the room with him, Pete said that of course I had done the right thing in my tack toward *Time*. But when we saw each other alone a short while later, he said, "You can't win this one."

Thursday, 4 February 1982

Jennifer, with morning-after breeziness, joked (heavily), "Do unto others as they would do unto you. I've spread the word in the press corps that you don't handle substance." I rejoined, "That's right. I'm just a sponge."

In his role as designated presidential liaison to organized labor, GB is to hold meetings with top union leaders at least quarterly. He appears before the AFL-CIO executive council in Bal Harbour[8] in twelve days, but he's not counting it as this quarter's meeting. So today he met with the man he considers a friend, Lane Kirkland, head of the federation, and some of his colleagues in the Roosevelt Room. (Kirkland used its old nickname "the Fish Room," dating back to when FDR kept an aquarium there.) Some unions

---

8. I once twitted Lane Kirkland how labor held its winter meetings in a Florida resort town, just like corporate executives do. He replied by telling a story about David Dubinsky, longtime head of the Ladies' Garment Workers' Union. Every so often, as a treat to himself, Dubinsky ordered a dish of fresh strawberries and cream at his favorite deli. One day, enjoying this meal in a seat by the window, he was spotted by a fellow unionist, who gave him hell for indulging in nonproletarian behavior. Dubinsky insisted that he had earned the right to this little bit of sybarism. "Bal Harbour is our strawberries and cream," Kirkland concluded.

that were pro-GOP in 1980—police, maritime, and building trades—were at the table, but their representatives let the southern-accented, cigarette holder–flourishing Kirkland speak for them.

GB led off by discussing Administration policy on Poland, the one great area in which organized labor and we are on the same side, except that the unions are more vocally pro-*Solidarinosc*[9] and anti-Soviet than is RR. Kirkland said we should adopt tougher stands against the USSR and the martial law regime in Warsaw, even if our erstwhile European allies refuse to go along. This means in particular cutting off credit to Poland and embargoing all trade (especially grain) to that country and to the Soviets.

GB was stating the dilemma of acting independently of our allies when the door opened and Ronald Reagan entered. He went around the table shaking hands with the union leaders, and he didn't miss us staffers along the wall. GB reviewed what had been said to that point, and RR (sitting at the head of the table, hunched forward and hands clasped) reassured Kirkland & Co. that the US is not backing down from the strong words he enunciated on Poland before Christmas. But, he cautioned, there is nothing the Soviets would love more than to split the US and its allies and "Finlandize" the continent. Then spoke the traditional Reagan: "We may never again in our lifetime have such an opportunity to crack the Warsaw bloc [*sic*], the Iron Curtain." With that, the President rose, swept the room with a few flashes of his twinkling eyes through two or three fixes of his broad shoulders and departed.

As part of "creative" scheduling, an effort to break free from merely reacting to invitations mailed and phoned in to the White House, Vice President Bush in 1982 began visiting military bases, in this case Pope Air Force Base and Fort Bragg in North Carolina.

Friday, 5 February 1982

We landed at Pope on a drippy, clammy day. Immediately the VP and staff boarded a C-130 transport alongside AF2. It was windowless, noisy, and had rack-type seats running lengthwise. The plane rumbled off and reached the desired altitude of 800 feet for a "jump." At a yelled signal, paratroopers in combat gear and painted faces stood and hooked their chute lines onto a taut overhead wire. To psych themselves and each other up, they rattled the teth-

---

9. Kirkland, whose wife was Polish, liked to use this word instead of Solidarity.

ers and gave war whoops. The doors opened, the line started, and in a matter of seconds all the guys were gone and we were alone.

This done, the C-130 landed on a dirt strip with a jolt. The rear bay opened, and jeeps waited on the red mud to take us to a viewing area. We looked up into a rainy sky as some C-130s dropped a couple of tanks and several quarter-ton jeeps. Then some long, prop-jet C-141s discharged 800 paratroopers. Even in today's weather it was a remarkable sight. The officer next to me couldn't contain his own excitement. "Good chutes! Good chutes!" he exclaimed.

We next boarded the Army's new UH-60A "Blackhawk" helos (a larger and more maneuverable improvement on the Huey) and zipped over the pines to a clearing. A soldier met us there and escorted us on foot to the Gabriel demonstration site of the Special Forces, the famous Green Berets. For the next hour or so we were back twenty years in time to those misty days of Camelot when tough, multilingual snake-eaters were America's perfect answer to communist insurgency around the world. The Green Berets are proud of this reputation, and they put on a show that was first class—but an obvious show nonetheless.

A brigadier welcomed us and led us to some bleachers underneath an umbrella-like parachute canopy. At his order, men of the demo unit marched out and barked well-practiced descriptions of their jobs. Half of these spiels were in foreign languages: Russian, French, Turkish, and Thai, the latter spoken by a black with a Deep South drawl. Next they demonstrated hand-to-hand combat with knives, pistols, and rifles, complete with screams in simulated crotch kickings and neck snappings. We gave them a round of applause.

Tuesday, 9 February 1982

In Houston, attorney Hal DeMoss,[10] GB's Texas campaign chairman in 1979–80, had a half-hour visit which I attended. Hal offered all help for 1984, leading GB to talk more on that topic than I've heard him do. Bush said he's "locked in" as VP while Jack Kemp[11] can move around the country. "Still," he

---

10. President Bush in 1991 would appoint DeMoss as judge of the US Court of Appeals for the Fifth Judicial Circuit.

11. Kemp was congressman from New York from 1971 to 1989, a candidate for the 1988 Republican presidential nomination, Bush's secretary of housing and urban development, and GOP nominee for vice president in 1996.

voluntarily added, "I've got Air Force 2 and a certain visibility and presence." Recently at the Republican Southern Leadership Conference in Orlando, GB related, Kemp was going around flatly saying that RR won't run for reelection in '84 and that people should start now to support him [Kemp]. GB said he thinks Reagan will run again and hopes the President will announce as much. I don't sense that GB is particularly worried about Kemp, given the congressman's arrogance and rather arcane, "frantic" expositions on the economy.

Thursday, 11 February 1982

NBC last night had a feature proving that GB had actually, publicly said "voodoo economics" in the Pennsylvania primary campaign of April 1980. In a press conference in Houston on Tuesday, GB denied ever having said it. Red-faced, the VP handwrote a note to NBC correspondent Ken Bode, saying "NBC—1, Bush—0." The network was so amused it showed the note on tonight's news.

People in the capital were astonished at Bush's flat disavowal of the phrase he made famous, unable to believe he had simply forgotten saying it or thought he could get away with lying about it. Speaker of the House Tip O'Neill said the VP had "a convenient memory." But George Bush is a man who lives in the present and the future, never the past. It is Barbara Bush and George W. Bush who have the steel-trap memories in the family. There was also an important extra factor at work. Now that he was Reagan's friend, colleague, and defender, Bush had thrust out of his mind all the unpleasantness of having run against him, as if it had never occurred.

The main event of the afternoon was Jennifer's and my meeting with Ed Rollins and Lee Atwater to go over vice presidential scheduling. The President's top two political aides are unhappy that GB agrees to do fundraisers for pals like [Congressman] Bill Young [R-Florida] who need no help at all. "You're wastin' the greatest campaign asset we've got," Lee said, temporarily forgetting a man named Reagan.

Tuesday, 16 February 1982

From *AF2,* en route to Florida, I called Barbara Hayward to ask if the new issue of *Time* had arrived. It had, with a full-page story by White House correspondent Doug Brew on the theme of a feeble tenure by VP Bush. There were also several paragraphs on Jennifer. I gave this fragmentary bulletin to all interested souls. This prompted an intense private conversation with BPB, who's had to put up with Jennifer for longer than the rest of us. Despite occasional rudeness from Jennifer, Barbara says they get along because they have to. BPB has "spies" who tell her what's going on, because she (and others) know Jennifer isn't going to tell them. But like all the other conversations about Jennifer I've ever had with anyone, Barbara and I were stuck with what to do about the problem. I predicted that it will take a "cataclysm"—an embarrassment to the VP or Jennifer worse than an unfavorable story in *Time*—to force her departure. Both of us agree that the word best describing Jennifer's relation to the world of Bush is "pathos." She can't survive financially or emotionally outside the VP's orbit.

We landed at the Fort Lauderdale–Hollywood airport, and drove forty-five minutes to the Sheraton Bal Harbour Hotel, site of the midwinter meeting of the AFL-CIO executive council. Council members—all but two male and all but two white, with many also serving on the Democratic National Committee—sat around a large square of tables, with GB seated to the right of Lane Kirkland. The VP made a vigorous defense of the Administration's economic policy, challenging labor to support such things as "the jobs amendments" to the Clean Air Act. There was a semidebate between GB and Sol (Chick) Chaikin of the International Ladies' Garment Workers' Union over the proposed "enterprise zones" in depressed central cities. Murray Finley of the Textile Workers criticized Republican rhetoric that all social welfare programs are "a mess." Conceding political verbiage inflation, GB nevertheless told the council they ought to recognize that Social Security *is* a mess. Albert Shanker of the extremely liberal American Federation of Teachers blasted US policy toward Poland as insufficient, prompting GB to say, "Don't try to tell me that Ronald Reagan is a dove." The final words were Kirkland's: taking advantage of a lively little joke session on "voodoo economics," he said that in his mind Reagan economic policies are "Jonestown economics"—a reference to the mass suicide of bizarre religious cultists in Guyana in 1978. It was unfair—and headline-making.

In Miami my main mission was to get a copy of *Time*, something I did in a bookstore in a mall adjoining the Omni Hotel. The story by Doug Brew was indeed bad, speaking of "a mysterious hold" that Jennifer has over GB and saying that due to conflicts with her, Rich Bond can no longer be counted on as a Bush loyalist. The rest of the story debunks the Far Right's contention that GB has extraordinary influence over the President—but does so by denying he has any influence at all. In the suite I gave the magazine to GB and Pete Teeley, who read it together, shaking their heads.

Saturday, 20 February 1982

Morgan Mason, an assistant to Ed Rollins, brought by his father, the aging but still highly distinguished actor James Mason. He related that near where they live in Switzerland is a rock formation that resembles GB! From the unpetrified version I heard nothing all day.

Monday, 22 February 1982

The highlight of the day undoubtedly was the visit the VP had with the brainy, funny Democratic grandmaster, Robert Strauss. Bush called me in to keep Strauss company while he tended to other business. We had a lively, if brief, chat about the responsiveness of local government versus the federal government. Strauss agrees that mayors and legislatures respond faster than the feds but that the quality of public servant still is much lower at that end than this. We had just gotten into a more philosophical discussion of the mood of America when GB returned and I took my cue to leave. The VP said later, "I would have sworn I was with someone who'd like to run for president."[12]

Tuesday, 2 March 1982

In our staff meeting we all laughed over an item in today's *Washington Post* in which Bob Jones 3rd (president of Bob Jones University, an ultra-fundamentalist institution in South Carolina) called GB "a devil" and RR "a traitor to God's people." But GB expressed a rare public concern for his own safety, worrying aloud that "some nut" might take it upon himself to rid the earth of the devil.

Wednesday, 3 March 1982

At 1:15, I rode with GB to the Hill, where he presided over the Senate during its deliberation on the fate of Sen. Harrison A. (Pete) Williams, a liberal Democrat who has represented New Jersey since 1958. Williams was convicted last year in federal court of soliciting a bribe in the so-called Abscam

---

12. Strauss never did run, saying of his fellow Democrats, "They could do worse—and probably will." He would be Bush's ambassador to Russia from 1991 to 1993.

case, in which an FBI agent dressed up as an Arab sheikh to entice Williams with offers of great amounts of money for wielding his influence. The question before the Senate isn't whether Williams is guilty but whether he should be expelled (requiring a two-thirds vote) or merely censured (requiring a simple majority). Only in the case of a tie would GB vote, most likely only on a procedural issue and most dramatically only on a Democratic motion to substitute censure for expulsion.

During our staff meeting this morning, I had wondered aloud whether senators might object to GB's voting at all, inasmuch as the Williams case is such an internal matter. But [congressional liaison] Susan Alvarado said he should, because "the vice president is a member of the Senate." Jennifer furiously argued against his being present for what she considers a lynching of Williams by self-righteous colleagues. But, as GB said to Senate parliamentarian Bob Dove when Dove came into the ceremonial office [just off the floor] to brief him, "I guess it's my dad's connection with the place, but I just feel I should be here." Dove and various senators strongly concur; he said VP Humphrey attended only the last two days of debate on the 1967 censure of Sen. Thomas Dodd (D-Connecticut), the last disciplinary case the Senate had to decide.

GB went up on the dais to preside, and I took a seat in the Vice President's Gallery directly opposite him. The public galleries were packed and periodically cleared in order to seat new shifts. As splendid a seat as it might seem, mine was actually the worst place in the Senate to see anyone other than the presiding officer. Even when I couldn't see a speaker, I could enjoy the atmosphere of the chamber—first used in 1859 and the site of vice presidential inaugurations until deep in the twentieth century. It was an occasion in which practically every senator was in his or her seat; even Pete Williams was present. Sen. Malcolm Wallop (R-Wyoming), chairman of the Ethics Committee, gave its report, after which the vice chairman Howell Heflin (D-Alabama) proceeded to demolish every possible point that might be raised in Williams's defense. Unfortunately, Heflin, a rotund southern senator in the classic mold, spoke so long that I was unable to hear the eloquent defense by Williams's manager, Daniel Inouye (D-Hawaii), as I had to head back to the White House.[13]

---

13. On March 11, Williams resigned from the Senate rather than face a vote for either expulsion or censure. Gov. Tom Kean appointed his and Bush's close friend Nicholas Brady Jr. as interim senator. Brady, who did not seek election to the seat, served just over eight months. He would be secretary of the treasury from 1988 to 1993.

Every so often I like going to the Capitol to appreciate GB's antique role in the place. I might add that for some folk there, including our own Hill staff, the VP's presence is an exciting embodiment of the Executive Branch. I detected great silent admiration from an elevator operator who inquired what the small, square, yellow pin in my lapel indicates.

Friday, 5 March 1982

For today's trip to Wisconsin, Chris Buckley had gleefully given me an envelope marked "Urgent for Pete Teeley." Inside were several stapled pages with a cover sheet announcing the document to be the text of a speech. But the subsequent pages were all blank, except for page 2, which read, "You're on your own now, you son-of-a-bitch!" I gave this to Pete the moment before takeoff so he had several minutes to go into shock. Later I gave him the real envelope.

Our entire route was blanketed in white, and Lakes Erie and Michigan were contrasts of sheet ice and pale blue water. Coming with us on the short leg from Green Bay to Milwaukee was the congenial, funny Gov. Lee Dreyfus, whose trademark is the red vest he constantly wears. As president of Wisconsin State University in its rambunctious years, Dreyfus was the target of an arrow unsuccessfully fired in anger. He defiantly began wearing the red vest as a dare to the assailant to hit him next time. Dreyfus is seeking a second term in November.

In the gracious old Marc Plaza, I went to the crowded two-room staff suite to find a Wisconsin feast: beer, pretzels, and cheese. The ballroom was decorated with red paper vests bearing the word "Again!" The same logo was on many a lapel pin. The menu was, for a political dinner, a stroke of genius: a traditional Friday evening Milwaukee fish fry, with wonderful deep-fried filets, French fries, chunky cole slaw, and pitchers of beer.

Better still was the governor himself, an instantly lovable man with a silly-putty face, dumpling figure, and smashingly funny speaking style. Dreyfus indeed is one of the few true characters of current American politics. He noted, for example, that "we may be in the snowbelt, Mr. Vice President, but when the snow melts, it becomes water. I've told [Gov.] Bill Clements he can have all the water he wants from Wisconsin—so long as it's in cans and has malt, hops, and barley mixed in with it." His biggest laugh, however, came when he asked, "How many of you guys my age can get your wife to wear a button that says 'Again'?" When Dreyfus is serious, he speaks with genuine enthusiasm and emotion about the diversity of his state's and America's people. He is in the best traditions of the liberal Republican movement that was born in Wisconsin. He was difficult for GB to follow, but the crowd was in such an upbeat mood that Bush got repeated applause.

One special assignment that Vice President Bush sought from President Reagan was the chairmanship of the South Florida Task Force, which coordinated federal efforts to interdict drugs coming into that state. He did so at the urging of his son Jeb (then a Miami businessman) and a bipartisan group of Florida officeholders. The task force not only enabled Bush to show concern for a major problem affecting Florida, it gave him a wholly justified reason to go there frequently and earn valuable political credit. It also gave Adm. Dan Murphy an action role of the sort that suited his operational background and which he had previously lacked as vice presidential chief of staff.

Tuesday, 16 March 1982

Aboard SAM 86972—the only top-of-the-line 707 that hasn't been injured lately—were Sen. Paula Hawkins (R-Florida) and the crafty Gerry Carmen, administrator of GSA and the Republican kingpin of New Hampshire. Paula still has her neck in a brace and undergoes traction eight hours a day, recovering from a bizarre, frightful accident several months ago. Panels from a fake wall on the set of a TV studio fell on her as she sat talking with the reporter. Hawkins is a feisty, fearsome lady—the first woman ever elected to the Senate entirely on her own, without succeeding a husband or having a famous father like Nancy Landon Kassebaum (R-Kansas).

In Miami, I escorted Paula and Gerry to our car for the US Coast Guard base at Government Cut. There we were met by senior Coast Guard officers and John Walker, GB's first cousin and assistant secretary of the treasury for enforcement.[14] Rear Adm. Benedict Stabile, commandant of the district and soon to be vice commandant of the Coast Guard, told us they have had some great initial success; just last week, a big planeload of cocaine with a street value of $1 billion was seized. The task force chieftains recognize, however, that the better they are, the cleverer the crooks will become.[15]

---

14. Walker was so outstanding as a federal prosecutor, as enforcement chief at Treasury, and as a district judge that no one alleged nepotism when President Bush elevated him to the US Court of Appeals for the Second Judicial Circuit in 1989.

15. Indeed, the success of the task force caused drug importers to shift their efforts from Florida to the porous land border between the US and Mexico.

Wednesday, 17 March 1982

When the VP's trip to Pittsburgh tomorrow was laid on several weeks ago, it was decided to visit a steel finishing plant at McKeesport. US Steel recommended the place because it had had no layoffs, though unemployment in the Pittsburgh steel industry grows by 100–200 a week, partly due to foreign competition. Today we learned that the plant will discharge twenty-five workers *tomorrow*, almost as if to embarrass the Vice President. The question at our briefing for the VP was whether to cancel the plant visit. Chris Buckley and Fred Bush, enraged at US Steel, were all for cancelling. Jennifer defended the original decision to go, and Thadd said we should enlist Lane Kirkland to bring the Steelworkers local in line so they won't boycott the visit. Fred argued to the VP that "Kirkland set you up before [with the "Jonestown economics" crack at Bal Harbour] and he'll do it again."

I kept my peace till the appropriate moment, when I said the VP should go and try to take advantage of a poor deal by showing compassion and using the grim opportunity to defend the economic program. I said that all year long the VP had spoken of avoiding "a wagon train mentality," hiding from potentially unpleasant confrontations, and now is such a time. I don't know what the final decision was, but I am confident the VP heard enough voices on the matter.

Thursday, 18 March 1982

I rode with Jennifer and the VP in the motorcade to Andrews. The VP definitely was tense, yearning to relax, but the US Steel layoff flap bothered him. He decided to keep the visit to the plant, saying, "I can't back out now."

After both nonpolitical and political events in Pittsburgh, we drove up the Monongahela River to McKeesport, a community that is the picture of economic depression, each glance at rundown buildings and hollow-looking people a news photo of despair. Yet only about twenty passive picketers from the Steelworkers local waited for us outside the gate of US Steel's Duquesne National plant, which makes steel tubing for the transport of natural gas. The layoff of which we learned late yesterday numbered 150 workers, but only for two weeks, making it more like a furlough than forever. This eased tensions enormously, especially when GB met and talked with a couple dozen employees in the plant. Still, the plant operates at only about half its capacity, largely due to the international oil glut and the corresponding decline in domestic energy production. For the tour, all of us were given hardhats with our names painted on. Fortunately, the USS logo was made of applied plastic and was easily removed without a trace.

With relief and contentment, we drove the short distance to Allegheny County Airport, to which *AF2* had been moved. The VP was delighted everything had worked out well, that on the same visit he had sounded both positive on the President's economic program and sympathetic with those who are suffering.

Friday, 19 March 1982

My luncheon guest today was that lovable liberal Democratic walrus, Mike Berman, former counsel and deputy chief of staff to VP Mondale and still a political strategist for him. Mike took me to lunch last summer, and today I returned the favor. Not only did I enjoy his company, but many permanent workers around the White House lit up when they saw him. Clearly Mike was one of the most popular of the Carter staffers, as opposed to Jim Johnson, whom Secret Service agents still mention in dark mutters. Mike made only one allusion to Mondale's "political opportunity in 1984." I asked, "Let's see: that's for county commissioner in Duluth, isn't it?"

Tuesday, 23 March 1982

[On leave in Puerto Rico,] I am surprised at how little I think about what's happening back in the office. Indeed, I force such stray thoughts from my mind whenever they enter. Now that I have the political charter on the VP's staff, working in the White House is no longer "a diet of whipped cream"; it's more like very rich cake—more substance but still not meaty. And, I should add from afar, one can still get heartburn from overeating it.

Tuesday, 30 March 1982

This evening I was delighted to welcome Jamie and Sue Bush[16] for a tour of the West Wing and dinner. Jamie gave a nonstop account of his father's Senate campaign and especially the caucuses a week ago tonight in Fairfield

---

16. He was the son of Prescott Bush Jr. and Elizabeth Kauffman Bush, sister of the admiral for whom I had been an aide in the Philippines. As a member of the Hingham (Massachusetts) School Committee in the early 1990s, Sue was the only Bush in public office between the George H. W. Bush presidency and the George W. Bush governorship.

County [home of both the Bush and Weicker families], where Pres beat Lowell Weicker 2 to 1 and won all seventeen delegates to the state GOP convention. The convention isn't until 23 July, a lot of time for a major party split to develop. Jamie said they're hoping Weicker will simply quit the Republican Party and declare he's running as an independent. Only in a three-way race could Pres hope to defeat Congressman Toby Moffett, the Democratic nominee.

Friday, 2 April 1982

The VP asked me to sit in on his meeting with Ed Feulner, head of the Heritage Foundation [a conservative think tank with great influence during the Reagan Administration]. Clearly Feulner wanted a perfectly private meeting and never looked at me throughout the half-hour conversation. GB led the discussion into the realm of New Right/Old Right, and Feulner led it into the Connecticut Senate race. He offered to be a "broker" between Pres Bush and the New Right types. GB reswore his neutrality, but he opined that "Pressie is the only choice" versus Weicker and Moffett. He cautioned, however, that Pres is more liberal on certain social issues (like abortion) than is Heritage.

It was a lovely warm spring day, the first of the season, and the awfulness of winter was a fresh enough memory to spark rejoicing over today's weather. Rejoicing was needed today, for there was bad news. Unemployment stands at 9 percent, according to a report released by the Labor Department, tying a post–World War II high in 1975. Also rising is the number of workers who have given up looking for a job and thus aren't even figured into the unemployment rate.

Also today, Argentina invaded and seized the Falkland Islands. Originally treated by CBS and others as an amusing comic-opera story, the takeover proved an embarrassment to Britain (which has no disposable forces in the South Atlantic) and to the US. Last night, President Reagan spoke for fifty minutes by phone with President Galtieri, unsuccessfully urging him to refrain from invading the islands. The threat of worsened relations with the US apparently proved not much worry to the Argentines.

Thursday, 8 April 1982

Chris Buckley came over to give Barbara Hayward and me autographed copies of his new book, *Steaming to Bamboola*, the story of his life aboard a Norwegian freighter. "For Chase," reads the inscription, "old maritime hand and friend."

Tuesday, 13 April 1982

At noon, Chris and I got sandwiches in the EOB cafeteria and went out on the fresh grass by the First Division Monument. Sadly, it was the only time we had ever gotten off by ourselves, and Chris announced that he will leave the staff in June to begin serious work on his second book (possibly a historical novel about Saint Paul[17]). It's really no surprise, because the task of grinding out vice presidential speeches is, well, a grind. [*Chris once described every speechwriting experience as "like waking up to realize the final exam began an hour ago."*] GB may not require more than a capable hack writer, though I would push for someone who (like Chris) can give his speeches the "red meat" that party audiences crave. Chris isn't persuaded that GB believes that "good speeches matter."

Wednesday, 14 April 1982

I was eating breakfast when GB called to say that Joe Straus 3rd (son of his good friends Joe and Joci Straus of San Antonio) was on his way up to the EOB office, a half hour early. I greeted Joe, a tanned, handsome, self-confident senior at Vanderbilt who would like to work on our staff. He is being considered for the letter-writing job in Domestic Policy, but Thadd Garrett is unsure whether he wants to hire Joe. "We have too many sons and daughters of the wealthy on our staff," he said, maybe not entirely in jest, referring to such folk as Boyden Gray, Chris Buckley, Kim Brady [daughter of Nicholas Brady], Liz Grundy, and Monie Murphy (niece of Henry Ford II). In reply I declared, "Contrary to what is said about this administration, we don't consider a person's background in deciding whether to give them a job. A rich kid has just as much chance as a poor kid."[18]

Thursday, 15 April 1982

I was the first guest to arrive for dinner at Henry and Jessica Catto's home in McLean. The dashing Henry (assistant secretary of defense for public affairs)

---

17. Actually, it was the first in a series of wicked political romps called *The White House Mess*, which he honored me by asking to read in manuscript.

18. Straus went to work for the commissioner of US Customs instead. In 2005 he was elected to the Texas House of Representatives from San Antonio, and in 2009 he became its speaker.

and I talked about Korea till Jessica came downstairs and other guests started arriving. And what a parade it was: Sen. Lloyd and B. A. Bentsen (D-Texas); the new Israeli ambassador, Moshe Arens; SecDef Caspar Weinberger and wife, Jane; columnists George Will, Meg Greenfield (who's also the editorial page editor of the *Washington Post*), and Rowland Evans; White House communications chief David Gergen and wife, Anne; Boyden Gray of the VP's staff; and Kathy Troia, Secretary Weinberger's speechwriter. (Dave today missed the President's helo to Andrews for a trip to Chicago. The press got a big laugh out of this. Anne said it wasn't the first time he had kept the President waiting—and hoped this incident would end his lifelong lateness.)

Kathy was seated to my left, and I was anxious to talk with her. But the ever-burrowing "Rowly" Evans wouldn't release me, talking over poor Anne, who sat between us. Evans and partner, Robert Novak, are anti–Jim Baker, pro–Jack Kemp, and disdainful of GB, so I had to watch myself. After dinner, during the stand-up coffee and liqueur session, I escaped from Evans and joined a group that included my hero, George Will. The best part of the evening, though, came when all other guests had left, and Henry, Jessica, and I sat around and talked about GB. Jessica worries that the right-wing attack on Bush is beginning, and she's right.

Saturday, 17 April 1982

[After returning from a campaign trip to South Dakota,] I very much like our visits to small states. They have the excitement that the VP causes in an entire population. In Aberdeen today, for example, people lined the sidewalks to wave—and Aberdeen is a Democratic stronghold. People act differently in places like Sioux Falls and Moorhead (Minnesota) when meeting the VP. I noticed at last night's reception that they were so nervous they looked away from GB as soon as they shook his hand. We also get to know an entire congressional delegation, such as South Dakota's, Iowa's, or Utah's.

Tuesday, 20 April 1982

I rode in GB's motorcade up to Capitol Hill for the swearing in of Nick Brady as the new senator from New Jersey. The ceremony, part of the opening exercises of a routine morning of Senate business, was quite brief. GB entered the chamber and immediately went over to shake hands with visiting Congresswoman Millicent Fenwick, who leads for the Republican nomination for the full term of Harrison Williams's old Senate seat, which Nick is filling only through November. When the clerk got to the spot on the roll call where "Brady" would come, GB (in the chair) read boilerplate language announcing Nick's appointment and summoning him forward to take the oath. Down the center aisle he came, escorted by the gangly and ambitious Bill Bradley (D), now the senior senator. GB stepped to one side of the dais, held out a Bible, and read the oath. All Nick had to do was say "I do" and sign an old bound book, as sustained applause filled the chamber. It was over in about three minutes, but it isn't every day that someone you know is sworn in as a US senator.

GB stayed on the Hill for a reception for Senator Brady in the Vice President's ceremonial office. He introduced me to Congressman Jim Courter (R–New Jersey), whom "the White House" (meaning Lee Atwater) has assured of both the President's and VP's support if he moves into another district to escape being paired with Congresswoman Marge Roukema (R). It's true the President will offer a letter of support, but we have never been asked to commit to Courter. Worse, in the new district Courter faces a challenge from Rodney Frelinghuysen, son of former Congressman Peter Frelinghuysen, a longtime pal of GB's. Only last week on Bush's instruction I called Frelinghuysen Sr. to assure him that the White House would follow its policy of neutrality in Republican primaries. Unfortunately, my source, in the Rollins-Atwater office, didn't himself know what was going on. Courter feels confused and betrayed.[19] This episode hints that the President's political staff has been throwing around the name of the VP. Knowing GB's sensitivity to having others determine his schedule, Ed Rollins this afternoon assured him, "We will never commit you to anything."

This meeting was followed by two hours of briefings on Asia [to which we travel Thursday]. It's still unclear whether we'll go to the PRC [China]. That depends on whether the Chinese acknowledge the visit as purely one of goodwill and frank exchanges of views rather than a climactic negotiation on arms sales to Taiwan. GB gave instructions to the State Department to "keep working this thing back and forth" while we're en route to New Zealand.

---

19. Courter won the new seat, lost the governorship of New Jersey to James Florio in 1989, and served on appointment of President Bush as chairman of the Base Realignment and Closure Commission. Rodney Frelinghuysen, scion of a New Jersey political dynasty dating back to the early days of the republic, won election to Congress in 1994.

Chapter 16

Luncheon with the Emperor

Those of us "manifested on the helo" had to bring our luggage to the White House the day before the great Asian adventure for eventual loading aboard Air Force 2. This allowed me to walk from my apartment house to the Naval Observatory on the day of departure for a twenty-day trip of 36,000 miles to six countries and two states carrying just an old TWA flight bag.

Thursday, 22 April 1982

SAM 86970, filled with people and baggage, lifted off heavily from Andrews at 8:50 a.m. for the seven-and-a-half-hour flight to Anchorage. En route I read a history of the opening of US diplomatic relations with Chosen or "Corea," a study of the 1934 and 1954 congressional elections, which Lee Atwater gave me, and the State Department–prepared briefing book. Our route took us over an endless Canadian plain marbled with still-frozen lakes. Later we passed over the magnificent Canadian Rockies, with perhaps the most spectacular scenery just before reaching Anchorage.

We landed at Elmendorf Air Force Base, to be met by Gov. Jay Hammond (R), a husky, bearded bush pilot. Our motorcade went the short distance to the Anchorage Windward Hilton, tallest building in the city, for a GOP fundraiser. The VP's remarks, written by Chris Buckley, noted that when Alaska joined the Union, the Texas state song had to be changed from declaring the state "largest and grandest" to "boldest and grandest"—"and Alaskans probably would still want to argue that."

Back at Elmendorf, *AF2* was all juiced up and ready for takeoff on the seven-and-a-quarter-hour flight to Tokyo. I didn't hesitate to take Dr. Ed Yob's advice to get as much sleep as possible to help our "circadian rhythm" bridge the enormous jump in time zones. Using eyeshades and a blanket, I shared a couch with Jennifer, her legs in one direction and mine in another.

Friday, 23 April 1982

Air Force 2 landed at Haneda Airport and taxied to an arrival spot jammed with press and security. Amb. Mike Mansfield—Democratic majority leader of the US Senate from 1961 until his retirement in 1976[1]—came aboard with the Japanese chief of protocol. We in the official party then lined up and disembarked in rank order. We shook hands with the Japanese official party and quickly boarded our cars. It was a thrill to be back in Tokyo, and the sights of the imaginative, tightly tailored city were wonderful.

The motorcade swung past the moat of the Imperial Palace; the grounds there and elsewhere were in mossy spring green. Then we entered the gates of the stupendous Akasaka Detached Palace, a replica of Versailles set far back from the street on a section of land as large as Buckingham's. The Akasaka was built for then–Crown Prince Taisho [father of the future Emperor Hirohito] in 1909. He never lived here, but Hirohito and his wife did, both before and after their enthronement in 1926. It was restored in 1974 to serve as the state guesthouse. It is a great honor for the Akasaka to be made available for GB's use; he is the first non–head of state to stay here. We entered the marble halls and climbed a red-carpeted staircase to the second floor. In a grand salon done up in gilt and painted ceilings, GB and BPB sat in golden chairs as the rest of us Americans lined up facing the official Japanese greeting party. The Japanese chief of protocol presented them to the Bushes, who rose. GB then presented each of us to them. We all made little bows from the hips.

Jennifer and I were then shown to our suites, containing giant bedrooms, everything done in fine fashion if not exactly to my taste. After depositing my carry-on items, I returned to the vice presidential quarters for the meeting GB had at 5:30 with Ambassador Mansfield and his "country team." An Asian scholar as well as a politician, the ambassador stressed that "the Japanese-American relationship is the most important bilateral relationship in the world, bar none." He added that to the Japanese, their ties with the US are the central focus of their entire foreign policy. As a consequence, they tend to overplay even casual remarks by congressmen and other US government officials. "They pay close attention to what we say, and they pay close attention to what we don't say," warned the embassy economics chief. This

---

1. The highly respected Mansfield was appointed ambassador by Jimmy Carter in 1977 and was wisely retained by Reagan throughout his administration.

was his way of telling the VP to use every one of the taking points they had
written for him.

Saturday, 24 April 1982

Chris Buckley and I went walking through the Akasaka Palace grounds on
a soft, sunny morning. He said I am "too literate a fellow" to be in politics
[*which I took to be a compliment*].

At 9:30, we members of the official party once again lined up in rank
order along a red carpet set within the extensive courtyard of the palace for
the arrival ceremony. A sheet of plastic was laid across the carpet so that
Prime Minister Suzuki's three-car motorcade wouldn't put tire tracks across
it. Once the cars passed, two men in green armbands hustled out to take the
sheet away. From the palace the VP and PM emerged to take the salute of
the honor guard. This done, they stepped down from a platform to troop the
line. As the two leaders approached a section of Japanese elementary school
children in their dark, military-like uniforms, the kids started waving paper
Japanese and US flags, which made a lovely fluttering sound.

At 11:30 our motorcade left for the Imperial Palace, passing by the Diet
Building, an ominous-looking structure almost perfectly designed to be the
backdrop for 1930s newsreels. On previous trips to Tokyo, I had always gazed
up at the forbidding yet beautiful walls of the Imperial Palace and dreamed
what it would be like to cross the moat and enter the grounds. Today that
dream was realized. The VP's motorcade, Japanese and US flags flying from
the limo's fender, crossed the outer moat and then the inner moat, climbing
a hill past one of the original pagoda-like buildings of the palace complex.
Then we entered the enclosure for the new ceremonial annex. It is modern
and elegant in the way Japanese architecture can bridge centuries. Modeled
after the imperial palace in Kyoto, it is built around a large pebbled courtyard.
The interior has highly polished black marble floors that look like pools of
water. Vast picture windows look out on a hillside planted with (blooming)
azalea bushes, massed to form figures of giant turtles—symbols of longevity.
For Hirohito, these must be good omens, for he turns eighty-one next week.

The Bushes were led by the vice court chamberlain to a private audience
with the Emperor. The rest of us were ushered into a waiting room, where
Japanese protocolaries gave us a last-minute demonstration of proper bowing technique. After a few minutes, we were led down a corridor and up into
an audience chamber. It looked out on a pool with a broad, swift-flowing

waterfall, multicolored gardenia bushes, and "islands" of reddish boulders with pebbles raked to give the impression of ocean waves swirling around them. Here we were introduced (and bowed) to various Japanese dignitaries, including the prime minister, the foreign minister, the speaker of the Diet, the chief justice, and former PM Kishi.[2] Once again, at some unseen and unheard signal, we all lined up in rank order and turned our attention toward the door.

GB's flat Fairfield County tones, in conversation with the Emperor, announced their approach. In a moment, the Bushes entered the room with Hirohito, Crown Prince Akihito, Crown Princess Michiko, and Prince Hitachi and his wife. The Japanese royal family was dressed as one might expect of their British counterparts: the men in striped trousers and the women in hats. The VP introduced the Emperor to the American party; each of us extended our hand and bowed slightly while smiling. (The bow was traditional Japanese courtesy, not an honor due royalty.) Hirohito, though aged and stooped, was a living embodiment of his caricatures of half a century back: He was small with bushy eyebrows, a little mustache, and round rimless glasses that glinted light. Perhaps hard of hearing and definitely shy, His Imperial Majesty greeted each of us the same: "So happy to have you with us!" These rote exclamations were dutifully translated each time by an elderly aide. Though not a historical actor in the same sense as his former prime minister Tojo, Hirohito was at least the man in whose name many acts of twentieth-century history were done. If it is not rare enough to meet an emperor (and, after the ouster and death of the shah of Iran, Hirohito is the only one left), it is rarer still to meet someone who once was a certified deity.

The entourage followed the royal family and the Bushes into the state banqueting hall, a vast room dominated by a wall-to-wall tapestry of clouds reflecting the rays of the rising sun. I sat between Ambassador Okawara [Japan's envoy to the US] and Shinichiro Tomihari, a pleasant member of the imperial court who speaks good English and carries the ancient title of master of ceremonies. The meal, served by a surging mass of waiters, was continental, except perhaps for the glâce shaped like Mount Fuji. (The Emperor

---

2. Kishi was a remarkable link with Japan's bad old days. A minister in the Tojo cabinet, he had signed the declaration of war against the United States in 1941. Although a "war suspect," he was never tried, and General MacArthur ordered him released. Kishi reentered politics and rose to become prime minister in 1957–60. During his tenure, the current US-Japan security treaty was negotiated.

reportedly favors western food to Japanese cuisine.) There were no formal toasts. As dessert was served, we all quieted as GB and Hirohito exchanged compliments from their seats and raised their glasses. As we rose, I was sure to pocket the menu card and place card, each topped with the sixteen-petal imperial chrysanthemum[3] in raised gold.

Mrs. Bush had a much more challenging time at table, the occasion for a hilarious story she tells in her Barbara Bush: A Memoir *(1994). She was seated next to the Emperor and found conversation with him to be extremely trying, as he responded to everything she said only with "Yes," "No," or "Thank you." At one point, in desperation, she noted how lovely the palace was; Hirohito thanked her. Was it new? Yes, he replied. What happened to the old one? she asked. Hirohito smiled and said, "I'm afraid that you bombed it."*

We passed into yet another receiving room, where coffee and cigars were served. I automatically waved off a waiter with an open box of cigars, prompting Mike Mansfield himself to come over and whisper, "Next time they pass the cigars, take one, if only for the band." He was right; the band also contained the imperial chrysanthemum. [I later gave it to Dr. Yob, a cigar smoker.]

A very busy protocol official suddenly appeared and said with a show of arms and teeth, "Please, Mr. Untermeyer: The Emperor!" Members of the court kept circulating guests up to meet and converse with His Imperial Majesty, who had his silver-haired interpreter with him. I wished the Emperor a happy birthday and praised the Akasaka Palace. He then bowed slightly and concluded the brief audience (as he did every one) with the same words: "I hope your stay in our country is an enjoyable one."

Next, the protocol man beckoned me to chat with the forty-nine-year-old Akihito, the heir apparent. Educated by American teachers, he speaks good English, and we had a pleasant exchange until the time came for us Americans to line up for adieux to the royal family. We said goodbye to Hirohito and the government officials before being escorted out to our cars, with a stop to look through the picture windows at the azalea turtles.

Into the cars, down the hill, across one moat, past a line of flag-waving Japanese, across another moat, and back to the Akasaka. The afternoon with the imperial family was a great honor for GB, who received the courtesies and

---

3. The national chrysanthemum has only fifteen petals.

attention of a head of state. The Japanese may have acted out of friendship at a time of tension over trade. But they may also believe that George Bush is indeed what NBC called him: the president-in-waiting.

Hirohito died in 1989, and President Bush attended the funeral. Akihito then became the 125th emperor of Japan.

Chapter 17

Rimming the Pacific

Sunday, 23 April 1982

At 7:00 we all gathered out front of the old Akasaka to board our vehicles for Haneda. The entire serving staff of the palace waved goodbye as our motorcade wound through the portico and away. On the two-hour flight to Seoul, we were given the glorious treat of passing right over Mount Fuji, getting a special perspective of its famous graceful slopes and irregular crater cap.

Our 707 came in over the hazy plain of central Korea and landed at Kimpo, just outside Seoul. Soldiers lined the runway like fenceposts every few feet. We in the official party came down the ramp and proceeded along the red carpet, shaking hands with the Korean PM and US ambassador Richard (Dixie) Walker. A Korea specialist, Walker is the oddest of Reagan ambassadors: a staunch GB supporter in the South Carolina primary who nevertheless got an appointment, though due to Senator Thurmond's patronage and not ours.

The route to and from the national cemetery was filled with people, mostly students in school uniforms, waving Korean and American flags. I'm bad at estimating crowds, but I imagine there were 100,000 to 200,000 out this afternoon. At the cemetery, we passed by foot through a pagoda gate and walked to a shrine where GB spread incense in three braziers. As trumpets sounded, we bowed our heads in remembrance of Koreans and Americans who fought and died together in 1950–53.

We returned to our cars and went back through the crowds into the heart of gigantic, bustling Seoul. We disembarked at the ambassador's residence—the very property that Lucius H. Foote, our first minister to Korea in 1883, had to buy because there was no place to rent. An original building remains, but the actual residence, built to a traditional Korean design, dates only from 1976. Here there was a briefing by Ambassador Walker's "country team." But DCM [deputy chief of mission] Paul Cleveland excluded Jennifer, Pete Teeley, and me. Walker is such a neophyte and so cowed by the VP's visit that he chose not to overrule his DCM. He told Pete that the briefing was "only for the people who count." My equanimity at this treatment is fueled by an almost Asian sense of taking the long view in life, and I still have a visceral conviction that I shall lead delegations and have a staff of my own one day. At such a time, being tossed out of Ambassador Walker's residence this afternoon will seem an amusing incident. So, in the words of then-Governor Henry Bellmon (R-Oklahoma), I shall "forgive and remember," patiently awaiting the time I may be in charge of presidential personnel and Paul Cleveland's papers for an ambassadorship arrive on my desk.[1]

Monday, 26 April 1982

I had breakfast with the head of the VP's Secret Service detail. In fifteen months I have observed that there are two kinds of agents. First there are the pols who are essentially achievers, who want to get ahead in the Secret Service and do. Then there are the proles, the ordinary guys who do their job well but are not out to hustle anything or anyone. They are by far the most fun to be with.

GB had breakfast at the ambassador's residence with some Korean dissidents. Then we proceeded to the US embassy for GB's standard remarks to Foreign Service personnel. Afterward I greeted BPB, who was temporarily standing by herself before wading into the crowd. As usual, she put me off balance. "Congratulations!" she said, and when I asked why, she noted that I had stayed at my assigned table last night at the PM's dinner rather than abandon my dinner partners for the staff table. That thought never occurred to me, but I imagine Barbara was referring to Jennifer, who dislikes talking with host nationals at state dinners. Regardless of whom Barbara had in mind, this little incident was a good sign that she remains strongly on my side.

The afternoon presented the opportunity to play tourist while other supernumeraries went shopping. The old Kyongbok Palace lies just behind the National Capitol and was easily reached on foot. Styled the National Folklore Museum, the palace grounds are like a very poor man's Forbidden City. Kyongbok means "Palace of Shining Happiness." The building where Korean kings worked was called "The Hall of Pondering Government." Cabinet ministers, on the other hand, convened in "The Hall of Cultivating Government."

We later all had tea with the speaker of the National Assembly before he opened the session. All except GB were shown to seats in the gallery of

---

1. For good or ill, I didn't get to savor this dish of cold revenge in 1989 when then–Secretary of State Jim Baker proposed the officious Cleveland to be ambassador to Malaysia.

the modern chamber, with members' seats arranged in a semicircle below us. Korea is a military dictatorship with extremely limited personal freedoms (mostly economic) and many democratic trappings.[2] The National Assembly is one of the latter; a third of the members are appointed by the president, and one imagines candidates of the two official parties don't dare question the government. When GB read the line in his speech "you represent the Korean people," Chris Buckley, the author, leaned over to me and said, "Ha-ha."

Later, I visited the Duksoo Palace. Like Kyongbok, it is down at the heels and dusty, yet it also retains the flavor of the time minister Foote arrived to present his credentials a century ago. There is an enormous seated statue of King Sejong the Great (1397–1450), whom the explanatory tablet credits with the invention of the Korean alphabet, improvement of printing types, invention of the sundial, water clock, and water gauge, the reform of classical music, the "readjustment" of the land system, and the encouragement of agriculture through the publication of the Six Codes of Economy. Just maybe he was also the creator of the government press office.

From Korea, Air Force 2 flew on to Singapore, a sentimental favorite since I first saw it as a junior naval officer during the Vietnam War. Only recently independent, Singapore in 1969 was a low-rise, bustling place not too different from other former British colonies in the neighborhood. It may not have been too different from what Lady Diana Cooper found in 1941: "I felt, when I first saw this pretty, feminine rococo town, that a modern world would not let it survive." But Singapore, not unlike Houston, Texas, is in a constant state of remaking itself, and much of what I describe below is today vanished.

Tuesday, 27 April 1982

AF2 passed over dozens of ships at anchor off muggy Singapore Island, to land at a little after 2:00. This place has grown phenomenally since I was last here [in 1970]. Perhaps more astounding than the skyscrapers are the land reclamations that have pushed familiar landmarks farther from the water than I remember them. Yet there remain streets in old Singapore's Chinatown with classic Southeast Asian architecture and allure, and the Singapore of today has not forgotten the importance of greenery. So, even in this afternoon's tropical rain shower, everything looked beautiful.

---

2. Korea moved toward full-fledged democracy in the following decade.

In the evening, we entered the lush, rolling grounds of the Istana, the old governor's palace, dominated by a magnificent white colonial structure built in the 1850s by prisoners from the Andaman Islands. (It is used only for ceremonial occasions; the president and prime minister live elsewhere.) The Singapore Army Band, in red caps and white tunics, played light airs on the front lawn. As my car drew up under the portico, a soldier opened the door and saluted. Enjoying my role, I nodded a greeting to the other troops as I mounted the red carpet into the palace itself.

There were leafy plants and banks of flowers inside the Istana, with open doorways leading out into a pleasant night patrolled by security men in dark suits and earpieces. In an atmosphere of warmth and friendship, we dined on a nine-course Chinese meal. The VP and PM Lee Kuan Yew exchanged toasts after course number 4. The PM noted GB's responsibilities, "more than any previous vice president," and set the agenda for their talks tomorrow by mentioning a wide range of concerns, down to GSA's proposed sales of surplus tin. GB gave a good response, properly praising this country and its PM.

Wednesday, 28 April 1982

Today I was up at 7:00 to behold a tropic sunrise through morning mist and clouds. The BBC World Service carried the announcement of GB's visit to China. Today's edition of the *New Nation*, published here in Singapore, was headlined "Bush to China." At a breakfast with the American Business Council, GB said, "America will no longer berate its friends and apologize to its enemies."

I had the entire rest of the day to reacquaint myself with Singapore. Leaving the Shangri-La Hotel, I walked down to the Singapore River, the most Southeast Asian spot in this city-state. Here, wide-beamed sampans [with eyes painted on the prows] come after lightering freighters anchored out in the roads. The godowns (warehouses) lining the fetid river receive merchandise off the barges just as they have always done, and to walk through the arcades of the old city is to sense again all the splendid sights, smells, and sounds of my days wandering this neighborhood.[3]

---

3. All gone—except that a few remaining "bumboats" survive to take tourists up and down a now-pristine river. An ultramodern container port, built on reclaimed land, allows cargo ships to dock instead of anchor out. The godowns are now quaint boutiques, and the preserved colonial-era buildings have been renovated to achieve a handsomeness they probably never enjoyed in their youth, looking not unlike a movie set.

Stepping over pieces of Chinese cabbage and around baskets of peppers drying in the sun, I inhaled the aroma of spices and incense and stared at rhinoceros horn on offer in apothecary windows. I sought out a cold orange drink in a shed among food stalls. These sheds have replaced the street vendors I remember fondly from 1969–70. Not yet ready for lunch, I sat at a small table, sipped the drink, and inhaled the unmistakable essences of charcoal and frying peanut oil. I continued poking around the narrow streets of the riverfront, crossing over on the nineteenth-century iron Cavenagh footbridge. There's an attractive promenade under drooping trees, and here I smelled copra on the lighters tied up in the stream. This is Empress Place, which sports a column commemorating the visit in February 1850 of the Marquis of Dalhousie, governor general of India. The legend (written in English, Chinese, Tamil, and Arabic-Malay) could apply to the Singapore of today: "He emphatically recognized the wisdom of liberating commerce from all restraints, under which enlightened policy this settlement has attained its present rank among British possessions and with which its future prosperity must ever be identified."

I returned to the promenade for a meal I've been yearning to have for over eleven years: fried hokkien mee, a plate of two kinds of noodles, shrimp, strips of chicken, and egg. I ate in a food stall with a view of the barge traffic. Afterward I went into the old business district, including one of the oldest streets in Singapore, Telok Ayer, where there are a 150-year-old Chinese temple, a Tamil shrine, and a mosque. At about this time (3:00 p.m.) the regular afternoon thunderstorm struck, and I had to seek shelter in an arcade on a side street. I read *Newsweek* and watched the water level rise in one of the deep (and dangerous) concrete drainage ditches. The rain's intensity ebbed but didn't really stop, so I pressed onward toward the Shangri-La. I got wet, if not soaked, but I can't think of a finer way to have spent my time. Nostalgia for *temps perdus* was richly satisfied.

Thursday, 29 April 1982

We landed at Darwin in the Northern Territory of Australia. Here we had to refuel and have the plane disinfected against insects. While we were still on board, a bloke in knee socks and shorts walked down the aisle, discharging two aerosol cans of bug spray at full blast. Inside a waiting room, over drinks, sandwiches, and cakes, the deputy lord mayor, a member of the sizeable local Chinese community, emphasized to us how young a population Darwin has. This, plus the climate and remoteness, means a highly casual way of life. The typical footgear, he said with Aussie color, are "Japanese riding boots"—or shower thongs.

Friday, 30 April 1982

In Canberra, Australia's capital, the Bushes drove off to call on the governor general, and the rest of us proceeded to the small, utilitarian but handsome Parliament House. Built in 1926, it will be replaced at the end of the decade. Inside, in King's Hall, a lobby that adjoins the House and Senate chambers, are portraits of recent prime ministers and governors general. I sought out the men's room, on whose door was stenciled "Male Members."

Outside, we took position in rank order behind a reviewing stand, facing cadets from Duntoon Military Academy, Australia's West Point. Prime Minister Malcolm Fraser stepped up to take his personal salute and then went down the line shaking hands with each of us. About then, GB's motorcade arrived, sending Secret Service agents springing from their cars. The VP and PM mounted the platform. "Guard of honor!" the cadet commander shouted in an accent that made it sound like "Goldwater!" The band played "The Star-Spangled Banner" and "Advance, Australia Fair" as guns boomed nineteen times.

In the Cabinet Room, the dour Fraser, so un-Australian in his Scottish parson's grimness, welcomed the VP and invited him to speak. GB gave an overview on the US economy and even more forcefully on RR's commitment to reducing nuclear stockpiles. Fraser, who sees himself as a world figure, quizzed Bush on China, on the imminent hostilities between Britain and Argentina over the Falklands, and on lesions in the Atlantic alliance over the Soviet threat. The PM (whose colleagues addressed him with just those initials) is, if anything, harder-line toward the USSR than are Ronald Reagan and Margaret Thatcher.

Emerging from Parliament House, we beheld a beautiful day. The sun had burned off the morning pea soup fog, revealing a perfectly blue sky and Canberra in all its green and autumnal glory. The poplars were ochre, and the maples were both silver and gold. We went to the Australian National Press Club, outside of which a small, noisy band of protestors chanted, "Out, out, US bases!" An Australian businessman had told me during breakfast, "There are two generations in Australia: the Coral Sea[4] generation, for whom

---

4. "Coral Sea" is a reference to the May 1942 naval battle, the first in history between aircraft carriers, in which US, British, and Australian forces halted a Japanese drive toward Australia.

America can do no wrong, and the Vietnam generation, for whom America can do nothing right."

Then we were off on the forty-minute flight to Sydney. In perfect weather, it lay before us, interlaced with finger bays. Sydney is unquestionably one of the world's most beautiful cities, ranking with San Francisco, Capetown, and Rio. Pete Teeley and I rode together to Government House, where the VP and BPB called on Governor and Lady Rowland. Set on a hill overlooking the harbor, Government House resembles a Norman castle. It has formal gardens and walls hung with portraits of British sovereigns—including, most noticeably, George III.

Tonight brought Sydney's annual Coral Sea Ball. Demonstrators a few floors below us chanted, "We remember Vietnam!" and "Money for jobs, not for war; US out of El Salvador!" From such things came apt vice presidential remarks at dinner to Australians of the Coral Sea generation.

Saturday, 1 May 1982

En route to Melbourne, I chatted with the affable Bob Nesen, the US ambassador to Australia, who was an assistant secretary of the Navy in the Nixon Administration. He looks exactly like what he is, a successful car dealer from California who was given a political plum. He's been a longtime friend and supporter of RR's, dating back to the 1960s, when as a county Republican chairman Nesen drove the then–General Electric employee to speaking engagements.[5]

Tonight, PM Fraser (a proud product of Melbourne) gave a dinner for the VP. There were anthems and "loyal toasts" by the PM to President Reagan and by the VP to "Her Majesty, the Queen of Australia." In his remarks, Fraser once again praised the resolve of RR, and to underscore the same point GB announced that earlier today the US formally sided with Great Britain over the Falklands, ending our sincere but frustrated efforts to negotiate a peaceful resolution of the problem.[6] The audience was thrilled, and cries of "Hear, hear!" went up for GB's comments.

---

5. Ambassador Nesen dearly wanted to become secretary of the Navy when his friend was elected president. But, with GB's strong support, John Lehman got the job. This difficult choice proved one of historic consequence for the Navy, and Nesen was given the not-inconsiderable consolation prize of Canberra.

6. This was the result of a major bureaucratic victory by the pro-British Caspar Weinberger over the pro-Latin Alexander Haig.

Sunday, 2 May 1982

Today was a free one here in Sydney, but first there was an event I attended with the Bushes, the only staffer to do so. The motorcade took us to St. Stephen's Uniting Church for services commemorating Coral Sea Sunday. It was an Anglican service with all the proper touches. The VP read the lesson; the minister told dry little jokes; bagpipers in full Scottish regalia played outside; and we sang "God Save the Queen," "The Star-Spangled Banner," "Battle Hymn of the Republic," and "Eternal Father" (the Navy hymn). I'm glad I went. It was, after all, why we came to Australia in the first place.

During an afternoon walk around Sydney, I rounded the point called Mrs. Macquarie's Chair and headed for the Opera House. Hundreds of people were outside, looking toward the water. I came closer and found what was going on: the return of George Bush to Man o' War Jetty, aboard a cabin cruiser with two police boat escorts. There was a little applause as GB disembarked and got in the limo. Mostly people gawked at the number of cars and security men that the United States requires to take its vice president away from a boat ride.[7] Able to appreciate the spectacle myself as an anonymous member of the crowd rather than as a passenger in the motorcade, I could sense the sheer power that such a show denotes. One of the Sydney papers today casually described the boss as "likely to be the world's most powerful man in a few years."

Monday, 3 May 1982

On the three-hour flight to New Zealand, I read both the classified and unclassified briefing books. The VP, the Admiral, and Assistant Secretary of State John Holdridge[8] are concerned over a blast in Beijing's *People's Daily* to the effect that continued US arms sales to Taiwan could damage relations with the PRC. It's nothing new, but coming now it raises the question of whether the Chinese plan to pommel GB and make an embarrassing scene,

---

7. By contrast, PM Fraser rode in the front seat of his official car with one followup vehicle. I once asked a Secret Service agent how presidents and vice presidents are protected abroad. "It's very simple," he answered. "When they come here, they do it our way, and when we go there, they do it our way."

8. Holdridge was second in command at the US Liaison Office in Beijing when George and Barbara Bush arrived in 1974. He served as ambassador to Singapore and to Indonesia before getting the State Department's East Asia–Pacific portfolio in 1981.

as they did on his ill-advised trip to Peking as a vice presidential candidate in August 1980. The VP was in fact under the impression that the Chinese would hold down the diatribes prior to his visit as a sign of goodwill.

We came in over the North Island. Below us were placid farms with white specks: sheep. Beautiful Wellington is contained within a bay and, with its nearby forests, rather resembles the US Pacific Northwest. The motorcade wound around the bay and into the green, park-like grounds of Government House, a Tudor-style lodge built in 1910 for New Zealand's governor general. The incumbent, Sir David Beattie, and Lady Beattie welcomed the Bushes and our entire official party with champagne and finger sandwiches. I found the New Zealanders even friendlier than the Australians, if that can be believed, even though this country seems far more conservative and English than the great neighbor 1,200 miles distant. This friendliness may be because New Zealanders are conscious of being little fellows on the world scene, especially vis-à-vis the United States.

The governor general [the official representative of the Queen] said he soon will embark on a four-week cruise around the islands to New Zealand's north to maintain friendly relations. The VP approved: "You never know when one of these little guys will sign an agreement giving the Soviets porting rights." New Zealand, I noted, can perform this liaison role well, because as a small country it can appear less domineering than the US.

Tuesday, 4 May 1982

Parliament House in Wellington consists of two buildings: one stolid and English and the other circular and eclectic. The latter is named "the Beehive." Here, Prime Minister Robert Muldoon—a short, scrappy fellow with a bulldog's face—welcomed the VP and escorted him into the Cabinet Room. On the wall, composed of multicolored slats of wood, hung a world map centered on Australasia. Looking at the map, I was seized by the thought that at that moment I was right down *there*, at the very end of the Pacific Rim we've been skirting for the past eleven days.

The PM began by calling the ANZUS [Australia–New Zealand–US] Pact his country's most important treaty, and in accordance with it his government won't ban US naval vessels with nuclear weapons from using New Zealand ports, as the opposition Labour Party wants. "Our involvement with ANZUS means we go all the way," he said. PM Muldoon is as interested in international economic affairs as his Australian counterpart is interested in foreign affairs. GB responded with his own great enthusiasm for this subject.

He stressed that the US will first "get its own economic house in order" and that "we are dealing with a principled president who's seventy-one and too damned old to change his mind on things." The 100-minute session also dwelt on trade (especially dairy issues) and the Falklands but, perhaps significantly, nothing on China. The New Zealanders look more to their immediate neighbor (and to the US and Britain) than they do to China, which has long been an Australian preoccupation.

In the state luncheon to follow, PM Muldoon spoke in measured tones about the US–New Zealand relationship and of the importance of the South Pacific ministates. He was "supported" by the leader of the Opposition, who spoke eloquently of young New Zealanders' desire for peace, saying that is why his party supports a nuclear-free zone in the South Pacific.[9] GB's Buckley-written reply was one of his best efforts on this whole trip, reiterating RR's commitment to a reduction of nuclear arms and wondering whether antiwar protestors truly remember the lessons of Vietnam, where today there is no freedom and no peace.

---

9. When the Labour Party won power in 1984, it declared it would allow US warships to use New Zealand ports only if they could certify they were nuclear-free. Operating under a "neither confirm nor deny" policy, the US refused, and eventually ANZUS broke apart, the US forging a separate (and close) defense relationship with Australia.

Chapter 18

Everything but the Quack

Leaving Wellington, Air Force 2 made a grueling thirteen-and-a-half-hour passage to Hangzhou, China, with refueling stops in Sydney and Darwin.

Wednesday, 5 May 1982

Around 9:30 p.m., *AF2* approached Hangzhou in the rain. We could see very few lights and nothing that looked like an airport. Suddenly the plane accelerated and raised its landing gear to come around and make another pass. We later learned that the airport hadn't switched on the runway lights! The second try was a success, except that the pilot braked so rapidly that loose items in the cabin crashed to the deck.

A steady rain was falling as we disembarked to meet US ambassador Art Hummel and the smiling and mostly elderly officials of Zhejiang province. GB went into the terminal to read a short statement and answer a few questions from the US press. Then we took off in a long, slow-moving motorcade, headlights on lowest beam. The scene was dreamlike: landing in coastal China in the rain and traveling slowly through groves of trees into and out of a dim central city and across a long causeway. On the other side was an island thickly grown with old trees and featuring some fanciful old-style buildings, all of which we saw through a veil of rain and mist. A teahouse-like structure appeared, flashing neon signs that said WELCOME and CAFÉ. It was pure Somerset Maugham. Chris Buckley would have loved it, except he detached in Wellington to return to the US to do book promotions.

Finally the cars stopped on a narrow bridge. We got out and walked the short distance to Guesthouse Number 1, where the official party is staying. We found our rooms down several corridors in the somewhat faded but still-gracious lodging. The only copy machine available to us is aboard AF2, so there are no schedules or room assignments with telephone numbers, as in every stop we make. Still, no one complained: We have arrived in China, and it's time for bed—almost 4:00 a.m. in Wellington, New Zealand, far below the equator.

Thursday, 6 May 1982

At 9:30 there was a major skull session in VP Bush's office, just off the bed-room at the entrance to the guesthouse. Out the picture windows was Hang-zhou's Inner Lake, separated from West Lake by an old green causeway. To discourage anyone from recording the conversation, GB played what he called a "burble," a tape of radio static. Sitting in my armchair by the wall, however, I could hear everyone perfectly. The WHCA folk later told me that burbles won't foil electronic eavesdropping, and Ambassador Hummel said that if the Chinese heard what was discussed, it would be helpful. As with yesterday's airborne conference, this one began with GB worried about his encounters-to-be in Beijing and ended with everyone excited and optimistic.

Later we boarded launches for a tour of the famous West Lake, which so entranced Marco Polo on his visit here in the thirteenth century. When we docked at the ancient artificial Island of Little Oceans (from which one sees the Impressions of the Moon above Three Deep Pools[1]), a member of the traveling press asked the VP if there would be an arrival statement.

GB deliberately chose the occasion of tonight's dinner given by the gov-ernor of Zhejiang province to read a carefully prepared statement that made clear the Reagan Administration supports a "one China" policy and believes Taiwan is a part of China. He had two audiences more important than those gathered in the Hangzhou Hotel tonight. One was the American and inter-national viewing public, which has been led to believe that RR is backing away from the Shanghai Communiqué of 1972 and the 1978 agreement to normalize Sino-American relations. The other, more important, audience are the leaders in Beijing, who might be inclined to lambaste the VP for what they think is a tendency toward a "two Chinas: one China, one Taiwan" policy. If so, they ought to have gotten the message tonight.

Friday, 7 May 1982

At the airport we shook hands with provincial and city officials and boarded *AF2* for the two-hour flight to Beijing. The Chinese originally wanted the VP to fly aboard one of their planes, but we stood firm. Thus, *AF2* got us and CAAC [the Chinese national carrier] got the press. As a face-saver, we

---

1. Other place names on the islet were Lotus Stirred by the Breeze at the Distillery, Listening to Orioles in the Waving Willows, and Observing the Fish at Flower Harbor.

took along a half dozen Chinese officials, including Han Xu (vice minister of foreign affairs)[2] and a People's Liberation Army officer in uniform. The debonair, English-speaking Han was invited to ride in the lounge—making for a scene in which we staffers took turns chatting with him in hopes of diverting his attention from conversations over classified cables that John Holdridge and Don Gregg [of NSC][3] were having only a few inches away. Meanwhile, Ambassador Hummel prowled the aisles tensely, and GB remained in his cabin.

Although China has just opened a vast new airport, when we landed in Beijing at 10:00 it was at the old Stalinesque facility I remember from 1977. Here we quickly got in cars (black Nissans instead of pearl-gray Shanghais) for the forty-five-minute drive to the Diaoyutai State Guesthouse on the western side of the city. Among the obvious changes from my last visit are a number of high-rise buildings, advertising, and a distinct absence of propaganda paintings. US and PRC flags flew from lampposts in Tiananmen Square.

Diaoyutai means "Angler's Terrace" because (according to John Holdridge) it was where the emperor and his ministers used to cast a ceremonial line in the water once a year. For the past twenty years it has been a patch of green and blue in the heart of Beijing, reserved for the top leadership and the most important state visitors. It isn't Hangzhou, but it is a visual relief from the Mongolian hardness of the rest of the city. We are lodged in Guesthouse Number 8, where each room is stocked with creature comforts like fragrant sandalwood soap.

The VP's motorcade departed at 7:15 for the Great Hall of the People, where PLA [People's Liberation Army] troops came to attention upon our arrival. We climbed the broad flight of red-carpeted stairs, turned, and went down a receiving line to shake hands with Premier Zhao Ziyang (our host), FM Huang Hua, and others. Then we entered the great banqueting hall, so familiar since President Nixon's visit a little over ten years ago. A PLA band played jaunty airs, including some American folk songs like "Home on the Range," "Shenandoah," and "She'll Be Coming 'Round the Mountain."

---

2. Immensely warm and pleasant, Han was a major laborer on the Sino-American relationship during the 1970s and 1980s. Soon after Bush's 1982 visit to China, Han came to Washington as ambassador.

3. Gregg, a career CIA officer, would shortly succeed Nancy Bearg Dyke as vice presidential national security advisor and would become President Bush's ambassador to Korea from 1989 to 1993.

Then came national anthems and settling into our seats. Mine was at table number 2, heavily populated with vice ministers; I was bracketed by those for petroleum and international trade. The food was rather good, but the conversation was somewhat strained by language, the interpreter being some distance off.

When time came for toasting, the band stopped and PM Zhao mounted a stage. His remarks were brief and friendly, with only this political message: "We both recognize that there exist several obstacles in the present Sino-American relationship. At this critical juncture, Vice President Bush, as entrusted by President Reagan, has come to discuss with us matters of mutual concern. This is no doubt an important visit. . . . We sincerely hope that the Vice President's visit will yield positive results." GB's reply was like his statement last night in Hangzhou, only it had a note of added resolve. When he finished, each toaster went through the ritual of moving around the table to raise a glass to each person. Then we returned to our cars for the ride home along a boulevard that now has (of all things) neon lights.

At the guesthouse, there was a stand-up huddle with the VP to compare dinner table conversations. The Chinese appear disappointed that GB has not come to negotiate. Someone in the huddle asked if the VP needed a toast for tomorrow's lunch with Deng Xiaoping, and John Holdridge [*perhaps forgetting the 1981 toast in Manila?*] said, "You can wing it." GB temporarily lost his worried look and grinned: "Yeah, I might be winging it back home!"

Saturday, 3 May 1982

Jennifer and I were driven to the Great Hall for the luncheon Vice Chairman Deng Xiaoping[4] gave VP Bush after their morning talks. As I later learned, what began as a "private visit" of only five minutes prior to the formal discussions became the discussions themselves. The talks also ran a half hour overtime, and Jennifer and I chatted with BPB until lunch was served. When the two men entered the enormous, beautifully decorated dining room, we all studied their faces. They looked somewhat drawn but smiled resolutely,

---

4. Expelled from power during the Cultural Revolution, Deng had been rehabilitated by the time Bush arrived as US envoy to China in 1974. Their personal relationship was forged during Bush's subsequent year in Beijing. Deposed by the so-called Gang of Four after Mao's death in 1976, the wily Deng quickly rebounded to become China's unchallenged leader until his own death in 1997. As the motive force for his nation's economic expansion in the late twentieth century, Deng may be remembered as a far greater figure in Chinese history than the destructive Mao.

as would two experienced politicians. Pete Teeley sat next to me and in a low voice expressed great worry about this stop in Beijing's being a "disaster" for GB.

GB was scheduled to accompany BPB to Coal Hill (overlooking the Forbidden City), but the motorcade returned instead to Diaoyutai. There followed immediately a meeting in the VP's suite for a discussion of where things stand now. (GB played a "burble" tape of recorded music.) The VP felt encouraged by his meeting with Deng which, while tough and focused on Taiwan, was milder than what he experienced yesterday with FM Huang. Once again the Chinese pressed the US for a date certain on which to cut off arms sales to Taiwan, something no US negotiator in Beijing can do, given the Taiwan Relations Act [mandating such sales]. GB's conclusion, though, was that he "can get out of town" without a blast from the Chinese declaring the visit a failure. Ambassador Hummel agreed but said a big blast is coming if GB can't persuade the President to alter US policy on Taiwan. I didn't gather from the discussion that Deng expects as much or that GB promised to do anything other than report on their conversation to RR.

I wonder whether the date certain is all the Chinese want or whether they will come up with a new "obstacle to our relations" after that. This wouldn't surprise me, for obviously Beijing wants *Taiwan*. It is typical communist intransigence to keep making an impossible demand in the hope that the dumb democracies will make concessions in the interest of harmony, peace, and gentlemanliness. I further believe that many State Department types like Holdridge have a career-long interest in the closest possible relations with Beijing (which they glamorize as "our strategic relationship") and are willing to sacrifice the security of Taiwan to achieve it. Once again, RR's instincts are correct. I hope GB keeps his own perspective on the matter— and I wish somehow he could have visited Taiwan once in his life to see what's at stake in all this.[5]

We were back in the Great Hall this evening for a reception officially given by GB after his discussions with Premier Zhao. We lined up in protocol order, and the Chinese came through in reverse order: vice ministers first, then Huang Hua, and Vice Premier Wan Li last. We official party folk were paired with ranking Chinese guests; my opposite was Hao Daqing, president

---

5. I had visited Taiwan once, as an admiral's aide in 1969, when the island was a smoky, low-rise, and rather impoverished place firmly under the control of Chiang Kai-shek and his Kuomintang party.

of the Chinese People's Institute of Foreign Affairs. CPIFA was our official host on the 1977 trip to China, and Hao gave a banquet in the Bushes' honor. I thought this would inspire a jolly jaw, but the rotund Hao was more interested in the buffet than me.

When the rather pro forma toasting was done, we scurried to our cars and were driven to the Wang Fu Jing Roast Duck Restaurant—known in the American community as the "Sick Duck" because it's located near the hospital. Huang Hua was the host, and the menu included [as the Chinese like to say] "every part of the duck except the quack." I enjoyed all of this, including such unorthodox morsels as the web, brain, and tail. The last two are the real *pièces de résistance*, and Mr. Cao of Chinese protocol and I agreed to split the servings. The brain is served in a roasted duckhead-on-the-halfshell and has the taste and consistency of *pâté*. The tail (a dab of cartilage with roasted skin) is delicious but oily and best eaten inside a sesame bun. Of course the main course was the sliced meat eaten in thin pancakes. When the chef made an appearance with the big, browned bird and paraded it around the room with great pride, we all applauded. Don Gregg unhelpfully proposed several *ganbeis* [toasts with potent mao-tai], but I survived on Mr. Cao's assurance that it isn't considered bad manners to refuse to drain one's glass every time.

The fitting end to the day and the trip was our route home. On John Holdridge's inspiration, we requested permission to cut through the Forbidden City. We slowly drove past towering walls and gates in full moonlight, a marvelous romantic spot.

Sunday, 9 May 1982

Huang Hua came by the guesthouse at 10:45 to bid GB farewell. We boarded the motorcade and departed, passing under the portico where the FM and his wife waved to us. At the airport, GB held a press conference, a tricky affair because he expressed optimism for his mission and yet refused to give reporters the reasons why he felt progress was made on Taiwan. The answer was one he couldn't give them: he never had any instructions to negotiate the issue and saw the value of the trip only in terms of conveying to the Chinese RR's feelings about the importance of our relationship.

We boarded *AF2*, decorated with cartoon signs proclaiming it "Aloha Two." Though no one was dancing through the aisles, the mood was definitely one of relief and anticipation of some holidaying in Hawaii before returning to the half-forgotten world of Washington.

Many hours later, across the International Date Line, "the Big Island" of Hawaii—twice as large as all the other Hawaiian Islands combined—loomed ahead of us. AF2 put down at Keahole Airport on the lava-blackened Kona (west) coast. The Bushes disembarked and were whisked away by the Secret Service to a private residence near the Mauna Kea Beach Hotel, where they can have absolute privacy. The rest of us had to stay on the plane till US Customs cleared everyone. There were thousands of dollars in duty to pay, owed mostly by the vanished Secret Service. Kim Brady wrote a personal check that freed everyone to reenter the US after an absence of two and a half weeks. [*There are advantages of having "rich kids" on staff!*]

The hotel was built as a Rockresort by Laurence Rockefeller, and it has the harmonious architecture and exorbitant prices of its kin. While I'm sure we're getting a discount, there's no reason why the taxpayers should put the likes of us up at such a joint.

Monday, 10 May 1982

At 2:00, advanceman Jim Remington drove me up to GB's rented residence in a small but posh subdivision called Mauna Kea Fairways. It was easy to pick out the VP's quarters: the limo and follow-up wagon were parked in the short driveway, other cars were massed nearby, agents in polo shirts and sunburns drifted in and out of the garage, and a special aluminum pipe containing sensitive communication cables ran along the ground.

After the usual light banter with the agents, I was escorted inside by John Magaw. Joe Hagin, the staffer who's closest to the agents, says the main reason John hasn't advanced in the Secret Service, despite his superb skills, is that "he's too perfect"—which I suppose means too serious, too straight, and too well-combed to be one of the guys.[6]

GB was in a bathrobe, about to take a nap, but he wanted to take the time to "debrief" on his conversation Saturday with Deng Xiaoping. He gave his impressions of that meeting and the whole China visit, and I asked a few probing questions relating to personality and emphasis. It all took less than a half hour, after which I went back down the hill to the hotel. In the staff office, I immediately transcribed my notes while the words were still fresh.

---

6. Later in the year, speechwriter Peter Robinson pointed to John and inquired, "Who is that agent who looks like God?" Overcoming his "handicaps," John Magaw became director of the Secret Service in 1992, director of the Bureau of Alcohol, Tobacco, and Firearms in 1993, and Undersecretary of Transportation for security in 2002.

The job done, I went to the secure room guarded by two Marines to lock up the monologue, which probably will end up classified secret or top secret.

Tuesday, 11 May 1982

A bus took us staffers to an oceanside factory where a huge, squat Marine helo waited, its rear ramp laid down like a tongue in the dust. This became "the helo to Hilo." It was definitely a field chopper, with two long rows of opposing benches. A corporal showed us how to use the life vests and helmets "in case we go down," a phrase he used with distressing frequency. We then lifted off on a fifty-five-minute flight around the northern end of Hawaii, over water all the time. The corporal motioned to me to come see something out the open rear hatch. We had passed around to the wet side of the island (and Hawaii is the rainiest place on earth), and there in rows were over a dozen tall, thin, white waterfalls tumbling down black cliffs directly into the ocean. Occasionally, a rich green alluvial valley indented these mountains, and everywhere there were rain clouds.

We landed at the Hilo airport, about twenty minutes before the VP's helo touched down. Both Bushes were refreshed and rested from their sojourn on the mountaintop overlooking the Pacific. Then AF2 lifted off for the mainland and home.

Thus ends a glorious trip, the longest taken by a president or vice president in recent Secret Service memory. Probably no other will quite compare with all its special features: lunch with Hirohito, meetings with both the Australian and New Zealand cabinets, boat trips in Sydney and Hangzhou, and finally Beijing. Often I think that the real power wielders in the White House, like [Jim Baker's top aide] Dick Darman, must envy our footlooseness. Like the "toffs" and "tarts" defined in Graham Greene's *The Comedians*, these staffers may think, "We have the responsibility, but they have all the fun."

Wednesday, 12 May 1982

I arrived at the White House at 9:30, ninety minutes after landing at Andrews and a half hour before João Baptista de Figueredo, president of Brazil. GB asked me to "perform the Hagin role" at the arrival ceremony, since Joe was at home, recuperating from the flight. This meant holding the VP's folder of sensitive papers so he could be hands-free in the receiving line. I stood just behind one of the curving staircases on the South Portico, enjoying a president's-eye prospect of the ceremony: the crowd and troops before me, the trumpeters above, the guest limousine, flags flapping, pulling in from the left as the fanfare swelled, and the twenty-one-gun salute fired as I faced the Mall. Then I went to the office to grapple with a three-week backlog of paper.

Thursday, 13 May 1982

At our staff meeting, Shirley Green mentioned that ABC is looking into our having stayed at the Mauna Kea Beach. There was general squirming, and I piped up to say there ought to be no debate over where the VP himself stayed. (The house rented for $500 a day.) "The question is whether the taxpayers should have paid $200 a day for my room." After the meeting, I told Dan Murphy we can't put GB at risk by staying in luxury spots where simple first class would surely do. "We can be right on all the facts—security, need for rest, need for privacy, etcetera—and still lose the political argument. Voters may not understand the defense budget, but they can understand hotels, meals, parties, and clothes."

The Admiral agreed with me on the need to be careful but said, "I resent your holier-than-thou attitude." The trouble was that I was speaking to a mustang [*up from the ranks*] admiral who says outright that people in government ought to take every penny they are due in per diem and hotel accommodations. The Admiral's sense of politics was formed during his service under Melvin Laird [a former congressman from Wisconsin and Nixon's first secretary of defense]. But Laird was a crafty old fox and was never in as exposed a position—or had a political future—like GB's.

Chapter 19

Just Your Typical Palace

Friday, 14 May 1982

On the helo to Andrews, GB said that last night he was in bed when the phone rang, and [Senate majority leader] Howard Baker said there might be some tie votes on the defense appropriations bill. None occurred, but GB was at the Senate from 11:00 p.m. till 4:00 a.m., unsuccessfully trying to sleep in his office just off the Senate floor. It would have been terrible under normal circumstances but especially so after returning from across the Pacific.

When we landed in Las Vegas, the VP and we senior-staff types took an evasive route to the home of singer Wayne Newton. Back in the 1950s, Newton won fame for his brassy style and boyish grin while singing in a high voice. Today he is just as popular, but his looks have changed: he wears a pompadour, black mustache, and flamboyant clothes open to the navel. Newton is one of few entertainers under sixty who is an active Republican and a strong supporter of RR's. Frank Fahrenkopf[1] is his lawyer and, working with Jennifer, wangled a vice presidential visit to Newton's ostentatious spread.

Behind a tall wall made of cement blocks, Newton has a huge house with pillars and porticos, ponds and peacocks, a garage full of Rolls Royces and various custom cars, and a stable full of Arabian horses. We trooped into the house for drinks and hôrs d'oeuvres. GB had to make conversation with Newton, his attractive Filipina American wife Elaine, and a strange-looking couple, both of whom are doctors to the great Wayne. I absented myself to explore the rooms. [In the study was a framed letter to Newton from Ronald Reagan, written by hand the day after the 1981 inauguration, apologizing to

---

1. Then Nevada state Republican chairman, Fahrenkopf chaired the Republican National Committee from 1983 to 1989 before becoming chief lobbyist for the gaming industry in Washington.

him for some glitch.] Out on the lawn [in itself a luxury and rarity in Las Vegas], Arabians were paraded for the VP to see, each horse with its own handler.

Afterward we proceeded down the tawdry Las Vegas strip to the ultra-excessive Caesar's Palace Hotel, a sprawling place that seeks to tie ancient Rome into the twenty-eighth century. The VP went immediately into a press conference with Gov. Robert List. As I stood watching, I felt a hand on my shoulder: It was [deputy chief of staff] Fred Bush, beckoning me outside. "The people he's having dinner with tonight are all Mafia," Fred said. His source was an advanceman, who took out the guest list for the $5,000-a-couple function benefiting the governor and ran his finger down it: "This guy's a contractor; this one's a real estate developer; and this one owns Caesar's Palace, for God's sake," he said. I replied that, to the best of my knowledge, it isn't illegal to be any of those things. The advanceman said some local friends had seen some negative comments about the owner of the dinner site, a man who had to sell his interest in Caesar's Palace to get a gaming license in New Jersey. That, too, isn't illegal. Fred insisted that only our photographer be present so that we could destroy all shots of the VP with such folk before he might sign them and send them to the mobsters for placing on their walls.

After the press conference, we followed after the VP to his suite, which was complete with whirlpool sunken bath, an automatic curtain enclosure for the bed and a mirror high above. Fred made his emotional pitch, which of course shocked and distressed the VP. "How do you know this? Who says so?" Bush asked. John Magaw had reports only on the owner of the dinner site, who wouldn't even be present. A couple of diners have ties of some kind (social or business) with underworld figures, but John said that is common-place in Nevada.

Bush asked that Governor List come to the suite. They conferred privately, and List reassured the VP. A short while later, GB asked me to come into a briefing John Magaw gave him on the guests. This calmed the issue, but it had been a bad scene. After the dinner, I went with the VP to the door to the suite. All had gone well, we concluded, and he added without explanation, "There's a lesson in all this."

Sunday, 16 May 1982

Flying in Ohio National Guard helos from Cincinnati, we landed at Miami University's small airfield, the rotors blowing the fluffy heads of thousands of spring dandelions. As the motorcade passed through the leafy streets of

Oxford, people stood in their yards and waved. There were handmade signs of welcome held by children, and US flags flew everywhere. It was a refreshing piece of Americana.

We ended up at the university, a state institution in red-brick Georgian style. The first event was an alumni association luncheon honoring Barbara Bush, whose parents and brother were Miami grads.[2] Her short ad lib remarks were ideal, and she remembered to recognize and praise Congressman Mike Oxley.[3] Mike afterward took a group of us on a tour of the campus, where he had been student body president. Passing by seedy frat houses where students in cutoffs lounged in the hot sun and drank beer, we reached Millett Hall. There we heard GB's commencement address, a fine little Buckleyan effort on the control of nuclear weapons.

Tuesday, 18 May 1982

Rich Bond came over from the RNC for lunch in the Mess, a good place to mumble. Rich said we could lose as many as twenty-two House seats this fall but possibly gain a couple in the Senate. Governorships will be a wipeout for the GOP, given retirements of popular midwestern governors. This, Rich added in a low voice, won't help GB in 1984, because his power base are such moderate leaders as Bob Ray (Iowa) and Bill Milliken (Michigan). Jack Kemp is busy speaking around the country and has attacked the RNC (= Rich) for giving financial support to GB but not to him. Rich said a de facto ally for GB is Interior Secretary Jim Watt, who for some reason hates Kemp. Unfortunately, Watt is quite unpopular these days.

Wednesday, 19 May 1982

At 5:00, I was driven to the Senate side of the Capitol. Howard Baker wanted GB on the premises to break any ties on a series of amendments to the budget and, by his mere presence, demonstrate the Administration's serious opposi-

---

2. The media still routinely describe George and Barbara Bush as "East Coast (sometimes New England) patricians," but in fact both were offspring of the Midwest. Barbara Bush's family was pure Buckeye State. George Bush's paternal grandfather was a businessman in Columbus, and his mother's family, the Walkers, were from St. Louis.

3. Oxley was elected to Congress with VP Bush's help in a 1981 special election. As chairman of the Committee on Financial Services, he coauthored the 2002 Sarbanes-Oxley law on corporate governance.

tion to them. When I found the VP, he was not in his chair but in his beautiful ceremonial office, where we went over the names of high-powered New York pols whom Sen. Al D'Amato was bringing to the VP's Residence this evening. The VP gave the senator a lift in the limo; the siren escort caused some people to take snapshots and others to put their fingers in their ears.

The house was filled with Republican county chairmen and county executives, the power center of the Empire State GOP, plus several members of the congressional delegation, including Jack Kemp. GB, BPB, and Al made brief remarks from the staircase. The VP and senator then left for the Capitol and the continuation of voting. Several chairmen told me of their support for GB in both 1980 and 1984, despite the man D'Amato calls "Golden Boy" (Kemp).

I stayed till after all guests had left. Laurie Firestone [Mrs. Bush's social secretary] and Kim Brady fumed about the filching of a half dozen ashtrays by one or more chairmen.

Friday, 21 May 1982

At a meeting of White House deputies, Lee Atwater echoed Rich Bond's prediction of the loss of twenty-two Republican seats if the election were held now. He said he was conservative in his estimates, giving us the worse side of the doubt. Lee assumed the economy won't improve but thinks the White House and GOP can blunt two important perceptual issues the Democrats are using: that RR is out to destroy Social Security and that he is "the rich man's president." We were shown some test commercials made for the RNC, which we all agreed were so bleak—showing unemployed workers in Youngstown and a farm being auctioned in South Dakota—that they might have been made by the Dems. Even the tagline was one-cheer: "Republicans are beginning to make things better."

Monday, 24 May 1982

I rode with "Big Marv" [the VP's son, Marvin] to Boston College, where GB gave the commencement address. It was an excellent forum; located in one of the heartlands of American intellectualism, BC is a blue-collar, ethnic campus not unlike Duquesne. There were no visible protests anywhere, a great surprise. Immediately upon entering the hockey rink (where the commencement exercises were relocated due to rain), I came upon the glorious Nancy Bush Ellis. We sat together throughout the proceedings, and she quizzed me intensively on the nuclear arms issue. A classic Lincoln, Mass., liberal, she is inclined to accept the logic of a nuclear freeze.[4] "I mean, don't we have enough bombs as it is?" she asked, whereupon I'd try once more to explain the strategy of relative strength and deterrence. Fortunately, her brother hit the nuclear disarmament issue full-on in his address, and Nan was so stirred by his flat pronouncement that RR will achieve an actual reduction of weapons by the end of his tenure that she led the applause that interrupted him.

The next phase was the day's pleasantest, again despite the rain. We went to the Ellises' home on Sandy Pond for some "private time" for GB. He lay down on a couch in the living room, warmed by a fire on this almost-autumnal day, and Nan urged the rest of us to relax in the glassed-in den, with its own fireplace and view of the pond. Later came the four Massachusetts state reps who cochaired the Bush for President effort in the Bay State in 1980: Andy Card, now a candidate for governor; Andrew Natsios, state party chairman; Leon Lombardi, unopposed candidate for lieutenant governor; and Paul Celucci, Andy's chairman. They are a bright, attractive, and impressive group of young guys.[5] GB clearly enjoyed the reunion. He has the gift of leaping over the generational divide without appearing foolish or condescending to younger people.

Tuesday, 25 May 1982

At 5:00, the VP met with Crown Prince Hassan of Jordan, the brother of King Hussein,[6] in the Roosevelt Room. Hassan has a beautiful baritone like his brother but speaks much faster. A monotonous and (to me) perplexing outpouring of names had a highly embarrassing consequence for the State Department protocol officer escorting Hassan: not only did this fellow's head plop down on his vest, he erupted in a snorting snore. His Royal Highness was too polite to take notice, and GB later claimed he didn't hear anything

---

4. The nuclear freeze movement demanded an end to further construction of nuclear weapons by the US and USSR. Their logic was such that when Reagan called for an end to nuclear weapons altogether—which one would imagine to be their goal—they denounced him for proposing something the Soviets would never accept, prolonging the status quo.

5. Andy, the quintessential Bush family loyalist, became deputy chief of staff to the first President Bush, Secretary of Transportation, and chief of staff to the second President Bush; Andrew became administrator of the Agency for International Development; Leon became a state judge; and Paul became governor of Massachusetts and US ambassador to Canada.

6. Shortly before his death in 1999, Hussein made his son Abdullah crown prince.

at all, but the eyes of the American diplomats at the table filled with horror and earnest appeals to me to do something. I got up from my armchair, walked at a half-crouch to the guy's chair, and gave him a couple of fraternal claps on the shoulder. He came awake. If I had committed such a *lèse majesté*, the embarrassment would have produced such a gush of adrenaline that I couldn't have gone to sleep for a week. Alas for the gent from Protocol, he soon nodded off again, fortunately in silence this time. His colleagues from State spoke in sudden, loud bursts in order to rouse him, but on he slept. The moment the meeting ended, they rushed over to wake him. Mitchell Stanley of the Meese office predicted the poor fellow "will be stamping visas in Senegal next week."

Wednesday, 26 May 1982

Jim Lilley,[7] our de facto ambassador to Taipei (as "director of the American Institute on Taiwan"), came by at 2:00. He said his respect and admiration for Taiwan has grown by being on the island, and he fears that the depth of US obligation there isn't fully appreciated by the State Department in their desire for closer relations with the mainland—my position precisely.[8]

Saturday, 29 May 1982

At a bookstore near the White House, I found a Penguin paperback edition of *The Travels* of Marco Polo. I was inspired to read about the first great China traveler when we were in Hangzhou—a place called Kinsai in the thirteenth century, which Polo proclaimed "without doubt the finest and most splendid city in the world." Written by a "romancer" named Rustichello of Pisa, who probably embellished the tales recounted to him in prison by Polo, *The Travels* remains a marvel. I wonder if the journey to China described in this very

---

7. A true American patriot and one of the most dedicated public servants of his day, Jim Lilley was a Chinese-speaking career CIA officer who headed the Beijing "station" when GB was there in the mid-1970s and accompanied us on the 1977 China-Tibet trip. President Reagan appointed him ambassador to Korea, and President Bush made him ambassador to China and assistant secretary of defense for international security affairs.

8. In August 1982, the US pledged in a joint communiqué with China that it would not sell arms to Taiwan indefinitely and would in fact reduce those sales "over a period of time." Yet as of the publication of this book, thirty years later, the US continues to sell weapons to the island.

volume might one day also dazzle a reader in a distant century. As much as I am appalled that it took the Polos three years to reach Peking, so might the reader of this journal 700 years hence groan at the thought of spending hour upon hour cooped up in a 707 jet to reach the same destination.

Monday, 7 June 1982

I attended a meeting in the office of Ken Duberstein, assistant to the president for congressional relations.[9] Along with fellow politicos Lee Atwater, Rich Bond, and others, I helped plot the final push for votes on a budget bill in the House. We went down a list of names, parceling out those with whom we think we (or our chiefs) have some influence. The jargon was exotic: we discussed getting "babysitters" for "Yellowjackets," "Gypsy Moths," and "Boll Weevils." The Yellowjackets, led by [Congressman] Bill Archer [R-Texas], are so conservative they don't want a deficit that even touches $100 billion. The Gypsy Moths are liberal Republicans, most from tough districts, who can't vote to cut social programs or to increase the deficit. And the Boll Weevils are the conservative Democrats who passed the President's economic program last year and whose votes are needed again. Ken said he'd like the VP to have private meetings with about twenty Moths and make about a dozen phone calls to some Weevils. [*This Bush did, showing again the value of a modern vice president as his administration's highest-ranking lobbyist on Capitol Hill.*]

Alejandro (Alex) Melchor, ambassador-at-large of the Philippines, called with an invitation to dinner. He was acting on behalf of Mrs. Roberta McCain, widow of the great Adm. John S. (Jack) McCain, CINCPAC [Commander-in-Chief Pacific] in my days in the Philippines. The dinner was in the elegant apartment house at 2101 Connecticut Avenue in the Kalorama neighborhood. I was met at the door by Roberta, still a southern beauty deep in her sixties, and by her twin sister, Rowena, who's even more beautiful.[10]

In addition to Alex and his shy wife, Charito, the guests were ex-ambassador Henry (Hank) Byroade and his sleekly handsome wife, Jitka. I

---

9. By the end of the Administration, Ken would be chief of staff.

10. Roberta's son, John S. McCain III, would be elected to Congress from Arizona later in the year and became a senator in 1986. He was the Republican presidential nominee in 2008. The sisters had accompanied "Jumping Jack" on official trips around his ocean and were known in the military as "Admiral McCain's R&R." When jokingly asked how he could tell the twins apart, the grandly gruff Admiral would say with a cigar clenched between his teeth, "That's *their* problem."

was transported back to that momentous era in my life when I was a naval aide and my present company were all potentates. We ate a substantial boiled dinner served by a retired Navy steward; conversation was fast-paced and filled with recollections. There followed a long period of coffee, liqueurs, and more talk. Byroade (who also served in Egypt, Afghanistan, and Pakistan, among other places) is deeply concerned about Israeli influence on US policy in the Middle East. The Byroades gave me a lift home, and I promised to put in a memo to White House social secretary Muffie Brandon for them to be invited to the state dinner for President and Mrs. Marcos in September.

Wednesday, 9 June 1982

In New York, we went first to the University Club for a $250-a-plate fundraising breakfast for Bill Green, Republican representative since 1978 of Manhattan's silk-stocking eighteenth congressional district. Green [a Gypsy Moth] has been very antagonistic to the Administration's budget policy, and as of Monday's meeting had been written off by Ken Duberstein as a possible vote. The room, decorated with grand portraits of university presidents, was filled with substantial-looking people. GB's remarks focused on China and on the widening Israeli incursion into Lebanon, but he finished with a flourish on the economy and the need to enact a budget that shows declining deficits. "We need your support," he told the audience. "And we need the support of your congressman." He later increased the public pressure by asking his listeners "to contact everyone you know in the House and call for action on the President's program." (Ken's office was delighted when I reported this to them.) What did Green do? He studied the uneaten scrambled eggs on his plate.

Leaving Forty-Third Street, we proceeded to the UN Building, pulling inside the iron gate and up to the front door. There the VP was met by Amb. Jeane Kirkpatrick. The nonstop feud between her and SecState Haig is in the news again. Haig refuses to talk directly to her, comparing her to "a company officer, with a corps in between." On the famed thirty-eighth floor, GB met with the new secretary general, Javier Perez de Cuellar. Down below, Buddhist monks from Japan beat drums for world disarmament.

In a holding room, I phoned Lee Atwater to find out how yesterday's "Dump Jim Baker" meeting in Dallas went. "It was a dud," he said. "Capital D, capital U, capital D, dud." Eighteen people showed up to hear Howard Phillips of the Conservative Caucus call Clymer Wright [a Baker foe from

Houston] "an American Dreyfus." This remark probably puzzled half the room and infuriated the rest for calling Clymer a Jew.

Thursday, 10 June 1982

While Bush was at CIA, Jim Cicconi [an aide to Jim Baker] dropped by to alert me that voting was in progress on the Latta substitute to the House budget resolution. We watched the vote on the tote board on the C-Span cable channel. The Republican-backed substitute carried 215–200, the result of 46 Democratic defections and only 16 Republican losses. Next, the House voted on the budget resolution as amended, and it won, 220–207. I phoned GB in the limo with the good news.

Sunday, 13 June 1982

Just before noon, Jennifer called to say the VP would be leaving for New Orleans from the Residence rather than touching down at Andrews from Maine. This meant he had come back early, and I immediately guessed the reason why: King Khalid of Saudi Arabia had died overnight of a heart attack at age sixty-nine, and undoubtedly GB the crisis manager needed to be back in DC. Jennifer confided that Judge Clark [the national security advisor] felt that GB should go to Riyadh for whatever ceremony or official calls are to be made there.

In the Crescent City, Lt. Col. Bill Eckert came into the reception [for Congressman Bob Livingston] with the word: the VP will go to Saudi Arabia, leaving at 7:30 tomorrow evening. [Secret Service detail chief] Wayne Welch was quite concerned; this gives him practically no time to advance the trip—to, of all places, the Middle East in the immediate aftermath of Israel's crushing the military arm of the Palestine Liberation Organization, probably ensuring reprisal acts of terror. Soon there was a clump of aides around the VP, partly to hear what was happening and partly to block well-wishing Louisiana Republicans. As soon as the VP finished his remarks, he dashed to a holding room telephone to talk with Nancy Bearg Dyke about the trip to "Saudi" (as oilmen call it).

We then boarded the motorcade for the short ride to the New Orleans Super Dome. Inside were about 40,000 Southern Baptists, gathered for their annual convention. The VP and [evangelist] Billy Graham and other Baptist divines came on stage. There was some gospel singing and a brief sermon by the Rev. Bailey Smith, president of the Southern Baptist Convention and the man who in 1980, with then-nominee Reagan sitting nearby, announced that "God doesn't hear the prayer of a Jew." Pete Teeley and I tensed for what the Reverend Smith would say this evening, but his message was only loud. He did make an oblique political plug, saying, "There is alive in the White House today the things we hold important."

GB's text was based in large measure on a memo recently sent him by *National Review* publisher William Rusher. It defended the use of the political system by what has been called "the religious right" to arrest a decline in moral and family values. The crowd interrupted him several times with applause, at one point in midsentence.

Monday, 14 June 1982

Today I was up at 6:00 and packed in one bag for a journey to far Araby—not really certain I would be going. In the White House, GB buzzed for Jennifer and me to join him and Nancy Bearg Dyke, at which time he read off the list of staff making the trip—including the three of us. Seats on AF2 were squeezed by the addition of a high-level official delegation: SecDef Caspar Weinberger, Sen. Charles Percy (R-Illinois), chairman of the Senate Foreign Relations Committee; Sen. Bennett Johnston (D-Louisiana), a member of the Appropriations Committee; Congressman Clem Zablocki (D-Wisconsin), chairman of the House Foreign Affairs Committee; Congressman Bill Broomfield (R-Michigan), ranking minority member of Zablocki's committee; Adm. William Small, the vice chief of naval operations, representing the Joint Chiefs of Staff; and deputy national security advisor Bud McFarlane.

There was no obvious reason for me to go, but as long as George Bush, vice president of the United States, wanted me on the manifest, I wasn't going to object. Even as I write, I have no idea what if anything I'll do in Saudi Arabia, but I value this opportunity as perhaps my only chance in life to go there the really right way.

The Republican state chairman of Illinois came in to see the VP, but he had to wait while Bill Clark reported to Bush the surrender of Argentine troops on the Falklands to Great Britain. GB came out to tell us, and [native Britons] Jennifer and Barbara cheered.

In the late afternoon, I returned home to change clothes. We received a protocol advisory saying that men should not wear "black" clothing, it not being appropriate by Saudi mourning customs. So, off went the pinstriped navy suit and on went a pinstriped gray. Then I went to the Naval Observatory, parking near the helipad and walking to the Residence. Tonight the Bushes hosted Sen. Richard Lugar (R-Indiana) and his "Ground Floor Group" of major donors. They arrived in three busloads, and I stood at the door and shook hands with many of them as they filed in. Indiana is almost an oddity: a thoroughly organized political entity ruled top to bottom by the Republican Party.

When the VP's limo pulled up, happy Hoosiers crowded around, and I took my chance to leave for the helipad. Secretary Weinberger arrived there by motorcade, popping out of his Cadillac without a briefcase and heading in my direction. I like to think that, if all goes well, I can be like Weinberger— going from Harvard student[11] to state legislator to protégé of a rising pol (RR in his case) to Cabinet officer. The VP came a short while later, and when the helo lifted off, we circled the Residence as a farewell to the waving folks below.

Already at Andrews were the rest of the delegation and the Saudi ambassador, who came to say goodbye. After SAM 86970 lifted off, a casually dressed GB emerged from his cabin to socialize with his confreres over a supper of cold seafood. Then everyone went off to bed: Weinberger is in the cabin with the VP; Percy, Johnston, Broomfield, and McFarlane are in the after-bunks; and Zablocki and Small are with Jennifer and me in the lounge.

Tuesday, 15 June 1982

Today I came awake at 8:30 British time (3:30 a.m. in DC) after three hours of semi-comfortable sleep. Clem "Zablocked" my legs from fully stretching out on the couch. We refueled at Mildenhall AFB in England, a place of red-roofed buildings with a high-flying spy plane parked discreetly to one side. Then we flew over Central Europe, the Med, and Egypt; the State Department's Arabic interpreter pointed out the Pyramids. En route I read *The Times* of London on the ceasefire in the Falklands and the fighting in Lebanon, plus both the classified and unclassified briefing material on Saudi Arabia. I talked politics with Representative Broomfield, a quietly likeable old congressman in the Gerry Ford manner, and chatted with Secretary Weinberger, the image of alertness and appetite for work.

---

11. The Secretary's son, Cap Jr., was a friend since college days, when we lived in the same freshman dorm. Our "proctor," occupying the ground-floor suite, was a second-year law student named David Hackett Souter, later a justice of the US Supreme Court.

As the sun began sinking over the desert, we touched down at the Riyadh airport, a combination commercial and military airfield. The VP and delegation were met by Amb. Richard Murphy, who was in Manila during last year's vice presidential visit. The air was hot but not oppressive; in fact, it was a welcome change from the over-air-conditioned cabin of AF2. Men in long white robes and burnooses [*the correct word for the Arabian head covering for men is* ghutra] swarmed around the ramp. The VP had a quick cup of ceremonial coffee with his greeters before proceeding into the city. Riyadh is a place of khaki-colored buildings (few looking older than ten years) set on a khaki-colored landscape. There is little of scenic or architectural interest. One appreciates Saudi Arabia for its economy, culture, and religion; only the T. E. Lawrences can appreciate it for its beauty.

The motorcade pulled onto the grounds of the Kubba ("Dome") Palace, the state guesthouse. Built for King Saud, who reigned from 1953 to 1964, it has been refurbished for use by state visitors. GB is the first such occupant. The Kubba is managed by the InterContinental Hotels chain. It can be called a newer version of the Akasaka Palace in Tokyo, albeit of traditional Arabic design rather than mock Versailles, and if anything it's bigger.[12] My suite is of such vast proportions that I removed the fruit basket and mineral water from the living room into the bedroom for easier access. And when the phone rang, I had to run from the bathroom–dressing room area to answer it in time.

After showering and changing, I embarked on an exploration of the palace. There are two gigantic halls in both wings, both used by lounging Saudi security men. Down one of these wings are two spectacular smaller rooms: one decorated in intricate multicolored Arabesque style, and the other completely covered, walls and ceiling, with fitted pieces of mirror that reflect a chandelier's dazzling light. Another room had a TV set showing a videotape from Saudi TV of the funeral services for King Khalid, beginning with the announcement of his death to his being borne down the ramp of his 747 on a litter, wrapped in simple desert robes. He was then carried in similar fashion through the streets of Riyadh.

Jennifer and I were invited to the VP's quarters, located below the dome of the palace, everything in baby blue, gold, and cream. Pete and Ambassador Murphy joined us for a regal little supper of Iranian beluga caviar, smoked

---

12. When we returned to Washington, a staffer in the VP's domestic policy office gushed, "Gee, I heard you all stayed in a palace! What was it like?" I'm afraid she didn't appreciate my attempt at humor when I answered with a shrug, "Oh, it was just your typical palace."

salmon, and truffled pâté. An Arabist, Murphy was the instant choice for this post when Secretary Haig fired his predecessor for making remarks critical of the Administration's lobbying efforts on AWACS last year. We talked, somewhat guardedly, of the Israeli actions in Lebanon. GB has long resented "the Jewish lobby" and particularly bridles at PM [Menachem] Begin's bloody ways. I am less aggrieved, perhaps because I despise the PLO [Palestine Liberation Organization] so much.

Originally, the VP was to leave at 9:00 p.m. to call on the new king, Fahd, but this was indefinitely delayed due to a stack-up of visitors. The Saudis wanted GB to be last so that his visit would be unrushed. It was therefore not until 11:20 that the motorcade mounted up. We went to what was described as the King's "working palace," a large, Arabic-to-nondescript building not far from the Dome. The interior was well but not lavishly furnished, with a big room rimmed by identical armchairs.[13] Here GB and the rest of the official delegation made a brief formal condolence call on King Fahd, Crown Prince Abdullah,[14] and other male members of the royal family. Afterward, Bush, Weinberger, Small, and McFarlane had a private audience with the King, and the congressional members of the delegation met with the foreign minister, Prince Saud, nephew of the King.

Bill Eckert, Cynthia, and I found ourselves sitting in a large lobby next to a row of Bedouins in bandoliers, cradling rifles between their knees. When the advancemen offered a ride back to the Dome, I snapped it up. Someday I may be exalted enough to meet privately with the king of Saudi Arabia; until then I need my sleep.

Wednesday, 16 June 1982

Today, when I got up at 6:30, the Saudi summer sun was already so hot that I was glad the Dome Palace staff had drawn the thick curtains last night. Breakfast was served in a large dining room. Congressman Broomfield and I went through the buffet and took a table together. I was complimented when he asked whether I plan to run for Congress someday.

Due to the cancellation of calls by the VP on two members of the royal family, we were able to leave Riyadh ahead of schedule. The motorcade left

---

13. This room, found even in modest Arab houses, is called the *majlis*, literally "the place for sitting."

14. Abdullah would succeed Fahd as king in 2005.

the Dome Palace, every cornice of which was perfectly visible in the glaring sunlight, and whisked to the airport. GB read a departure statement expressing US grief over the late King Khalid. Then we all dashed through the heat to *AF2*. Low sand dunes were our farewell to Saudi Arabia as they had been our welcome.

During the long journey home, we refueled twice: at Rhein-Main Air Base near Frankfurt (the first footfall for me on the soil of my ancestral Deutschland) and again at Keflavik in Iceland. The party was met by Amb. Marshall Brement and by Rear Adm. Ron Marryott,[15] commander of Iceland Defense Forces. We crowded into a conference room for a classified briefing on US defense relations with Iceland. The tiny nation (with less than one-quarter million people) holds an extremely strategic location astride Soviet air and sea routes into the Atlantic, and yet the proud Icelanders have never liked the relatively large presence of even an ally's forces on their territory. US military personnel, for example, are forbidden to live off the base, supposedly for fear of diluting the ancient Icelandic culture.

We left Keflavik and flew along the coast of Greenland. A mountain chain, completely covered with snow and made painfully bright by the sun, appeared on our right. To the left, ice floes and an occasional iceberg drifted off in cloud-like swirls into the turquoise sea.

Our two-day trip came to an end at 10:00 p.m., some eighteen hours after leaving Riyadh. At the Naval Observatory, Barbara Bush gave each of us a welcome-home kiss. Once again a long foreign trip proved that fatigue, not time zones, causes jet lag, and by getting ample rest in flight one can survive the zones (seven in all today).

It has become standard comedy fare to assert that the job of a vice president is to attend funerals. George Bush even added to the shtick by saying his slogan was, "You die, I fly." But a foreign funeral is like the one for your Aunt Tillie: it's not for the dead but for the living. Bush's attendance at funerals (as well as inaugurations and other state celebrations) were superb opportunities to meet other leaders, particularly the new leaders with whom the US would have to deal, as was the case in Riyadh and on three future occasions in Moscow. A CIA officer once told me, only half-joking, "George Bush put together the coalition that won the Gulf War at all the funerals he attended as vice president."

---

15. Later in the decade, as assistant secretary of the Navy, I would work with Marryott when he was superintendent of the Naval Academy.

Friday, 18 June 1982

The Republican National Committee held its main business meeting today at the Washington Hilton. Out in the lobby, Lee Atwater introduced me to the conservative writer John Loftin, one of the anti-Bush/Baker leaders. "When is George Bush going to hire some Reaganites?" he asked before moving off. I wish I could have answered: we are *all* Reaganites—certainly after 16 July 1980 [when Reagan chose Bush as his running mate], and we're more loyal than a lot of folks who were Reaganites before then.

Ed Rollins addressed the RNC after lunch. In his well-meaning way, Ed dropped a couple of lines ripe for quoting out of context: "We've got a seventy-one-year-old president who would rather be out in Santa Barbara riding horses then being beat on by the Democrats. . . . We're ten feet from the peak of Mount Everest, and if we lose this November, we go all the way to the bottom." Somehow Ed, an extremely savvy fellow, lets himself say potentially explosive things like this.

Wednesday, 23 June 1982

GB saw a succession of visitors this afternoon, including ex-congressman Wilbur Mills (D-Arkansas). For many years a titan on the Hill as chairman of the House Ways and Means Committee, Mills today came as a humble lobbyist for increased US agricultural development aid to Egypt. GB has remained a loyal admirer of his onetime committee chairman, despite the personal embarrassment that caused Mills's downfall in 1974, because Mills was so fair to him as a junior member of Ways and Means back in 1967–71.[16]

But the greatest visitor of them all was PM Margaret Thatcher of the United Kingdom. She arrived ten minutes early, before the President had returned from a reception in the East Room, so GB met her at the entrance to the West Wing and brought her, Secretary Haig, and outgoing ambassador Sir Nicholas Henderson into his office. When they emerged, Barbara Hayward gave a misty-eyed little statement how "we all admire what you did [in the Falklands]. It was truly wonderful." The PM modestly praised the British armed forces. "Nico" Henderson then noticed on the wall a seascape

---

16. As a freshman congressman, Bush became a member of what's invariably called "the powerful tax-writing Ways and Means Committee," a rare occurrence before or since. Mills had resigned his chairmanship after a drunken night on the town with a Washington entertainer named Fanne Fox, aka "the Argentine Firecracker."

by Worthington Whittredge, an American artist of the Hudson River school, titled "Thacher [*sic*] Island off Rockport, Massachusetts." Mrs. T studied the painting for a few moments before announcing to her ambassador, "I must go govern it someday!" Then they were all off to the Oval Office.

Thursday, 24 June 1982

There were two groups of pols who came by the West Wing this afternoon. The first were Iowa Republican congressmen Tom Tauke, Jim Leach, and Cooper Evans, all GB supporters in 1979–80. Each wants the VP to do a fundraiser for them, Leach warning that conditions for the GOP in Iowa are as bad as they were in the disaster years of 1964 and 1974. GB agreed to doing the three events plus something for gubernatorial candidate Terry Branstad. Leach then launched into a critique of the Administration's policies on nuclear arms control. President of the [moderate-liberal Republican] Ripon Society, Leach is admired by GB as "thoughtful" and "cerebral." That means he's a soft-spoken liberal.

The Iowans were followed by George Deukmejian, attorney general of California and our gubernatorial nominee. The quiet, broad-smiling "Duke" brought his family, chief aide, and former Reagan speechwriter Ken Kachigian. The 8 June Republican primary was noteworthy for the victory of moderates like Deukmejian for governor and [San Diego mayor] Pete Wilson for the Senate. But Deukmejian doesn't think that's any portent for the future of California politics. As they left, Duke's aide told me they hope to get GB to the state because "he's very popular out there."[17]

Friday, 25 June 1982

When I returned to the office a few minutes after 3:00, Secret Service agent Larry Kumjian, standing outside the door, asked what was going on: "People are rushing all around here." I saw Teeley, Boyden, and Barbara Hayward in with the VP watching television, so I joined them to learn the blockbuster: a few minutes before, President Reagan announced the resignation of Secretary Haig and the nomination of ex-Labor and Treasury Secretary George Shultz as his replacement. No details were given, but undoubtedly it was the predictable end to everyone's patience: Haig's with the White House for not

---

17. Bush would in fact be (in 1988) the last Republican presidential nominee to carry California.

letting him be "vicar of foreign policy," and the White House's with Haig for his constant fits of pique and arrogance. The Israelis and Western Europeans may be sorry to see him go, but no one in the West Wing is. Shultz will be a respected "team player" (the big phrase in the Reagan White House) who will fit in nicely with the other members of the Administration's foreign-policy ball club: GB, Cap Weinberger, and Bill Clark. Out of the Haig resignation ought to come some commentary how much influence GB has on foreign affairs and how much the departure of his self-made rival Haig will underscore, if not enhance, his position.

Monday, 28 June 1982

GB called from the car to ask me to watch the *NBC Nightly News* and see a Marvin Kalb report on the Haig departure. I did: Kalb said Haig was "irritated" that on our Saudi Arabia trip, GB and Cap Weinberger allegedly sympathized with the Arabs against Israel in Lebanon, undercutting Haig's pro-Jerusalem stance. The Israelis and Jewish Americans are concerned that Secretary-designate Shultz and Weinberger are anti-Israel, or at least not pro-Israel. There's no doubt that GB and Weinberger (not to mention Chuck Percy) were upset over the bombing of Beirut and probably communicated that to the Saudis. GB is carping more and more in private about "the Jewish lobby," making me wonder whether his voice grows louder because he realizes how politically potent it is and he's irritated at how much heat they're putting on him.

Tuesday, 29 June 1982

At 8:00, I arrived at the Metropolitan Club for dinner with Scott Thompson. He's been chosen as an associate director of the International Communications Agency [soon to revert to its old name of the US Information Agency]. Scott feels, as I do, that the US is resurgent in world affairs, helped by the victories of its allies Britain and Israel and by the remarkable circumspection of the Soviets. "It's been the best three weeks for the US since [the Cuban missile crisis of] 1962!" he asserted.

Eventually we got around to talking of the Untermeyer future. Without stating any specific ambition, I allowed that I would like an assistant secretaryship. Scott is confident I can get such a spot, and he advised to "go for the ones with troops. Sometimes there's a tradeoff, and what a job may lack in title it makes up in troops."

*Scott did not refer literally to armed forces but metaphorically to deployable re-
sources of any kind. He felt—and in time I would come to agree totally—that one
should seek an appointment in which to do things, not merely to issue papers, take
trips, and hold meetings.*

Sunday, 18 July 1982

Ron Kaufman called to report that yesterday Connecticut state GOP chairman Ralph Capacelatro endorsed Sen. Lowell Weicker for reelection. This
was both shocking and significant, for Capacelatro was a prime force in en-
listing Pres Bush to run against the hated Weicker. This could cause a stampede to Weicker at next weekend's convention. Pres's campaign has been
faltering this past month largely due to ineptitude. I related this to GB [by
phone] when he returned from boating [in Maine]. Refreshed and exhila-
rated by the run on the water and eager for a run on land with his weekend
guest, PM Lee Kuan Yew of Singapore, GB's fine mood was dulled by the
Connecticut report.

Wednesday, 21 July 1982

SAM 86970 was in the shop, suffering from another ailment, so we had
86971 instead for today's trip to Atlanta and beyond. Joe Hagin is increas-
ingly nervous about all the breakdowns in our twenty-five-year-old 707s.
Yes, we should get newer and better long-distance aircraft, but it would be
politically hard to do so before the 1984 election. Till then, we have to hope
there'll be no crisis.

Landing at Hartsfield International in Atlanta, we proceeded to the
campus of [predominantly black] Morehouse University and its new Basic
Sciences Building, which GB this morning dedicated. Mayor Andy Young
made a noisy and late arrival. Despite their obvious differences over foreign
policy and the role of the ambassador to the UN [which he was under Jimmy
Carter], Young is someone GB likes and counts as a friend.

Across a small street, a band of demonstrators paraded with homemade
signs. They were almost all young whites, and their rote chants were "Money
for jobs, not for war!" "We want jobs, we want peace, US out of the Middle
East!" "They say cut back, we say fight back!" and the now-standard "Reagan,
Reagan, he's no good; send him back to Hollywood!"

Paul Coverdell, one of our favorite young Georgians, rode in the limo with the VP, and I rode in a car driven by his father-in-law, a retired Shell executive.[18]

Friday, 23 July 1982

Flying back from a political appearance in Springfield, Illinois, the Bushes were in a tense, expectant, wistful mood. This was the eve of balloting for the Senate nomination at the GOP state convention in Connecticut. The current thinking is that Pres will get the minimum 20 percent of the delegates he needs to qualify for the September primary (GB and I both guess 30 percent) but nowhere near enough to draw the contributions needed to beat Lowell Weicker at the polls. GB spoke dourly of "Pres having to make some tough decisions this weekend"—apparently whether to drop out.

Saturday, 24 July 1982

Before I got into bed, GB called to ask if I had any reports on the Connecticut GOP convention. I hadn't, but fortunately Ron Kaufman called with the results not long thereafter: Weicker, 609 votes; Bush, 321, or roughly 34 percent. I immediate phoned GB, who answered saying, "I got it!" We both puzzled over what Pres will decide to do. Had he gotten only 20–30 percent of the delegates, a challenge to Weicker in the primary would be wrong and foolish. But had he gotten over 40 percent, it would have been irresistible [to enter]. Ron hopes Pres will quit the race, now that he has obtained an honorable minority vote.

Monday, 26 July 1982

GB had me return a call from Pres Bush, in which he said he wanted to speak with the VP before making up his mind on continuing the Senate race. GB later said he told "Pressie" to make his decision independent of how it might affect him (GB). In large part, GB feels guilty about not helping his older

---

18. Then a state senator, Paul Coverdell had been the Bush for President chairman in Georgia in 1979–80. He would serve as director of the Peace Corps under President Bush. His election to the Senate in a special election after the victory of Bill Clinton in 1992 was the first of an unbroken series of GOP triumphs ending in the party's taking the Congress in 1994. Coverdell, much respected, died in office in 2000.

brother, who always helped him in his political campaigns. The truth is that if Pres continues the race, worsening the GOP split [in Connecticut] and causing us to lose the Weicker seat, GB will be blamed. My vote, therefore, is for Pres to drop out.

I took advantage of a wisp of responsibility given me by Jennifer: to think of something the VP could do Sunday morning in San Antonio. Shirley Green [who's from San Antonio] and I came up with the idea of his attending church in Mission San José, followed by a Mexican breakfast on the West Side with Louis Terrazas and other Latino friends. Jennifer thought this was great. Louis will find out whether it would be all right to invade San José, whether the priest would radicalize the proceedings, and what should be the involvement of Archbishop Patricio Flores, a delightful personality but a confirmed liberal activist.

Tuesday, 27 July 1982

I escorted Chris Buckley's successor, Peter Robinson, over to my office, where we talked for an hour about the VP's Texas speeches and speechwriting for GB in general. Peter is a serious young man who went to Dartmouth and then Oxford. He came to us through the *National Review*. I tried to impress on Peter that he has to make GB sound more conservative than he is.[19]

The main news event of the day was Prescott Bush's decision to drop out of the Connecticut Senate race. For a while he wanted to contest Weicker in the September primary, but (as [his wife] Beth told me), "It was a lack of money. We have a $250,000 debt. If we won the primary, the money would be there for the fall campaign. That's the sad thing." Pres was more bitter; he flatly predicted that Weicker will lose to Toby Moffett. Actually, this strengthens Weicker and GOP chances for retaining the seat. [*I was right.*] Weicker may be an insufferable ass, but a worse fate would be to elevate a cynosure of liberal activist youth of the 1960s and '70s. It was a sad day for Bushes. Pres becomes the third member of the family to be bested in electoral contests: GB and George W. of Midland were the others.[20]

---

19. After doing his best for the VP, Peter moved on to the presidential speechwriting staff, where his greatest triumph was penning Reagan's famous "Mr. Gorbachev, tear down this wall!" speech in Berlin in 1987.

20. Prescott Bush Sr. also lost his first race for the Senate in 1950, and in 1994 Jeb Bush would lose his first race for governor of Florida. Bushes have a way of bouncing back on their second tries, although Prescott Jr. never tested this by running again for public office.

Wednesday, 28 July 1982

After speaking with Louis Terrazas about arrangements for Sunday morning in San Antonio, I called His Excellency Archbishop Flores. He said he has plans to be in Corpus Christi that day but will see about changing them. Though I am an admirer of Flores, I worry whether he (or Father Tom, the parish priest) will take advantage of the VP's presence to do some lecturing on the poor and disadvantaged. Flores was quite sweet in our conversation, playing the humble-friar role, which roused my suspicions somewhat. *Vamos á ver.*

Friday, 30 July 1982

GB had me get WHCA to run a tape of a segment on NBC's *Today* show on the late GOP tussle in Connecticut. Pres Bush had the best line. Trying to explain Lowell Weicker's animus against the Bush family, he said laconically, "I guess Lowell is just jealous of George." GB actually cheered when the faces of his brothers and son George appeared on the screen.

Sunday, 1 August 1982

In San Antonio, I took my bags downstairs and went "across the alley to the Alamo" to stand, alone, gazing at the shrine. Then we drove to San José, perhaps the second most famous mission in San Antonio. Shirley's and my idea for the Bushes to attend services there this morning was indeed divinely inspired. The Bushes sat down front in the classical but simple mission church with the president of the parish council and his wife. We staffers sat in the rear; Mary Gall, a good Catholic girl, helped me with the missal. A small choir of teenagers sang, accompanied by a guitar, and Franciscan priests celebrated the Mass. By happy coincidence, today was the start of La Semana de las Misiones [Missions Week], commemorating the history and religious meaning of San Antonio's five missions.

At the end of the service, the celebrant of the Mass announced Archbishop Flores, who entered from the side and welcomed the VP and Mrs. Bush with kindly words and a book about the missions of Texas. Neither in these words nor in the priest's homily was there any lecturing on Reagan Administration cuts in aid to the poor. Archbishop Flores joked about having an Episcopalian at the service and asked the VP to say a few words. In his response, GB spoke of Jeb and Columba's two kids [George P. and Noelle]:

"I'm not sure if they are New England Episcopalians or Mexican Catholics, but I know they're wonderful kids and close to God." The Bushes exited with the Archbishop, who stood with them during an unplanned photo op in front of the church. Thus ended an event that brought universal rave reviews.

We next proceeded to the popular Mi Tierra restaurant in the Mercado district for a brunch organized by Louis Terrazas for about sixty Mexican American businesspersons and professionals who were supporters of the VP. When the brunch ended, we were somehow ahead of schedule, so the pilot made "lazy circles in the sky" over the Gulf Coast en route to Victoria. GB invited forward retired Army sergeant Roy Benavidez, who last year was awarded the Medal of Honor by President Reagan for his bravery under fire in Vietnam. Benavidez has become a celebrity, a potent recruiter for the Armed Forces, and a favorite on Republican platforms. As we made our approach to Victoria, he graphically described his bloody encounters with the Viet Cong. On the ground, Benavidez took out his medal and attached its baby-blue ribbon around his neck at the throat. "It's not often you see a Medal of Honor," I noted with wonder, "let alone a Medal of Honor winner."[21] Benavidez replied: "I'm not a hero. The real heroes are the guys who gave their lives or are in veterans' hospitals."

In early August, Vice President Bush took time off from campaigning for Republican candidates to attend the inauguration of Belisario Betancur as president of Colombia.

Thursday, 5 August 1982

This morning, GB received an hour-long briefing on Colombia by two officials from State and two Latin America specialists from CIA. Representation at the inauguration will be disappointingly low-level, limiting the goodwill that GB hopes to spread in post-Falklands South America. No one knows very much about Betancur. He was such a perennial presidential candidate that information gatherers never thought it worthwhile to establish contact with him.

---

21. In my Pentagon days not far ahead, I learned that those who hold the Medal of Honor recoil at the notion they have "won" it, as if combat were a footrace. The correct verb is "awarded" or "received" and the correct noun is "recipient" or "awardee." The reason, as suggested in my conversation with Benavidez, is that most all recent Medals of Honor were awarded posthumously.

Friday, 6 August 1982

"Home Sweet Airplane" (SAM 86970) waited for us at Andrews. On board was Sen. Bob Kasten (R-Wisconsin), chairman of the Senate Appropriations Subcommittee on Foreign Operations and (with the VP and Amb. Tom Boyatt) a member of the official US delegation to the Betancur inauguration. He's a bright, able fellow and without question a master politician, one of the great successes of the 1980 election [in which he defeated longtime Sen. Gaylord Nelson]. Early in my DC experience, I felt almost abjectly inferior to young members of the House and Senate. That was when I was a recently resigned member of the Texas Legislature. But after eighteen months of getting to know congressmen and senators on trips, I have regained my self-respect. I don't deny them all due honors as aggressive vote-getters, but in so many cases it's obvious they are where they are by a lucky combination of circumstance and cosmetics.

Tonight, in Bogotá, I attended a small but elite dinner given by the Colombian-American Chamber of Commerce in honor of Senator Kasten. I rode there with Juan Woodroffe, a young DC banker from Puerto Rico whom Elizabeth Dole [head of public liaison at the White House and wife of Sen. Bob Dole, R-Kansas] asked to include on the trip. At the presidential palace, outgoing President Turbay hosted a dinner to which only GB went. I'm sure ours was the second-best show in town.

The Cámara de Comercio owns a beautiful house built of rich woods in the English colonial style that was popular in the Bogotá of the 1940s. I sat next to Jaime Lizarralde, longtime representative of Celanese Corporation in Colombia and a man of effusive charm. We had a good talk, mostly in Spanish. My *español* received glowing compliments—especially significant because Bogotá has the reputation throughout all Latin America of speaking the clearest and most grammatical Spanish. Lizarralde said this is due to the city's relative isolation over the centuries.

I enjoyed myself very much, glad to be performing a useful role on this trip. Bob Kasten told me during the stand-up coffee session that he much preferred to be freed of his official responsibilities so he could "go out on the town and get into trouble." I laughed nervously, knowing that he probably wanted a companion on such an adventure.

Saturday, 7 August 1982

GB spoke to embassy employees and had "bilaterals" with the president of Ecuador and a couple of foreign ministers before the indoor ceremony for

Belisario Betancur. In the evening, the ambassador and his wife, Tom and Maxine Boyatt, gave a reception in honor of the VP attended by all delegations to today's inauguration. The most interesting thing that happened there was an impromptu discussion GB had with the Nicaraguan delegation. It was intense, with the VP telling the [communist] Sandinistas not to bother their neighbors and that the US has no quarrel with their country aside from this.

Monday, 9 August 1982

The VP invited Jennifer and me to join his briefing from presidential pollster Dick Wirthlin. The report from the field is discouraging but not hopeless. The President's personal popularity remains high (as did Eisenhower's), but he gets poor marks in his ability to manage the economy and foreign affairs. The current battle to pass new taxes to shrink the deficit[22] is "the most serious political challenge of the Administration," Wirthlin said, because RR has to fight rebellious elements within the GOP like Jack Kemp. If he loses, he will be seen as unable to lead his own party. All day today, tomorrow, and onward, the President and VP are meeting with congressmen in the grimmest spate of lobbying yet in the Reagan Administration. GB is concerned about a total collapse of confidence by the financial community if we fail, shooting up interest rates. Kemp, heedless of deficits, obviously hopes to revive his antitax constituency.

If this all weren't so dangerous it would be fascinating. I don't accept the argument of people like William Safire of the *New York Times* that this is a battle for the future of the GOP. If we are in a depression in 1984, Kemp will have to explain his role in the debacle, and GB will be hailed as the man who warned against "voodoo economics." But the Democrats would win in any event.

Wednesday, 11 August 1982

GB called me over to the EOB office for the last of his meeting with Bob Teeter, his 1979–80 pollster. He called me a "political advisor," whereas political *liaison* is more accurate. Bush went over the list of past and planned

---

22. That Reagan pushed for a tax increase to narrow the federal deficit a year after his historic tax cuts goes unmentioned in modern conservative dogma.

political events this year, noting "there are some I've done for friendship and"—dropping his voice to a mock-conspiratorial level—"there are others I do for a reason we won't mention." Playful though it was, it was the first time I'd heard the VP allude to using his 1982 travel schedule to build for 1984. During the rest of the morning, he met with Republican congressmen, encouraging them to support the tax bill.

Of all my activities during the rest of the day, nothing was as memorable as taking a call from Sen. John Heinz (R-Pennsylvania), making another attempt at getting the VP to a fundraiser. This is ridiculous, because Heinz is probably the safest Republican senator up this year. But (as I later told Ed Rollins), Heinz "poured on the charm like ketchup." He pleaded for help to relieve the pressure he has of paying two-thirds of his annual income (or a total of $300,000) just to service the interest on what he borrowed [to run] in 1976. Rollins is hard against anyone's doing anything for Heinz, especially since the President helped him in May. So, Ed will write him another letter, expressing the hope "I won't take forty-five arrows while the VP changes his mind." I told Ed, "There's not any room in your back for forty-five more arrows."

Thursday, 12 August 1982

I had a private talk with Admiral Murphy about [a senior State Department officer] who has been attached to our staff for a year because State doesn't have a job for him. [*Such persons are called "floorwalkers" in Foggy Bottom.*] This is a sore subject with the Admiral, who said, "If he's so goddamn good, why doesn't State want him? It's like those goddamn civilians who come to the Defense Department, and some lieutenant commander seems like a genius to them because at least he knows something and they know nothing. After a while they realize the guy isn't as smart as they thought."

At noon I went to the Metropolitan Club for a periodic lunch with Judge Wilkey. He had with him one of his former clerks, Bill Barr, a sleepy-eyed but smart fellow who now is in the Office of Legal Policy in the White House.[23] Back at my desk, I returned three calls from a frantic Senator Heinz, outraged at my saying Ed Rollins will decide whether the VP will do a fundraiser for him. The senator threatened not to support the tax bill. I oozed sweetness,

---

23. Barr would become US attorney general at the end of the first Bush Administration.

knowing that Ed will ooze bluntness. [*With Ed Rollins's blessing, Bush agreed to sign a fundraising letter for Heinz, which I drafted.*]

Later, in Virginia Beach, we went to the convention center for a $50-a-person rally for Congressman Paul Trible, who has one of our best shots for picking up a Senate seat this year. GB delivered Peter Robinson's stock speech badly, such that Peter, standing next to me, was in anguish. On the sidewalk outside the convention center and on AF2 heading back to DC, he worried that "I'm in over my head." I assured him that wasn't so and offered some suggestions. These were all ad lib, but perhaps in them is the making of strong speeches. It caused me to regret anew that GB isn't consistently a good stump speaker, able to calculate his remarks for each audience without a text.

Saturday, 14 August 1982

Our destination in Chicago was the CBS studios, where GB was taped for the Phil Donahue show in support of the "revenue raiser." Donahue is a red-faced Hibernian with a trademark mop of prematurely white hair. He strides restlessly around his audience of women as if it were a private harem. He pretends to be the voice of Everyman, spouting populist-liberal clichés about big business and the Pentagon. GB was on the show to plump for the tax bill, reaching out to the largely middle-class, apathetic audience. It was the idea of [former White House political director] Lyn Nofziger, and the jury is still out on whether it was a good one. Although GB gave and took extremely well, responding to as tough a TV environment as probably any president or vice president before him, it was still unseemly for someone of his rank to be treated the way he was. There was derisive laughter (with the camera focused on members of the audience shaking their heads in disgust) or aggressive questions followed by partisan applause. It was the longest hour I have ever been through, and for GB it must have seemed triple. From a political basis, the appearance probably helped win him respect for the way he handled a hostile situation, but it was probably of little value in stirring up support for the tax bill.

Aboard *AF2* for the ride to Columbus, where he's a candidate for Congress, was John Kasich. He's a thirty-year-old state senator running against Bob Shamansky, an old fellow who won one of the very few seats to go from Republican to Democrat in 1980. John is aggressive, cocky, and completely consumed by his race. The effect of talking one on one with GB in the lounge was practically hallucinogenic for Kasich. We gave him other favors during the day, like rides in the motorcade and a brief TV taping. Should Kasich be elected (and he has an excellent shot), I expect him to be pro-Bush. He'd better.[24]

In Columbus we drove to the relatively new Aladdin Temple Shrine Mosque. It was the scene of a gala for Gov. Jim Rhodes, retiring after the second set of four-year terms that began twenty years ago. The hall was packed with Ohio Republicans. It was a roast of Rhodes, delivered by various luminaries such as Ohio State football coach Woody Hayes, Cleveland mayor George Voinovich (who once served as Rhodes's lieutenant governor), Bob Hope, and GB. Some were good, most weren't, but all seemed genuinely fond—and fearful—of the honoree.

In manner, speech, and political muscle, Jim Rhodes is a throwback to nineteenth-century American politics. No one ever knows what he will say or do. Responding to his roasters, he took the occasion to broil Jack Kemp, while praising GB for his loyalty to the President: "That's why I'm proud to have George Boosh here tonight instead of some congressman who wants to run for president." GB was the ante-finale, inexpertly delivering some Ray Siller one-liners.[25] When he finished, the rear curtain opened, revealing the huge Ohio State Youth Choir, who burst into the "Battle Hymn of the Republic." Rhodes snatched the baton from the director and thrust it at GB, who waved it around a bit before being shoved by Rhodes into the alto section. The baton passed to other pols before Rhodes took it back for the closing crescendo.

Monday, 16 August 1982

I gave a former participant in my Institute of Politics study group a special tour of the West Wing this evening. It was special because the Oval Office had been made into a studio for the President's address to the nation on the tax bill. A stern-faced technician sat at the *Resolute* desk[26] while light-

---

24. Kasich was the only Republican to win a Democratic House seat in 1982. He was a major leader of the Republican-controlled House after 1994, rising to chairman of the Budget Committee. In 2010 he was elected governor of Ohio.

25. Siller, a devoted Bush friend and supporter, was for many years the gag writer for late-night TV host Johnny Carson. He was often asked to write humor for the VP. His technique was to take a hot topic (like a movie star's breakup with her boyfriend or a baseball player's blowing a game) and then write numerous riffs on it in the hope that one would prove a laugh getter.

26. This most celebrated presidential desk was made from the timbers of a British vessel named *Resolute*, which an American ship recovered in the Arctic. Queen Victoria gave the desk to Pres. Rutherford B. Hayes in 1880.

ing adjustments were made; he was the central-casting image of a Nixonian president. We watched him with amusement on a monitor in the adjoining Roosevelt Room. Suddenly, the "president" leapt out of his seat, to be succeeded by the genuine article, looking rosy-cheeked and lilting in his Irish way. We saw the actual speech on the TV in the VP's office. RR presented the case for the tax bill as clearly and as cheerfully as it could be done, another triumph of his art.

Wednesday, 18 August 1982

Rich Bond called to alert us that he was severely chastised by national chairman Dick Richards for giving an interview to the *Wall Street Journal*. In it, Rich (described as "brash") gloated over ways the rich RNC and congressional campaign committees can "nail (congressmen) to the wall" if they don't vote with the President on the tax bill. In a rare moment of contrition, Rich called his statement "boneheaded" and said, "I must have been taking stupid pills."

Tonight I went to the 8:00 concert by the Marine Band on the West Front of the Capitol. It was a grand way to ring out a summer in Washington. The sun set in a broad wash of reds, oranges, and purples behind the Washington Monument, and as the sky darkened the illuminated monument and the Capitol took on a two-dimensional magnificence. The band performed such works as Wagner's *Flying Dutchman* overture, Charles Ives's variations on "America," a medley from *Mame*, and *Rhapsody in Blue*, concluding with the "Marine Hymn," everyone standing. Evenings like this cause people to fall in love with Washington.

Thursday, 19 August 1982

The day closed with the televised vote of the House on the tax bill. From the start, it was clear the President's (and everyone's) lobbying had paid off: 103 Republicans voted with the Administration versus 89 who didn't—including all Texas Republicans. I can't understand why Tom Loeffler (R-Texas) would go over to the rebels; he's part of the House Republican leadership. Trent Lott, the whip, is philosophically in tune with Kemp & Co., and yet he remained loyal. Perhaps Tom senses that power in the caucus is about to shift from [House Republican leader] Bob Michel [R-Illinois]. Democrats, goaded by their leadership, split 123–118. It was another victory for the President. Because of the nature of the issue, no one was exactly jubilant in the West Wing, but everyone was happy with the win.

In anticipation of such strong government response to the deficit, continuing a decline in interest rates, the stock market yesterday traded 133 million shares, breaking the record by 40 million shares. Over the past three days, the market gained over 40 points. It's not time yet to sing "Happy Days Are Here Again," but we're hopeful.

Friday, 20 August 1982

The President left for California around 11:00, and the VP departed for Maine half an hour later. Instantly the West Wing became an empty shell. Workers wasted no time in removing all the furniture from the Oval Office and ripping up the vinyl flooring to lay down hardwood. There used to be a corkboard floor in the Oval Office, but legend has it that President Eisenhower's golf cleats tore it up. I noticed the activity and was able to walk in when just the famous *Resolute* desk remained atop the oval carpet. All the other furnishings were in the Roosevelt Room, making it look like a very special rummage sale.

Lee Atwater called to "haul ass ovah heah." He gave me the names of three [Republican] congressmen whose votes on the tax bill were bought with promises of getting the VP into their districts. A fourth managed to get a Bush commitment and then voted against us. I later reached GB in Maine, and he instructed me to let Atwater know he doesn't consider those pledges to be actual *commitments*, that the congressmen's requests will have to be processed the normal way. "We can't let them get started doing that," he said with some irritation.

Sunday, 22 August 1982

[On leave in Dallas,] I went to a brunch at the Brook Hollow Golf Club hosted by [longtime Bush backers] Sally and Bill (Billy Mac) McKenzie. Already there were Kay and Ray Hutchison. She still seems worn and somewhat bitter after her unsuccessful race for Congress, though Ray is reputed to be even less forgiving of [the winner,] Steve Bartlett.[27] Kay and I had a fast, near-private conversation, the first in a long time. When she asked what my plans are, I leapt at the chance to expose the idea of leaving GB after November to

---

27. The Hutchisons met while both were serving in the Texas House in the early 1970s. Kay would recover from this loss to be elected state treasurer in 1990 and US senator in 1993.

seek a responsible job. This was but the latest instance of making her my big sister in politics. Earlier occasions were in 1973 and 1975, when I wanted to run for the legislature, and in 1978, when she encouraged me to get involved in the Bush campaign rather than run for the state senate. Kay enthusiastically endorsed such a move, saying, "You've never run anything." That truth sounded brutal even when coming from a friend. Kay also seconded my thought of seeking a position at Defense, because it would carry long-term benefits in either business or government. After watching my idol, Cap Weinberger, on TV this morning, I find myself willing to take a lower-level job in the Pentagon (say, a deputy assistant secretaryship) so long as it enabled me to learn a lot, run something, and possibly advance.

Thursday, 26 August 1982

In Houston, I took the Southwest Freeway into Fort Bend County, arriving at the new home of state representative Tom DeLay[28] and his beautiful, lanky, funny wife, Christine. We watched the news (the stock market registered another record-setting day in volume) and then drove out through the lovely green expanse of the county to the DeLays' favorite barbecue spot. Tom eagerly told of plans [in the next legislative session] to best his longtime foes, the trucking lobby, and obtain the deregulation of trucking.

In a subdivision clubhouse I was the guest speaker at a gathering of about fifty Fort Bend Republicans. Tom gave me a long and generous introduction. In reply, I said, "There are some people you like being liked by, and that's the way it is for Tom and me. You know, Tom is in the pest control business. I won't enter the old argument whether there are too many lawyers in the legislature, but it's for sure there are too *few* pest controllers!"

---

28. I first met Tom before his election to the legislature in 1978. He was elected to Congress in 1984, becoming majority whip in 1995 and majority leader in 2003. While the latter post is officially second in importance to that of Speaker, Tom was widely considered the most powerful House member until his resignation under legal allegations in 2006.

Chapter 20

Nonstop to Idaho Falls

Sunday, 5 September 1982

In Miami, GB met with the leaders of the Cuban-American National Foundation, a group primarily devoted to winning congressional approval of Radio Martí, a US-based station that will broadcast into Cuba. The foundation's chief is Jorge Mas Canosa, a real evangelist for Martí.[1] On several occasions, GB asked me to make a note of Mas's requests, including write an insert into tonight's speech, vowing defiance of a recent trial-jamming of US radio by Cuba. This received a standing ovation in mid-speech, commenced by the Cubans.

Tuesday, 7 September 1982

On our third visit to New Orleans in less than three months, all we did was drive to and from the baroque old Sanger Theater, where the general convention of the Episcopal Church of the US was being held. A man with a "Staff" placard motioned me inside—to face 3,000 Episcopalians singing hymns but all looking my way. As the Bushes shook hands backstage, the rest of us joined in the singing. John Allin, presiding bishop of the Episcopal Church, introduced the Bushes, and GB played heavily on his allegiance to and grace from the church. Then he addressed the issue of nuclear disarmament, a tricky topic for an audience mostly composed of committed (but polite) suburbanite liberals. Perhaps Bush implanted some useful doubt in a few minds, emphasizing RR's commitment to "a verifiable *reduction* in nuclear arms." He may thus have undercut the President's remanent image with some folk as a bomb-loving jingo.

---

1. Jorge Mas modeled CANF after AIPAC, the extremely effective pro-Israel lobby group. By dominating anti-Castro Cubans in the critical swing state of Florida, Mas made himself a political powerhouse. I worked with him when, as director of Voice of America in 1991–93, I had supervisory authority over Radio Martí and its equally jammed counterpart TV Martí.

Later, our destination in Canton, Ohio—home of William McKinley—was Hoover Park (named for the local vacuum cleaner company, not the president) and Congressman Ralph Regula's annual fundraiser, the "Rally for Ralph." He turned out 2,500 people to eat grilled steaks, corn on the cob, and apple pie. Regula didn't need the help, but he had "rolled" the VP, claiming he was on the [White House] priority list, which he wasn't. The band played "The Yellow Rose of Texas" and "Deep in the Heart of Texas" in endless succession. GB closed his remarks with what may become the season's coda: "I believe Ralph Regula will be reelected in 1982, and I believe Ronald Reagan will be overwhelmingly reelected in 1984!"

Wednesday, 8 September 1982

Thadd Garrett dropped by, and we despaired over the constant misspellings on the VP's schedule. Today, for example, it showed GB meeting with "the speaker of the Israeli Conesat," which I thought was either the upper house of parliament or a satellite corporation. The actual word is *Knesset*.

Thursday, 9 September 1982

GB returned a call from his old political friend Peter O'Donnell, former GOP national committeeman from Texas. O'Donnell urged GB to do an event for Governor Clements in addition to the campaign curtain-ringer on 1 November. GB reacted in a revealing fashion. He was quick to tell O'Donnell that he had agreed to do an event for Clements that his campaign cancelled. Now they *really* want me, he was glad to say. [*Though not actively hostile, Bush and Clements were never close. As the first Republican governor of Texas in more than a century, Clements' reelection was important to the national GOP.*] Like any other human being, GB wants to be wanted, and he is much in demand this year. That's why he doesn't explode at his being used by the White House as a reward to congressmen who voted the Administration's way on the recent tax bill.

Saturday, 11 September 1982

Air Force 2 landed at Andrews about 4:15 after a campaign trip to Minnesota, but the day's politicking wasn't through. We boarded two Marine helos for the flight across northern Virginia to Sen. John Warner's horse farm at Atoka. Every year since 1977, Warner has hosted a "country supper" benefiting the

Virginia Federation of Republican Women. The choppers landed in a cow pasture where we were greeted by Sen. Warner and escorted to the farmhouse, where a receiving line of Virginia GOP dignitaries waited. I said hello to many of these, but I missed meeting [actress] Zsa Zsa Gabor, who reportedly was stationed in the kitchen.[2] GB was geared up for the sort of full-voiced harangue required of the occasion, and the crowd of about 3,000 loved him. By contrast, Congressman Paul Trible, our Senate candidate, sounded as forced and fake as always. The helo crossed the Potomac above the Cabin John Bridge. It was strange returning to the Observatory in broad daylight.

Sunday, 12 September 1982

On the forty-five-minute ride on *Air Force 2* to Philadelphia to help Congressman Charlie Dougherty, GB talked with Alan Baron. He's a former aide to several Democratic senators and ex–executive director of the DNC [Democratic National Committee], who now publishes the *Baron Report*, the best of the many political newsletters I read. Baron believes the two political parties have realigned—the Democrats becoming ideologically liberal and the Republicans ideologically conservative—leaving at least half the electorate alienated. The only ongoing class conflict in American politics, Baron noted with a gleeful glint, is within the GOP: New Mexico conservatives, for example, distrusting the George Bushes with their established wealth. As a veteran of suburban politics in Houston, I agree with Baron, but GB denied the premise. "Texans know that I made my own way in the oil business," he insisted. Unfortunately, that's neither politically nor factually correct: GB still is an outsider to most Texas Republicans, and he could never have gotten started in the oil business without the assistance of his "Uncle Herbie" Walker. Baron pushed Bush to say, hypothetically, whether a moderate could win the 1984 presidential nomination in the event RR doesn't run. GB said yes. After Baron left, GB called him back to meet me as "our staff brain— which shows what kind of shape we're in."

In Philadelphia, I rode with a young police officer named Tom who normally chases heroin pushers. He proved interesting company as well as an instructor in the local dialect. For example, I have always pronounced Schuylkill (the river) as "school-kill," whereas Tom says it's "Skookle." Also, in Philadelphia, Dougherty is pronounced "Dockerty."

---

2. Two months later, Warner's marriage to Elizabeth Taylor ended in divorce.

The motorcade proceeded a short ways up the Skookle to the Best Western Hotel. There Congressman Dougherty—a maverick who in 1978 became the first Republican elected to the House from Philadelphia in twenty-two years—held a series of meetings for GB with key people in his Northeast Philly district. The best was with labor leaders who were as wildly anti-Administration as they are pro-Dougherty. They were real salt-of-the-earth unionists who told the VP what it's like having plants close and jobs lost to foreign competition. "Soon we won't have anyone in this country who will know how to make a railcar or a ship," said a UAW [United Auto Workers] official. The men obviously admire GB, and one said, "We wish you were there [in the Oval Office] instead of the guy who is."

Monday, 13 September 1982

Back again in Philadelphia, Jennifer and I were driven by a young used-car salesman who actually referred to us as "youse." We crossed the Delaware on our own bridge and soon arrived at the Halloran Plaza social hall in Pennsauken, New Jersey. There GB attended functions for Congressman Chris Smith, a hard-punching twenty-nine-year-old freshman who got his start in the right-to-life movement. The ballroom was practically empty for a long while as diners at the $50-a-plate fundraiser drifted in. The Smith campaign invited police officers, hotel staff, and even the mummers band to sit and eat. (A Philadelphia specialty, mummers get their unique sound by heavy use of banjos, saxophones, and a glockenspiel.) We ate barbecued chicken, spareribs, and corn on the cob and drank pitchers of beer and root beer. Mummers strummed, a state senator yakked, and Chris Smith introduced his whole family. But GB gave the audience the sort of anti-crime, pro-America oratory they wanted to hear. Everywhere we go, Republican audiences still cheer lines about giving the President a chance to "turn this country around."

In mid-September, I did something unusual: Instead of traveling with Vice President Bush on a speaking trip, I made one of my own—to address the Montgomery (Alabama) Kiwanis Club.

Tuesday, 14 September 1982

I was given a tour of the historic state capitol, on whose steps Jefferson Davis was sworn in as president of the Confederacy, and presented with a certificate proclaiming me an honorary "lieutenant colonel aide-de-camp" in the Alabama State Militia. Then I was driven to the downtown Whitley Hotel for the Kiwanians' pickup southern lunch. I sat at the head table and patiently waited through all the preliminaries (prayer, pledge, "America," announcements) as I had done so many times before as a candidate and legislator. My twenty-minute speech was extensively covered by local radio and TV. I began by telling about my Alabama heritage and quoting what my mother's uncle F. D. Graves always said when asked if he were related to Gov. Bibb Graves (1927–31 and 1935–39): "When Bibb Graves is out of office, we don't claim kin to him, and when he's in office, he don't claim kin to us." Then I gave a general report on the Administration's foreign and domestic policies. Because the audience was conservative and in large part Republican, all I had to do was reinforce old feelings about the President.

After the luncheon, a state trooper drove me to the air terminal. Soon Gov. Fob James arrived, his jacket off and tie askew. He is a short, square former All-American [halfback] at Auburn who built a manufacturing business before leaving the GOP to run for governor as a Democrat on a strong conservative platform. Earlier this year he announced his retirement, saying he only wanted one term. He told me he has no desire to run for public office again.[3] With the governor was his son Fob 3rd, a Mobile lawyer with the intense lean looks (and political philosophy) of Lee Atwater. We boarded the state's seven-seater Cessna Citation, dubbed *First Lady*, and headed to Asheville, North Carolina, to pick up the actual first lady, Mrs. Bobbie James. The governor and entourage were going to Washington, where he will file a writ of mandamus asking the Supreme Court to hear a directed appeal on a decision by a federal district judge setting aside a prayer-in-schools bill drafted by Fob 3rd. The Jameses are evangelical Christians, and Mrs. James does a lot of speaking around the country. "I prayed to God for twenty years I could get prayer back in public schools," she told me with a warm smile, "and now I'll be standing with my husband as he tries to do just that."

The jet came in over the Potomac past the illuminated splendor of Washington. No matter how many times I see this, I'm still awed; it's like the opening of a movie. Sensing that my hosts wanted to go to their hotel and have dinner together, I said goodbye and took the Metro home. It was a fine and

---

3. In 1994 James switched back to the Republican Party and won a second four-year term as governor.

memorable day. I can't say I have gotten used to flitting around the land with vice presidents and governors, for that suggests conceit. Rather, the comfortable feeling I have about it all underscores my sense of balance—neither blasé nor delirious but still grateful for my good fortune.

Monday, 20 September 1982

At 4:00 I met with Ed Rollins and a group of well-informed young political heads. Topic A was (in Ed's words) "How to Survive 10-Percent-Plus Unemployment." Analyst John Morgan said "you can bet the farm" that dreadful statistic will be achieved and possibly surpassed in the Labor Department's next monthly report on 8 October. We fear it may knock a hole in the generally optimistic attitude voters have now toward the economy. Our conclusion was that candidates should try to keep on the offensive, asserting that "Reagan means jobs." Nancy Sinnott of the RNC gave poll results that show Democratic voters are 15 percent more committed than are ours: "They can't wait for November 2nd."

Peter Robinson came over, and we had a good talk before watching the news. The President announced he is sending the Marines back to Beirut to keep order. This worries me, for there's no obvious end to our staying there, and ancient sectarian feuds doubtless will lead to the death or injury of at least some Marines.[4] RR himself said that "outside force" won't help the muddled Lebanon situation.

Tuesday, 21 September 1982

The VP asked Michael Gail [the White House staff liaison to the Jewish community], Shirley Green, Lt. Col. Mike Fry, and me to attend his meeting with the potent Conference of Presidents of Major American Jewish Organizations. Jack Stein, formerly of the White House staff and a past "president of the presidents," had put the session together, and it included such heavyweights as [current Conference chairman] Howard Squadron of the American Jewish Congress. Generally the group supports President Reagan's decision to have US Marines share in the restoration of order to Beirut. But

---

4. Thirteen months later, a terrorist bomber killed 241 Marines as they slept in their barracks. The surviving contingent was later withdrawn.

they worry that the Administration's obvious dislike for PM Begin will cause us to turn against Israel. "Why punish Israel for one individual?" asked Frieda Lewis of Hadassah. GB, who can get choleric on the subject of Begin, was grateful for her pointing out the political problem of Begin's personality.

Later in the afternoon, the VP received someone totally unrestrained in his criticism of Begin. This was Edgar Bronfman, CEO of Seagram's and president of the World Jewish Congress, who—at least until his members slap him down—is all in favor of what RR is trying to do in the Middle East. Bronfman said, "I've been fighting Begin for years. He's a self-fulfilling prophecy: he's convinced the world hates Jews, and he's doing his best to see that it does." GB judiciously kept his opinion to himself in both meetings, but he recognizes the US must deal with the democratically elected government of Israel, which has been Menachem Begin's since 1977 and into the immediate future.

Sunday, 26 September 1982

Perhaps my chief political deed of the day was calling GSA administrator Gerry Carmen, the Republican boss of New Hampshire, to get his "advice" whether the VP should campaign for gubernatorial nominee John Sununu. Hugh Gregg, GB's former campaign manager there, had already recommended it, and the VP had already agreed to do it, but I urged a pro forma consultation with Carmen before proceeding further. I even counseled GB to make the call himself, but he declined. It was a successful conversation, Gerry enthusiastically endorsing a Bush appearance. With the national press paying more attention than they should to our Iowa trip, anything involving New Hampshire must be handled with extreme caution.

We landed at Dubuque at 4:20, to be met by Congressman Tom Tauke, an up-front Bush supporter elected in 1978. At the fence were demonstrators, many of them striking workers from a local steel plant—two of whose executives were hosting tonight's twin Tauke receptions. Eastern Iowa, on the Mississippi, has beautiful hills and trees that are beginning to turn colors. Completing the autumnal mood are fields of corn so ripe the ears can be seen on the stalks. We went to a motel where GB held a press conference and denied this trip is an exploratory one for himself. He could truthfully say it was for his friends Tauke, Cooper Evans, and Jim Leach. Later, Ken Bode of NBC tried to get me on camera flipping through the pages of the briefing book, but Pete Teeley vetoed it.

Monday, 27 September 1982

Aboard *AF2* for the short hop northeastward from Des Moines to Waterloo was the state's junior senator, Chuck Grassley. He and I chatted across the aisle till GB invited him to sit with him and talk Iowa politics. On a day clouded by only a few light puffs, we approached Waterloo over a multicolored tableau of rich farms with houses and barns at orderly distances from each other. This is just before harvest time, and Iowa bespeaks the bounty of agricultural America. The VP was met by Grassley's successor in the House, Cooper Evans, a prosperous farmer acclaimed for his decency. I observed to Chuck that "Cooper is the kind of man that Jefferson wanted in the Congress."

A throng of sign-waving and booing demonstrators met us at the Conway Civic Center. When GB spoke, I sat down next to Pete. He leaned his head toward mine and said with exasperation, "He doesn't know anything about all these [farm] programs he's talking about." Pete worries that national reporters like Ken Bode will catch him on this, even if the typical GOP fundraising crowd doesn't. It is true that GB often is a caricature of his own "preppie" image. Just moments after Pete spoke to me, the VP said, "I have the neat feeling that the Soviet Union knows we're serious about the nuclear balance."

Later, at the airfield in Moline, Illinois, GB was met by his friend Jim Leach, liberal Republican congressman from the First District. Leach is blond, pudgy, slow-moving, and "thoughtful"—meaning he votes against the President. We crossed the mighty Mississippi back into Iowa and proceeded to the highly successful hog farm of Roy Keppy, a Bushbacker. The motorcade traveled an unpaved road through a field of ripened corn and pulled up at a relatively modest farmhouse. Masses of small children were penned up under a tree, and on the other side of the yard ten piglets were penned up with their enormous mother. Inside, GB met with a group of corn farmers who were mostly interested in expanding exports. They admit they are victims of their own success, having achieved big yields.

I grabbed a ham sandwich which I ate en route to the next event, a meeting with local labor leaders in a small motel. This was like the meeting in Philadelphia on the twelfth, except that Iowa unionists are less rowdy. They are no less interested in jobs, because the area's farm machinery companies have been laying off workers. GB was able to tie unemployment to high interest rates. He probably didn't change any minds, but he scored well personally as always.

Tuesday, 28 September 1982

When we landed in Kansas City, Missouri, we were met by Gov. Kit Bond, Attorney General John Ashcroft, and today's honoree, young Congressman Tom Coleman. We agreed to do this stop in exchange for Tom's vote on the August tax bill. Just as GB was saying, "We care deeply about unemployment," a "Welcome VP Bush" banner behind him came unstuck and fell. "May the Lord strike me dead!" he exclaimed.

With the governor and attorney general along, we took off for Springfield about 2:00. The VP talked with Bond, and I spoke with the quieter, more sincere Ashcroft, a gospel singer when he's not lawyering. The word is that he'll run to succeed Bond in 1984 and that Bond will oppose Sen. Thomas Eagleton (D) two years later.[5]

Pete, Cynthia, and I rode in a car driven by a grumpy fellow I took to be a police officer but who is the mayor of Sedalia, Missouri. Surprised, I asked him how he happened to be recruited as a motorcade driver. "Hell if I know," he replied.

Thursday, 30 September 1982

On the flight to California, I was interviewed by Dave Broder [of the *Washington Post*]. He was curious how political events are decided by the VP's office and whether there is to be a "higher political visibility" out of GB before the election. When I relayed this to GB, he accused David Gergen (the author of the suggestion) of leaking his own not-yet-adopted idea.

In San Francisco there was a major-donors fundraiser for San Diego mayor Pete Wilson, GOP nominee for the Senate against Gov. Jerry Brown. The mayor, both here and at tonight's dinner, said, "What I want to see is eight years of Ronald Reagan followed by eight years of George Bush"—the boldest and biggest veiled endorsement that GB has yet received. Both Wilson and Bush blasted a thirty-second Brown TV spot that urges Californians to "vote for your lives," bluntly implying that Wilson's opposition to the nuclear-freeze proposal means he's for incinerating the world. GB scored well

---

5. Ashcroft was indeed elected governor in 1984, serving through 1992. Two years later he was elected to the Senate. Defeated for reelection in 2000, Ashcroft was US attorney general during Pres. George W. Bush's first term. Bond was elected to the Senate in 1986 when Eagleton retired, and served twenty-four years.

with the friendly audience; like Davenport, Philadelphia, and Greenwich, this is "Bush country."

Saturday, 2 October 1982

Aboard *AF2*, GB, Jennifer, Ed, and I conferred in the lounge on the end-game of the 1982 midterm campaign: where GB ought to go in the last few unscheduled days. Ed said anything can happen in the next month and that if we lose thirty or more House seats (which he doesn't now predict), "there's no way we can keep from losing some Senate seats." So he recommends that GB plan on helping incumbent senators, most of whom have not until now been seen as needing help.

We landed at Point Mugu and embarked on a fifty-five-minute motor-cade up the famed and fabulous Pacific Coast Highway to Santa Barbara (really Montecito). I was lucky to be on the left side of our borrowed Cadillac and see the sparkling, turquoise, calm Pacific in all its beauty.

Our destination was the pink stucco mansion of Mr. and Mrs. Stewart Abercrombie. Facing the mountains rather than the sea, the estate was *très Californie*, complete with a pool of live swans and one certified movie star (Robert Mitchum). It was so exclusive that we bladder-strained staffers were thrown out of the main house for using a bathroom.

Ed Rollins stayed behind in Santa Barbara, and his place in our entourage was taken by Tony Dolan, one of the President's principal speechwriters, seconded to the Second Man for the duration of the campaign. Though I don't quite trust Tony (brother of Terry, executive director of the National Conservative Political Action Committee), I admire his brains and welcome the chance to get to know him better—with caution.

When *AF2* landed in Palm Springs, it was met by former First Lady Betty Ford and ABC's *Good Morning America* host David Hartman. They all went off to the Fords' residence in Rancho Mirage, where the Bushes are spending the weekend. The rest of us went to the sprawling Gene Autry Hotel, grateful for this day and a half off in midcampaign.

Sunday, 3 October 1982

The car carrying Jennifer and me came to a sliding iron gate marking off the compound shared by the Fords and zillionaire Leonard Firestone. We reached the Bushes' room just as President Ford was leaving; we shook hands with him at the door. A prime topic of our mini–staff meeting was David

Broder's piece in this morning's *Washington Post* based on his trip with us to San Francisco. GB objected to the theme that the White House (= David Gergen) wants to build up his "visibility" in the fall campaign. There are some critical, but not unfair, observations of GB's lack of a killer instinct in political oratory.

GB asked for the Sit Room [the White House Situation Room] to "dex" [*a primitive form of fax*] us the story. The only trouble was that the machine was in the conference room, which Ford was using in lieu of his own office, the set for *Good Morning America*. That didn't bother the President, who kept puffing his aromatic pipe and studying the schedule for his next political trip. Neither was he disturbed by the difficulty the Sit Room and I had with the two-page transmission. When I finally got it, I made a point of showing it first to an appreciative Ford, who later signed an embossed business card for me.

Monday, 4 October 1982

We staffers reached the Palm Springs airport as a desert sunrise began. The Bushes arrived a short while later, and we were wheels-up at 7:00. Our direct route to Bismarck took us over some of the wildest and least-populated territory in the US. Breakfast was served, and GB conducted a speechwriting session with Pete Teeley and Tony Dolan. The latter recommended that GB, in every speech for a congressional candidate, challenge the Democratic opponent to pledge to keep the third year of the 1981 tax cut and the "indexation" of taxable income. He calls it "taking Bush pledge" and envisions its being used in a national offensive against the Democrats.

Ex-VP Mondale issued a challenge of his own: for GB to debate him. I feared GB might accept, enhancing Mondale's standing at great risk to his own. But at Teeley's suggestion the challenge was to be shrugged off with the quip, "We *had* a debate. It was in 1980. And they lost." (This is figurative; there was no Bush-Mondale debate two years ago.)

We came in over the Missouri River valley, its banks yellow with autumn color. Bismarck is a small, pretty place, and today's weather was on the crisp side of pleasant. The chicken-and-mashed-potatoes GOP fundraising lunch was an uncomplicated, good-spirited affair in the homely traditions of the Dakotas. After the meal, the motorcade proceeded to another motel, where the VP attended the official dedication of a gas pipeline. As I learned in our visit to Fargo last March, these motels are like midwinter resorts, with indoor pools, game rooms, and even gambling.

Tuesday, 5 October 1982

It was a hazy, warm, Indian summer afternoon in Detroit when we landed. Our first destination was in the city's large black ghetto, rarely visited by a high-ranking official of the Reagan Administration, with its unemployment rate estimated at 35 percent. We rolled up at the big workshop operated by Focus Hope, a private job training program run by a Father Cunningham, of whom Pete Teeley is a fan. This was all fine—except that chief Secret Service agent Wayne Welch mustered the so-called CAT (counter-assault team) guys, whose big automatic weapons were clearly visible under their windbreakers. Horrified at this unnecessary show of force, I asked Wayne why his regular agents' Uzi submachine guns, kept at the ready in shoulder bags, weren't sufficient for the site. And if they weren't, why didn't he veto the event as unsafe? Wayne contended that the workshop, with I-beams, sheds, and benches, was "like a ship," a collection of a thousand hiding places. He didn't apologize for what he did, and I hope he realizes there is a limit to the latitude our pro–Secret Service staff is willing to give him. When we left the ghetto, Wayne jumped in the control car—to direct the CAT in case of attack?—and was tensed till we were safely on our own cleared expressway.

I returned a call from Lee Atwater, who was agitated over a report (from Rich Bond?) that he is suspected of telling David Broder the VP needs to attack the Democrats more. Perhaps protesting too much, Lee said, "I'm the best friend you've got among the conservatives." I shall have to placate him, something that would be easier if I truly felt Atwater *is* our friend.

Wednesday, 6 October 1982

On today's trip to North Carolina were Sen. Jesse Helms, the high priest of the New Right, his wife, Dot, and Mrs. John East, wife of the junior senator, who would meet us in Raleigh. An opponent of GB's selection for VP two years ago, Helms asked to accompany us every step of the way in North Carolina, which is very significant. He is already in a tough reelection race [for a third term] in 1984, when he is sure to be challenged by Democratic governor Jim Hunt.[6] Despite his hard-line politics, Helms is the image of the courtly southern gentleman and conveys the aura of a real US senator.

---

6. Helms defeated Hunt and all subsequent Democratic challengers—though never by land-slides—until his retirement from the Senate in 2002.

Observing him at close range is the best aspect of this, my forty-sixth trip of the year.

In Winston-Salem (just "Winston" to locals), I showed GB the list of questions he would be asked at the R. J. Reynolds tobacco plant. Most of these were technical queries about tobacco and smoking. Appalled, the VP exclaimed, "How could my staff have thrown me in with some guys who'll ask me questions about tobacco?" The candidate for Congress swore off responsibility, as did Boyden Gary, descendant of a president of RJR. The answer, of course, lies with Jennifer and the mysterious way she alone constructs trips. It's ludicrous for one person who lacks interest in politics, policy, or press to have total authority in scheduling.

The multifaceted, mirror-sided Reynolds corporate headquarters is not far from downtown. There, in a swank boardroom, GB met with the directors of the company. These gentlemen slowly rocked back and forth in plush, rust-colored chairs, occasionally asking a weighty question. The first was why Congress (with the Administration's support) doubled the excise tax on tobacco. This obviously irritated the VP, who snapped, "You've got plenty of experts around this table who know the answer to that, because you all lobbied so hard on that one." He was not defensive on that or subsequent queries, but clearly the event had no benefit to GB and only passing current-events interest to the snooty tobacco men. We then made a quick tour of the plant, which makes and packages 435 million Winston cigarettes a day.

At a congressional fundraiser in Raleigh, GB was in top form, using for the first time a refrain crafted by Peter Robinson. Patterned after FDR's famous 1940 slam on "Martin, Barton, and Fish," the VP's speech repeatedly assailed "Walter, Teddy, and Tip" [Walter Mondale, Sen. Teddy Kennedy, and House Speaker Tip O'Neill]. Later, on the plane, Senator Helms acclaimed it "the best speech I've ever heard you give, George." That encomium means a lot, especially if Helms spreads the word.

On the ground about 11:00, we drove to Hendersonville, founded by another ancestor of Boyden's. We are staying at a Holiday Inn, a first in the Bush vice presidency. The sign on my door welcomed me to "South Western North Carolina."

Thursday, 7 October 1982

On the flight to Birmingham, Alabama, [GOP leaders traveling with Bush] talked exuberantly about the governor's race over drinks. They had a new poll showing the GOP nominee, Mayor Emory Folmar of Montgomery, only three points behind George Wallace (42 to 39 percent). Folmar (pronounced "FALL-mur") must be given all national Republican help, they implored, to keep Wallace from reviving his national constituency and take redneck voters away from Reagan in 1984.

We went to Boutwell Auditorium, where over 3,000 people, an amazing turnout, were in full cry. Folmar, a lean, hard-charging businessman and ex–military officer, was giving them an old-fashioned southern political harangue. It was a hard act for GB to follow, but he performed with appropriate zeal using words written by Vic Gold, an Alabamian brought back just for this trip. Bush compared the Alabama governor's race with the one for president two years ago—"new versus old"—and threw at Wallace an invocation the ex-governor had made famous: "Send them a message," by electing Emory Folmar. The folks went wild.

Monday, 11 October 1982

Aboard the C-9 was the man we were off to New York to help, Congressman Guy Molinari of Staten Island. With him were his wife, Marguerite, and daughter Susan. Molinari has been paired with Democratic Congressman Leo Zeferetti of Brooklyn. He worries that gubernatorial candidate Mario Cuomo will attract his fellow Italos to the Democratic ticket. Noting that today is Columbus Day ("as observed"), I suggested to Molinari that he might give the VP some appropriate words or phrases in Italian to say at lunch. Molinari smiled and said, "I don't speak any Italian."[7]

Later, in Wilmington, Delaware, we went to the Hotel DuPont (built in 1911), site of all events for this evening for Delaware's congressman-at-large, Tom Evans. He was first elected in 1976 and was an early backer of RR. Despite this admirable access, Evans is in deep trouble because of his dalliance with lobbyist Paula Parkinson. (The joke is that "Tom has Parkinson's disease.") His opponent is the popular young state treasurer, Tom Carper. Not an admirer of flashy types like Evans, I wouldn't mourn his departure, but tonight he was our hero.[8]

---

7. Molinari won reelection and served in the House until 1990, when he became borough president of Staten Island. He was succeeded by Susan, a New York city council member, who held the family seat until her resignation in 1997.

8. Evans lost to Carper, who was elected governor of Delaware in 1992 and US senator in 2000.

Tuesday, 12 October 1982

Just in time for the election, the stock market is way up, over 1,000, and interest rates are coming down. These have taken some of the edge off 10.1 percent unemployment. In-house political brain John Morgan said today he now expects GOP losses to be within fifteen seats.

Wednesday, 13 October 1982

In Old Saybrook, Connecticut, our destination was an inn named the Whitehouse, site of a fundraiser for Tony Guglielmo. Running a second time against quirky liberal congressman Sam Gejdenson, Guglielmo gave a speech that charmed the Bushes. Tony said his father, a postal worker, and GB's father, "also a federal employee," both gave their sons a respect for public service. On the flight back to DC, GB several times told Frank Clines of the *New York Times* that Guglielmo's remarks "pumped me up" for 2 November. He compared this concentrated, two-month spate of campaigning with an athletic competition, "a challenge" to the body, nerve, and spirit.

Thursday, 14 October 1982

At the White House I devoted two hours to catching up on deskwork till time came to board the motorcade for Andrews. Reluctant to get in the limo without an invitation, I got in a staff car and was reading the briefing book when Jennifer joined me, asking, "Are you boycotting him, too?" She was spitting mad at the VP that Ann Devroy, White House correspondent for Gannett News, had been manifested for tomorrow's four-day, three-state campaign swing. Devroy was the author of the notorious profile on Jennifer last January, after which Jennifer said she made GB swear "on his mother's life" that Ann would never come on AF2 again. But Pete Teeley won with the commonsense argument that the vice president of the United States cannot exclude Gannett from his plane in deference to his scheduling assistant; to do so would *really* invite a story. All day, Jennifer was unspeakably furious at GB, shooting deadly looks with a concentrated stare, muttering aloud, "I can't stand people who lie. . . . Weakling . . . What would your father think when your mother dies?"[9]

En route back to Washington after a day campaigning in Newburgh and

---

9. Senator Bush had already died (in 1972). Dorothy Walker Bush would live until 1992.

Tuxedo, New York, she exploded anew at him on the plane, causing a complete scene. GB engaged me in conversation to keep from having to stare at her staring back at him, and we kept up our self-protective banter on the helo.

Friday, 15 October 1982

With Ann Devroy (whom I rather like) on board, AF2 flew to Cincinnati. I was struck by the beauty of the old Queen City. We proceeded to the Cincinnati Club on Garfield Square for events benefiting Charles (Rocky) Saxbe, a state rep running for attorney general. Rocky, a red-haired ex-Marine, is the son of Bill Saxbe, former attorney general of both Ohio and the US, as well as a former US senator and ambassador to India. The Bush-Saxbe family friendship led to our helping Rocky today; he and George Strake [running for lieutenant governor of Texas] are the only nongubernatorial, noncongressional candidates GB is helping this year.

The luncheon was held in a big, high-ceilinged hall dominated by a mural, executed in 1943, of the founding of Cincinnati. It was a reminder of the era when this city was at its zenith, before Los Angeles became the cynosure American city. The stuffy audience didn't respond at all to GB's "Walter, Teddy, and Tip" refrain (unlike the Hasidic Jews last night in Tuxedo), and it has now lost favor with him and BPB. But he attacked the Democrats as "the party of fear, gleeful when unemployment hit 10 percent. They want to exploit the suffering to win on fear."

After a dinner in Toledo, AF2 flew on to Chicago. The night was so clear that the city appeared out the window as a vast computer graphic, each street brilliantly outlined in lights and the Loop buildings vividly three-dimensional in their velvet cloaks.

Saturday, 16 October 1982

In the staff office I greeted Cathy Bertini, a highly attractive young woman who's running for Congress against longtime incumbent Sidney Yates in a gerrymandered district on the north side of Chicago.[10] Cathy had a "photo op" with the VP, bringing an older woman who works for a suburban news-

---

10. Defeated for Congress, Bertini was appointed an assistant secretary of agriculture by President Reagan. In 1992, on the recommendation of President Bush, she became director general of the United Nations Food and Agriculture Organization.

paper. This lady kept snapping away, to the point of blocking BPB from leaving the bedroom. When Cathy suggested that Barbara be included in the pictures, the woman said to me in horror, "I didn't know that was Mrs. Bush! I thought it was someone important."

Tuesday, 19 October 1982

After lunch, I went into GB's private office in the West Wing to discuss a few items. In a talkative mood, he voluntarily recalled the way Jennifer blew up last Thursday, saying he ignored her verbal abuse (which was horrid) "because I know her so well." He praised the way I didn't rise to her continual baiting of me as "Captain Courageous," reluctant to fight over every little aggravation. GB and I are both pols, and pols—at least those who play it safe and straight—pick their battles. We agreed that Jennifer's is a sad life and a sad case. She can at times be "fun," GB said. "That's why I like having her around. Otherwise, I would fire her ass."

Thursday, 21 October 1982

In New York, I strode back to the Waldorf and put on my black-tie rig. Then I went downstairs for the thirty-seventh annual Alfred E. Smith Memorial Foundation Dinner, the famous affair sponsored by the Archdiocese of New York benefiting their health-care facilities. A tenor sang Irish songs, and Terence Cardinal Cooke gave thanks to many souls before introducing GB. The occasion calls for humor, and while some of the VP's gags fell flat, he got off one self-deprecatory winner: "I've been campaigning around the country for a lot of candidates whose biggest problem is name recognition. I know exactly how they feel. Frankly, I get tired of the President's calling me 'Schweiker' all the time." It was almost certainly a Ray Siller joke.[11]

Friday, 22 October 1982

The latest survey data show that a number of GOP incumbents once deemed absolutely safe are now in trouble, and the White House political consortium

---

11. The joke referred to Richard Schweiker, a liberal senator from Pennsylvania whom Ronald Reagan announced he would make his running mate if he won the 1976 Republican presidential nomination. At the time Bush spoke, Schweiker was secretary of health and human services.

(Jim Baker, Ed Rollins, Lee Atwater, and Rich Williamson) has ruled that GB needs to make a final sweep to shore these guys up. Some of the places the political shop wants him to go are normally solid Republican territory: Southwest Virginia, Utah, Idaho, and Palm Beach.

"Make no mistake about it," Lee said with a mixture of exasperation and fear, "we're on the defensive." Part of the defensive strategy is to distort our own expected losses. "We're gonna say that anything less than twenty [lost House] seats is a Republican victory; that twenty to thirty is a wash; and anything over thirty is a defeat," Lee said. When I asked what has suddenly happened to alter his yearlong optimistic scenario of losses only in the midteens, Lee said it was the September unemployment rate of 10.1 percent finally sinking in. "I've been in politics so long, I oughta remember the rules," he said, mad at himself. "There's a lag factor in these things of about ten days."

This pessimistic mood hasn't reached the press yet, which is not beyond the leakful Rollins operation. But once the VP's travel schedule is announced, the situation should become obvious. I left the meeting with Atwater with a queasy feeling in my stomach, a fear that the great unraveling may be about to begin.

Saturday, 23 October 1982

Our passage to Las Vegas was over the vast, pink-tinted Grand Canyon and Lake Mead. When we landed, we were met by clothing merchant Chic Hecht, our candidate against twenty-four-year incumbent Sen. Howard Cannon. Hecht is a bantam-sized fellow with a funny voice. As GB's friend and local political counselor Walt Casey told me, "We can win if we can just keep him *off* TV."

Separated from the main entourage, I got lost for a while in the buzzing, whirling casino of the Imperial Palace hotel. This proved useful, for I asked a strolling female change-maker to give me a dollar in quarters for the slots—not for the ones in the room but for the ones in the laundry machines at 2800 Woodley Drive in Washington. Now I can do sheets!

Monday, 25 October 1982

From Tucson we came into rain-soaked Newark and proceeded through the refinery belt of New Jersey to New Brunswick, there to attend the final fundraising hits for Congresswoman Millicent Fenwick in her race for the Senate.

At the press conference, GB was flanked by Mrs. Fenwick, Sen. Nick Brady, and Gov. Tom Kean—showing that the aristocracy still has a place in American government.

At the dinner that followed, Millicent Fenwick (a name out of Trollope!) spoke in warm, confident tones in a classic upper-class accent. Once a *Vogue* model, she still has the look of a woman of style fifty years ago: tall, with square shoulders and no chest. In her few words, she challenged her opponent [Frank Lautenberg] to tell what he'd do to balance the budget. Tired and perhaps a bit weary of his own familiar lines, the VP didn't make his best effort. But the strongly pro-Bush audience didn't notice.

Despite stormy weather, the helo whisked us from Andrews to the Observatory by 11:30. The atmosphere in the darkened cabin was splendid, but it's time for me to move on—to one of those buildings on the Mall over which we flew. The picture in my mind is clear: CU sworn in as assistant secretary of (blank) by Judge Malcolm Wilkey, as Secretary X looks benignly on. *Houston Post* and *Chronicle* please copy.

Tuesday, 26 October 1982

In northern New Jersey, GB held a "press availability" for liberal congressman Cap Hollenbeck. Queried, as expected, how he could support someone who's voted against the Administration, GB gave the now-standard reply, practiced in the districts of many a reservation leaver: "We don't want a rubber stamp. If we did, we wouldn't find it in this guy. We admire and respect his independence. He represents 1/435th of the country, and he does it superbly." Hollenbeck, whose independence has stung on more than one occasion, beamed his baby fat at that.

Wednesday, 27 October 1982

On the helo, GB was in bouncy spirits, which he ascribed to "a homestretch feeling" about the 1982 campaign. Approaching Stuart, Florida, north of Miami, we could see a good-sized crowd at the rally for our congressional candidate. Closer inspection, however, revealed that a good chunk of those present were IBEW [International Brotherhood of Electrical Workers] supporting his Democratic opponent. Some of their signs read: "Save a Tree—Burn a Bush," "Reaganomics Has Bush-Whacked America," "Bush Is a Thorn in Our Side," and "Busch Is a Good Beer, Not a V.P." At the rally, the protestors booed and occasionally chanted, "Jobs! Jobs!"

Thursday, 28 October 1982

It was a 100-minute flight across the Gulf to the pine forests of Jackson, Mississippi. GB continued to insist that this was a trip for the party, not for our US Senate candidate, Haley Barbour. "There are personal reasons," he kept repeating. This hints of some surprisingly strong ties between the Bush family and Haley's eighty-one-year-old opponent, John Stennis, who became a senator in 1947, the year Haley was born. The tenor of the whole visit turned out to be strongly pro-Barbour if not exactly anti-Stennis, which was fine, because Haley (in Lee Atwater's view) is a man for the future even if "Judge" Stennis whips him this year. It's good for GB to have another southern conservative political operative on his side.[12]

We drove to Smith Park, right across the street from the Governor's Mansion. There GB addressed a spirited, integrated rally that featured Haley and all three House candidates. The patriotic audience responded to every applause line the VP gave, such as how "the United States is acting like the United States again" under Ronald Reagan.

Friday, 29 October 1982

We left at 9:00 on what I called the first nonstop flight from Jackson to Idaho Falls. The Ozarks were rust-colored and the Rockies white. En route I lost an argument with GB. I recommended holding off our departure from Houston on Election Day till about 9:00, fearing an "impolitic" traffic snarl caused by intersection control if we leave any earlier. But the VP wants to vote promptly at 7:00 [when the polls open] and be off to Hobby Airport, refusing to believe that this could disrupt much traffic. I later talked with Wayne Welch of the Secret Service, urging him to urge the Houston police to do the absolute minimum intersection control on Tuesday. He said he would.

In Idaho Falls, we drove to the Civic Auditorium, which is attached to the high school. The stage was filled with straight-laced, older party officials, but the audience were mostly full-voiced teenagers. A master of ceremonies caused the crowd to break into a chant of "Batt! Batt! Batt!" I thought they were yelling, "Back! Back! Back!" until the VP walked on staged with our

---

12. Haley became Republican national chairman in late 1992, brilliantly leading the GOP to its historic midterm victory two years later. He gave up a lucrative practice as a Washington lobbyist to run for governor of Mississippi, where he served with distinction from 2004 to 2012.

gubernatorial candidate, Lt. Gov. Phil Batt. Sen. Steve Symms acclaimed GB as "the man most loyal to Ronald Reagan in Washington."

That evening in Boise, Secret Service agent Fred Fukunaga told me of an incident only twenty minutes before: GB had been having dinner with Sen. James McClure[13] and his wife at a local restaurant when sentries sighted two young men, one with a rifle, walking outside. In time-tested Secret Service procedure, agents pounced on the VP and removed him to the hotel. Joe Hagin told us, "My heart is still racing," not from any attempt on the VP (there wasn't one) but from the general tumult of the Secret Service's reaction. Later investigation revealed the men to have been involved in a family dispute with probably no knowledge that the vice president of the United States was even in town. I phoned the suite to offer my services in calling Bush family members. GB said he had already spoken with BPB and didn't think further calls were necessary.

Saturday, 30 October 1982

I studied the harsh man-made geography of Los Angeles as we swooped over the mountains and down to the coast, landing at Los Alamitos Naval Air Station. The VP was met by the man he had come to help, Congressman John Rousselot. Not long ago, the mere thought of GB's campaigning for Rousselot (or of Rousselot's wanting GB's help) would have been hilariously absurd, for he is an archconservative, a member of the John Birch Society in the woolly days of the early '60s. But now he has been forced to run in a new district that is heavily Mexican American in east-central LA, and we've got to keep him in Congress.

The motorcade went through dreary industrial and blue-collar residential streets to Cudahy and the Clara Street Park community center, where GB held a press conference. Asked about last night's incident in Boise, the VP praised the Secret Service and said, "The only thing I saw was the armpit of a Secret Service agent." He later gave that agent, Guy Caputo,[14] a gift: a can of Right Guard deodorant.

In Pico Rivera, another Mexican American suburb, we rolled into the International Club, a ballroom that was the site of a "Viva Duke!" rally for gu-

---

13. McClure and Bush were both elected to the House in 1966. He was senator from Idaho from 1973 to 1991.

14. Caputo became deputy director of the Secret Service.

bernatorial candidate George Deukmejian. Though the crowd was less than 400, it was a spirited affair with mariachis and a buffet of guacamole, refritos, and tostadas, on which I concentrated. Pete Wilson and the Duke himself gave speeches that showed how much they are forcing themselves to sound original and enthusiastic when in a state of exhaustion. GB was better but not at his best. Still, as I've been observing of late, if Deukmejian is elected, "GB will own another governor," as he now does Tom Kean of New Jersey.

When we returned to Los Alamitos, we found AF2 decorated in Halloween streamers, posters, and trick-or-treat bags filled with candy. Pete Wilson permitted himself a fleeting look of surprised, suppressed pleasure upon entering the cabin. On our quick flight down the coast, he and I talked across the aisle. I asked what will happen to San Diego city government after Tuesday, when he probably will defeat Jerry Brown for the Senate. "Turmoil!" he said with a trademark, weary lift of his eyebrows. For Jennifer, I drew a portrait of Wilson: a dead fish resting on a block of ice.

Monday, 1 November 1982

Today I was up early enough to spend the last fifteen minutes of our stay out on the beach by the magnificent Hotel del Coronado. Brown pelicans flew over the Pacific, its waters catching the pink-purple of dawn. Farther out, a submarine prepared to enter port. My vigil was noted by Barbara Bush, standing on her balcony. "I thought we might have to leave you," she later said.

In Dallas, at the old Union Station, there was a get-out-the-vote rally for Governor Clements. I stood next to his aide Ray Huffines, who predicts victory tomorrow by 55 percent–plus. The Governor was calm and confident, but in his remarks he acknowledged that God still has a role to play in the proceedings.

On the flight to Houston, the forward cabin of AF2 was for forty-five minutes a special speck of Texas Republican history, containing George and Barbara Bush, Bill and Rita Clements, John Connally, and John Tower.[15]

---

15. After Tower, an obscure college professor, won Lyndon Johnson's Senate seat in a 1961 special election, Connally returned to Texas from Washington to run for governor and preserve the old conservative Democratic hegemony in the Lone Star State. This included using all his influence to elect Lloyd Bentsen to the Senate over George Bush in 1970. Three years later, Connally switched to the GOP and made a famously unsuccessful race for president in 1980.

Connally was downright affable, calling me Chase and asking a long series of questions about races throughout the country. I didn't have the daring to ask what thoughts went through his mind this morning as we left Union Station, for our route took us right past the old Texas School Book Depository and the grassy knoll alongside which he and President Kennedy were shot nineteen years ago. Clements, all eager for his big win tomorrow, could hardly sit still.

My predictions for tomorrow are that we'll lose two seats in the Senate (retaining control), twenty-three seats in the House, and seven governorships. That won't be good, but it will be spectacular for such a grim year economically.

Tuesday, 2 November 1982

Today, the big day, I read the Houston papers before going down to the motorcade. At the Precinct 274 polls a short distance away, the Bushes struggled with the punch card voting system, which is difficult even without cameras rolling. Other voters waited patiently, having had to pass through a Secret Service metal detector just to enter the building.

To my horror, the Secret Service or the Houston police took us on the West Loop [the busiest stretch of road in Texas] en route to Hobby Airport, disrupting more traffic than if we had simply trekked in on Memorial Drive. During our return to DC, the last leg of the year's political campaigning, Jim Doyle of *Newsweek* came forward to talk off the record with GB. It was poignant to be discussing the 1982 midterm elections while 33,000 feet below us the American people were voting. Doyle said the Democrats concentrated more on winning back control of the Senate than on gaining House seats. The cabin crew came in with a cake decorated with a picture of the plane and "Campaign '82—38,466 miles." (That's the total just since Labor Day.)

In the evening I went to RNC headquarters on Capitol Hill. The general gathering was on the fourth floor outside Chairman Dick Richards's office. It was a typical election-night party: a lot of talking, eating, and little news. The nerve center was down on the first floor in Ron Kaufman's office. There the young GOP brain trust—Ron, Rich Bond, and others—received returns in a frantic atmosphere in a small room crowded with people and machines.

The news was (as expected) bad but not disastrous. Millicent Fenwick lost in New Jersey and [ex-astronaut and senator] Harrison Schmitt lost in New Mexico. But Paul Trible won in Virginia and Chic Hecht in Nevada, so it'll be a wash in the Senate. ABC says Republican losses in the House are eighteen seats,[16] greater than normal for a first off-year election and a blow to RR's coalition but by no means a rebuke. The scariest report of the night was that Governor Clements was losing. There was the further shocker that he failed to carry Harris County [which contains Houston], only the third time in twenty years this has happened to a major GOP candidate. [*Maybe the closure of the West Loop that morning had made commuters mad enough to go vote Democratic!*] We lost seven governorships in all, so my predictions were pretty close.

Wednesday, 3 November 1982

The President, with GB at his side, put a rosy spin on everything, celebrating the Senate's complexion and rationalizing losses in the House and governorships as either predicted or normal. The national media agree that the midterms weren't a disaster for the GOP or a rebuke to RR, but everyone concedes that Reagan's governing majority in the House has been lost.

Thursday, 4 November 1982

In the quiet time today I did some statistical work on the election results, determining that GB helped a total of 120 candidates, 59 of whom won and 61 lost. If George Strake and Rocky Saxbe, candidates for office below governor, are excluded, the tally is an even 59–59.

At 3:30, GB asked Jennifer and me to attend a meeting in the Cabinet Room of RR's "regional political directors." These include such titans as Gerry Carmen of New Hampshire, Frank Whetstone of Montana, Don Totten of Illinois, Roger Stone of New York, and Clif White, a mogul of the 1964 Goldwater campaign. The President and VP entered from the Oval Office to applause on this the second anniversary of their election. RR looked good in a dark suit and red tie, but for the first time I noticed that his hair is graying. (Well, at seventy-one, he's overdue.)

The prime topic was the extraordinarily close governor's race in Illinois, in which [incumbent Republican] Jim Thompson trails Adlai Stevenson 3rd

---

16. The final results were twenty-six seats lost.

with votes still being counted.[17] Everyone knew what *that* can mean in Illinois. The President joked, "I had an uncle in Chicago who got a silver cup for never missing an election in fifteen years. Of course, when he got it he had been dead for fourteen years."

More seriously, RR said he was pleased with the way Tuesday's election turned out—the official White House view that belies the body blows we took in Texas, New Jersey, and the whole House of Representatives. We need to "use the year between elections to educate the people," the President said, particularly on unemployment and Social Security, citing a list of statistics. He mentioned how he had planned to address the nuclear freeze issue in one of his Saturday radio talks but pulled the script when reports came that our candidates cringed at that issue's being given higher attention. This inspired blustery old Clif White to say, loudly, "Mr. President, always go with your instincts, because they're right! Don't let the so-called experts around this stinking town say afterward what they think you ought to have said. Follow your instincts, and we'll win 1984 by so big a vote they won't know what hit 'em."

A man who looked Hispanic spoke up, saying how much the GOP needs to broaden its base among women, minorities, and labor. But the broaden-the-base theme is a red flag to conservatives to whom it means liberalizing the GOP with Nelson Rockefellers. Grumped old Frank Whetstone, "We've already got the base! All we have to do is keep it."

Friday, 5 November 1982

I got to the White House in time to greet my breakfast guests: Congressman Mickey Leland and his "special lady," Alison Walton. Mickey called yesterday to invite himself to breakfast to introduce her, and since the RNC will pay for it (no doubt to its consternation), I said sure. Alison is quiet, serious, and serene, a good match for Mickey if she can control him.[18] Mickey told of the massive phone bank operation paid by Senator Bentsen, Lieutenant Governor Hobby, and Governor-elect Mark White that worked wonders, especially in the minority community. Mickey has long feuded with White and thus has mixed emotions about Mark's election. Now Mickey has the problem I've had for the past four years: pretending he likes the governor of Texas.

---

17. Thompson eventually eked out a victory.

18. Mickey and Alison were married the following year.

Tuesday, 9 November 1982

At lunch today in the Mess, Scott Thompson of US Information Agency confessed that after talking with a KGB defector he's less worried about the Soviet strategic threat. "Having Ronald Reagan as president is worth 350 SS-20s [Soviet missiles], and having a succession crisis [in Moscow] is worth another 350 more."

Chapter 21

A Funeral in Moscow, via Africa

Scarcely a week after returning to Washington from two solid months on the campaign trail, Vice President Bush set off on a major swing through Africa—with a dramatic and unanticipated side trip.

Wednesday, 10 November 1982

As I did before April's trip to Asia, I walked to the Observatory, reaching the hill just as the helo came out of a soft yellow sky. All passengers on Marine 2—the Bushes, the Admiral, Jennifer, Kim Brady, and I—smiled bravely at each other, knowing we were off on the most challenging trip of the Administration, both diplomatically and physically.

Old reliable SAM 86970 is completely filled with passengers, food, gifts, and luggage. The stewards had to appropriate one of the rear lavatories for bags. Tightly packed into the forward lounge are Peace Corps director Loret Ruppe and her husband, ex-congressman Phil; black Republican and businessman Art Fletcher; Dr. Benjamin Payton, president of Tuskegee; Dr. Louis Sullivan,[1] president of Morehouse Medical School in Atlanta; Admiral Murphy, Jennifer, and I.

We lifted off from Andrews at 7:00 a.m. on the longest single leg of the trip: almost seven hours to the island of Sal in Cape Verde [off the northwest coast of Africa]. It is a level and utterly desolate island on which is located the international airport. Cape Verde became independent of Portugal in 1975, and though it lists eastward in international politics, it is also pragmatic, dependent on money from South Africa to maintain the airport [to refuel its airliners] and on the US and émigrés Cape Verdeans for aid.[2] As we taxied,

---

1. In 1989 President Bush would appoint the able and convivial Lou Sullivan as secretary of health and human services.

2. About 300,000 Cape Verdeans live in the US, chiefly around New Bedford, Massachusetts. Needing to replace crew members lost at sea, nineteenth-century whaling ship captains

Joe Hagin reported that the plane was being chased by a pack of dogs. GB met with President Aristides Pereira—a refueling stop classified as an official visit—and the rest of us were led into the un-air-conditioned restaurant for refreshments. Using my pidgin Portuguese, which is nasalized Spanish with a lot of "zh" sounds, I chatted with a young man who's an appointed member of the island's governing council. He told me that Cape Verde hasn't had more than a sprinkle of rain in thirteen years, and sadly, the would-have-been rainy season ended last month. The US has a desalination project on Sal, and at the airport GB was greeted by a flag-waving contingent of American construction workers.

Around 8:15 p.m. we all rose and went to the VIP lounge for GB's departure statement, delivered alongside the Marxist foreign minister. Then came the hour-long flight to Dakar in Senegal, our first real landfall on the last populated continent we had yet to visit. Our nighttime introduction to this old exotic city was reminiscent of Saigon, with white French colonial buildings and villas, masses of trees, boulevards, and the lights of ships at anchor.

Thursday, 11 November 1982

Today I arose at 7:00 and opened the curtain to see a calm ocean with a pale pink sheen. Two French warships slowly rounded Gorée Island, and as they entered port, a gunfire salute was sounded. I ate some croissants and brioche with strong black coffee and read of the VP's visit to Senegal in *Le Soleil*.

Then I came downstairs for a tour of Dakar with Jennifer and Thadd. We saw rich areas, poor areas, and baobab trees, proof that I really am back in Africa.[3] The Senegalese we saw on the streets wore stylish clothing of all colors. Dakar, a city of one million, somehow lacks the crush of asphyxiating exhaust fumes and destitute humanity so typical of Third World capitals. Both Jennifer and I consider it one of the loveliest places we have ever seen, its natural and architectural beauty complemented by the graciousness of its people.

We returned to the hotel with just enough time to wash before the next

---

recruited sailors in Cape Verde, just downwind from New Bedford. A black American with a Portuguese surname and a Massachusetts accent almost certainly is a descendant of one of these sailors.

3. When I traveled "Cape to Cairo" in 1971, I developed a fondness for the distinctive, triangular baobab, which legend says God uprooted and replanted upside down to teach it some humility.

tour. I ran into Jennifer in the elevator lobby, and her first words were, "Did you hear? [Leonid] Brezhnev has died." I have no remorse for the aged Soviet supremo, hero of Czechoslovakia, Poland, and Afghanistan and promoter of Cuban and Vietnamese adventurism. But in a way I never would have guessed a mere two years ago, the news had a direct personal impact. Would GB be yanked away from Africa to represent the US at the funeral? The decision, needless to say, was for others to make and others to worry about today.

We *touristes* were taken to the former French naval base, where a Senegalese patrol boat was at our disposal. We rode topside, passing by merchant ships and the French frigates, out through the breakwater toward Île Gorée. Mocking its brutal role in history, the little island is exquisitely beautiful. One end has a small, round fortress built by the Dutch, and another end has a high bluff with rusty naval guns from the World War II era. In between are lovely pastel houses, trees, and flowers, sandy alleys each more picturesque than the last, and absolutely no motor vehicles. Gorée contains poor families who have lived there for generations as well as houses of such personalities as the Aga Khan and the Gilbey's gin heir.

The island's infamy springs from its role in shipping slaves to the Americas. Here, hundreds of slaves at a time were inhumanly warehoused till the slaving ships arrived. We were shown La Maison des Esclaves by a guide who minced no words in describing the barbarities endured by the unfortunate captives waiting for the ships into which they would be crammed. Only the strongest survived the wait and the voyage—a testament to the genetic fortitude of American blacks. (Thadd heartily agreed.)

Later I attended a meeting the VP had with some human rights activists, the only business event of his day. Across from me sat Elliott Abrams,[4] the thirty-five-year-old assistant secretary of state for human rights, who had just spoken to the distinguished Senegalese lawyers and parliamentarians. He and I noted that neither of us used the headset for the simultaneous translation of their statements in French. GB spoke animatedly about the Reagan Administration's commitment to human rights, aimed at results and not just "making a speech at the United Nations." He derided the notion that the

---

4. Later named by President Reagan as assistant secretary of state for western hemisphere affairs, Abrams was a vigorous advocate for the noncommunist Contras fighting the Sandinista regime in Nicaragua. Caught up in the so-called Iran-Contra affair, he pled guilty to misdemeanors for which the first President Bush pardoned him. The second President Bush made Abrams his principal National Security Council assistant on Middle Eastern matters, in which role I would work with him as ambassador to Qatar. Though this relationship was rocky, I have always saluted Elliott as a soldier in the conservative cause.

US, through economic sanctions, could end apartheid in South Africa or force South African withdrawal from Namibia. Several Senegalese criticized our desire to "link" progress on Namibia with the withdrawal of the Cubans from Angola. GB didn't retreat on this. Likewise he defended our nation's belief that human rights come before economic development, as the socialists believe. The Africans have a concept called *droits des peuples* [people's rights], which are collective rather than individual. GB obviously enjoyed the challenge of the friendly confrontation.

On the way out, I asked Lt. Col. Bill Eckert what the chances were that our travel plans might include Moscow, and he replied, "The Admiral thinks they're 90 percent, and the VP thinks they're a little better than 50–50." Although GB believed that the President should attend Brezhnev's funeral, he relished the chance to go himself, not unlike thirteen months ago when Sadat was killed. He got his wish. A short while later in the hotel corridor, Pete Teeley called to me, "Have you got your cold weather gear?" It appears that we shall depart Lagos on Sunday for Moscow and Monday's funeral, then somehow resume our Africa itinerary. What a wild—and spectacularly unique—trip![5]

Friday, 12 November 1982

The motorcade left the hotel at 8:00 and went to the US embassy, where GB spoke to embassy staff and foreign national employees. "If you think *this* invasion force is big," he said with a wave of his hand toward us staffers, "you should have been in China when Henry Kissinger came to visit." At the airport, we passed through a cordon of honor of Senegalese zouaves. They were striking in peaked red turbans with golden palm medallions, red capes, blue trousers with elaborate white piping, and drawn epées.

AF2 took off over the Atlantic and headed for Nigeria, passing around the great bulge of Africa rather than fly over a prickly country or two. On the four-hour fight, Elliott Abrams sat next to me, a great opportunity to become acquainted with that terribly bright and ambitious fellow. He was an aide to Sen. [Daniel Patrick] Moynihan [D–New York] in late 1980, when he decided to use all his "neoconservative" connections (such as his mother-in-law, Midge Decter, and her husband, Norman Podhoretz, editor of *Commentary*) to be-

---

5. Bush would attend the funerals of three successive Soviet leaders: Brezhnev in 1982, Andropov in 1984, and Chernenko in 1985.

come assistant secretary of state for international organization affairs. He figured it was a place a political appointee could have a policy impact. He was right, but he jumped at the chance to become Assistant Secretary for Human Rights, again correctly concluding it would be a better place "to get some ink."

While Elliott and I talked, Admiral Murphy came up, bent down and put his hand on my knee. "You're going to Moscow," he said, to which I replied, "Thank you, comrade." Elliott was obviously impressed and said, "I don't know whether to congratulate you or not." Such is the peculiar nature of my job that I get the trips, while the Elliotts of the Administration get the status, the responsibility, and the ink.

Toward 3:00 p.m., we came in over the thick forests and muddy rivers west of Lagos, followed by the city's expanse of rusting roofs, a trademark of the tropics. GB was met by his counterpart, Vice President Dr. Alex Ekwueme and an honor guard in green uniforms and tufted caps. The band—disappointingly tinny, hardly in the great British Army tradition—bleated out the national anthems twice, both before and after GB trooped the line. Then came the motorcade into the city, which lies on an island. It looked in an advanced state of decay, with masses of fetid shanties stuck between office and apartment blocks. Yet despite its squalor, Lagos is far from the hellhole it is universally reputed to be; anyone who has traveled in these latitudes has seen worse.

We arrived at the US embassy, where the VP spoke from the heart to American diplomats and their families, truly serving in a hardship post. When he gave them a quick report on the national economy, I feared for a moment he would spring back into the campaign stump speech. Ambassador Tom Pickering[6] later held a cocktail reception at his residence for the VP. The elite of the Nigerian political and journalistic establishment was present, and I enjoyed introducing myself to people. Nigerians, like Chinese, are easy to meet because they have an American-like sense of self-confidence.

Saturday, 13 November 1982

I went up to the Admiral's suite, where [vice presidential national security advisor] Don Gregg was briefing the VP on the proposed joint communiqué.

---

6. Among the ablest American diplomats of his time, Pickering also served as ambassador to Jordan, El Salvador, Israel, India, and Russia. President Bush in 1989 made him ambassador to the United Nations, where he was one of the toughest customers of my Presidential Personnel shop.

"I think communiqués are a pain in the ass," said GB, taking a swig from a tall green bottle of Sprite. "You struggle over every semicolon, no one reads the thing, but still you're committed on paper."

Waiting for the motorcade to go to the dinner in honor of the VP, Elliott Abrams expressed regret that GB, in his remarks two days ago in Dakar and at a signing ceremony today, practiced "relativism" in stating the US view on southern African issues, making too much allowance for his listeners' point of view. Abrams, who comes from the school of thought which holds that one must always be "tough," said we should just flatly state our position and say we are persuaded it is correct.

Throughout the meal service we were entertained by folklore dancers from different parts of Nigeria—long, vigorous, and often downright lascivious dances that GB rather enjoyed: he moved his eyebrows up and down in excitement when he caught Jennifer's and my glances. The real excitement, however, came in VP Ekwueme's toast. Rather than give the usual platitudes about strengthening bilateral relations, he chided the US on its policies toward Namibia and South Africa—"a low blow" in the opinion of Assistant Secretaries Crocker[7] and Abrams. The Nigerians applauded and the Americans sat still. GB read his prepared toast, word for word, without rising to the taunt; fortunately, it mentioned American commitment to the independence of Namibia. (Since the episode last year in Manila in which GB ad-libbed a toast, he now reads his texts as written by the State Department and translated into English by our speechwriter.)

Sunday, 14 November 1982

After a brief departure ceremony, we lifted off at 8:00 a.m. for the six-hour fight to Rhein-Main Air Base in Germany. We flew over the reddish-brown Sahara and then the Mediterranean, blue flecked with white. When we landed, those not continuing on to the USSR [including Messrs. Abrams and Crocker] were taken away in a bus to the base hotel, to be lovingly looked after by the Air Force. The USAF outfitted the rest of us with warm parkas, long underwear, and padded sox.

Aboard *AF2* was a uniformed Soviet air navigator, who guided us into Moscow. In his honor, Wayne Welch posted shifts of agents at the door of

---

7. Chester Crocker, assistant secretary of state for African affairs from 1981 to 1989.

the vice presidential cabin, though GB later went forward to greet him. The plane took off into the setting sun and then made its turn to the east on our mission to Moscow. Imported from Langley was Bob Blackwill, a [CIA] specialist on Soviet political affairs, who gave the VP a highly valuable and fascinating analysis on the post-Brezhnev period. Toward the end of the flight, the Admiral called all the staff into the lounge to say "the whole purpose of this trip is to get him (the VP) to the funeral and back. The rest of us will just stand by." He instructed us not to have any contact with Soviets who might approach us, and he warned that anything we say will be overheard by someone or something.

Toward 9:00 p.m. Moscow time, our plane began maneuvering jerkily on its approach to Sheremetevo Airport. Nothing was wrong, though, and we made a perfect landing. Out of the night rose a modern air terminal limned in colored neons that said (in the Cyrillic alphabet) MOCKBA. Beside it were two tall flagpoles, each flying a Soviet flag at half mast in the steady wind. When we came to a stop, we were met by a long line of cars in which rode Secretary of State George Shultz and Amb. Arthur Hartman (our host in Paris last year). As the American delegation descended the ramp, Bob Blackwill held back to watch which Soviet officials greeted the VP, a clue to how Moscow is treating his visit.

On the half-hour ride into the city, Bob gave me pointers on what we were seeing. The closer we got to Red Square, the more interesting the architecture became, especially the baroque nineteenth-century buildings. The streets were empty, store lights were on, flags with black streamers hung from façades, and divisions of soldiers barricaded the approach to the square, block after block. We caught a glimpse of the Kremlin and the magical St. Basil's Cathedral as we turned toward the illuminated Bolshoi Theater. Not far away we stopped before a mock-Regency building called the House of Unions, bedecked in special red and black flags of mourning and a large portrait of Brezhnev, one of only two pictures of him we saw anywhere along our route.

While we dutifully followed instructions and remained in our cars, GB and Secretary Shultz went inside to pay respects at Brezhnev's bier. Advanceman Doug Doyle later told us the place was crammed with flowers, especially in the Hall of Columns, where an embalmed Brezhnev greets callers face-on, his head elevated above his feet. The Soviets stopped Bush and Shultz as they turned to leave, leading them over to someone presumed to be Mrs. Brezhnev.

When the two officials emerged, the motorcade sped away to Spaso House, residence of US ambassadors since the establishment of diplomatic relations in 1933. There I greeted Tom Nassif,[8] deputy chief of protocol, who had arrived with Secretary Shultz. Tom and I were taken to the dreadful apartment block within the embassy compound where many embassy employees live. We are staying in the flat of Curtis (Curt) Kamman,[9] the political counselor of the embassy, and his wife, Mary. This is a special treat, for it personalizes a quick trip to the USSR. Though it was 11:00 p.m. when we arrived, Mary greeted Tom and me with bouncy hospitality, giving us tea, cheese, and cranberry cake in the kitchen while talking about life in Moscow.

Monday, 15 November 1982

Toward noon I walked the very short distance to another entryway in the grim, grim embassy building. An ancient elevator took me to the ninth floor, where a Marine guard admitted me. Curt Kamman then escorted me to an office dominated by a large Soviet black-and-white TV, around which were clustered all the embassy's young Kremlin watchers. After a quick hello to everyone, I stood behind a chair to view the funeral of Leonid Brezhnev. The only Americans in Red Square were George and Barbara Bush, Secretary Shultz, Ambassador Hartman, an interpreter, and Lt. Col. Bill Eckert.[10] My setup was the next best thing to being there—and a whole lot warmer.

The TV set showed Brezhnev's coffin being pulled in front of Lenin's tomb by an armored personnel carrier. The casket was open, and the grotesque-looking body was elevated. A huge Soviet army band played Chopin's funeral march over and over. Husky soldiers lifted the coffin, with the country's top leadership close in, providing the impression they were the actual pallbearers. When the body was put in position before the mausoleum, the official mourners mounted the squat, small building. The guys in the office with me perked up and grabbed their pads. "Here it comes! Here's the lineup!" one shouted. [The order in which the leaders stood indicated who outranked whom.] The undisputed man of the hour was Yuri Andropov, for fifteen years

---

8. Nassif was later ambassador to Morocco.

9. Kamman was later ambassador to Chile, Bolivia, and Colombia.

10. As he always did, Bill tightly clutched "the football," a briefcase containing the top secret codes required to authorize a nuclear strike. Only the creators of the classic Cold War comedy *Dr. Strangelove* could imagine a scene in which George Bush, attending a funeral in Red Square, would excuse himself from the proceedings in order to rain missiles down on his own location.

head of the KGB and named general secretary of the CPSU [Communist Party of the Soviet Union] soon after Brezhnev's death. Next to him were [Nikolai] Tikhonov, the premier; [Konstantin] Chernenko, whom Andropov had just vanquished; and FM Andrei Gromyko.

After a string of eulogies noted for their extraordinary brevity (including one by a worker in the Moscow Calculating Machine Factory), the band resumed Chopin's dirge, the mourners descended the side steps, and the body was moved beside the Kremlin wall. Observing an old Russian custom, family members came forward to kiss Brezhnev. The coffin was closed, and long white strips of cloth were slipped under it for lowering into the grave. An attendant standing at the head had difficulty, and in a shocking instant the coffin fell into the frozen earth. There was nothing for the family and the leadership to do except toss handfuls of dirt onto the casket. The Kremlinologists around me laughed that some of the top officials "couldn't do it fast enough." At that instant, bells, auto horns, factory whistles, and saluting batteries sounded throughout Moscow, followed by several minutes of silence. Then, as the band played a snappy march, the leadership remounted the tomb for a pass in review.

Curt and Mary invited me home for lunch of cabbage soup and cold cuts served by the Kammans' buxom Russian maid, Julia [*almost certainly KGB*]. Mary had an interesting description of the way Soviet society works. "It's like an American high school of the 1950s," she said. "The principal said you had to dress a certain way—no jeans, no long hair—and if you followed the rules you had no trouble. But if you got to thinking that, by God, you *were* going to wear jeans or leave your hair long, the principal cracked down on you."

After Mary showed Tom Nassif and me around Moscow by foot and subway, we squeezed into Uncle Sam's, the embassy snack bar, where an excited staff heard from GB, Secretary Shultz, and Ambassador Hartman. They had just arrived from the Kremlin and a private meeting with Andropov—a hugely important occurrence.[11] Then the motorcades left for the airport.

Even before our 7:00 p.m. takeoff, GB called for Bob Blackwill to come forward. While several of us listened in fascination, Bush debriefed us on the meeting with Andropov. He thinks it was a sincere effort by the new Soviet

---

11. On each occasion that he attended the funeral of a Soviet leader, Bush was the first foreign dignitary to meet with their successors, most notably Mikhail Gorbachev in 1985. When Walter Mondale assailed Reagan for being the first president since Herbert Hoover not to meet with his Soviet counterpart, RR replied with his trademark tuck of the head, "Well, they kept dying on me."

leader to establish high-level contact with the Reagan Administration. Bob speculates that Andropov may have also wanted to demonstrate to his own colleagues and his people that he is a world figure. GB gave Bob some of the "atmospherics" (how people looked and what the setting was like), adding with a sort of wistfulness, "I wish I were like Untermeyer. He remembers everything." (I don't, but it's useful to have the reputation.)

Stuffed flounder was served for dinner, during which GB and BPB told about the past twenty-four hours, surely among the most remarkable in their lives. For example, they detected not one bit of sorrow from ordinary Muscovites they saw in the streets. Then the Bushes retired for the night. When we landed at Rhein-Main, we refueled and picked up our fellow travelers to resume a trip to Africa that's not even halfway over.

Tuesday, 16 November 1982

At some wee hour, *AF2* landed in Cairo to refuel. A few in our group disembarked to take mint tea with Egyptian protocol officers, but I stayed in place, sleeping on a litter of cushions on the deck just off the main traffic route. By this means I was able to get an enviable seven hours of sleep en route to Zimbabwe.

Toward 11:00 a.m. we came in over the tranquil green high plains of southern Africa with their wide-canopied trees and clustered native villages with thatched huts. At Harare (formerly Salisbury) airport we had a large welcome: the deputy PM, a well-drilled honored guard, troupes of dancing children, the entire diplomatic corps, and a fine band that played a rendition of "The Star-Spangled Banner" I had never heard before. It was either a danceable version out of the big band era or something written down from hazy memory. All this and Chet Crocker, Elliott Abrams, and the Ruppes, too! The weather was delightful, but the approximately 5,000-foot elevation made for quick sunburning. My face glowed by day's end, and Elliott was a positive beet.

This evening, PM Robert Mugabe hosted a dinner for Vice President and Mrs. Bush. I was seated with the PM's principal private secretary and his chief political advisor. Both carry the title "comrade," which is given to all government officials and to blacks in general. I asked these gents the application of traditional Marxist-Leninism to Africa. Mugabe's political aide said that while the PM calls himself a Marxist, this only means he is more concerned about people than capital. To be sure, Zimbabwe [in its two years of independence] has yet to nationalize anything. Of course, if it did, that would kill off any hope of western aid. So for now, Mugabe is a pragmatist more than anything else. In his long toast, which he read in a high voice, the PM praised the US for its help to Zimbabwe and its dedication to finding a solution in southern Africa. GB responded by restating our position and praising Mugabe as a world statesman. My dinner partners were "reassured."

Wednesday 17 November 1982

Mugabe, normally a stone-faced man, seems to have been genuinely charmed by the Bushes. [At dinner tonight] he even referred to them as "lovable." The PM vowed that his country, "regardless of the system we take, will never become a totalitarian state."

Bushian charm did not work any permanent magic on Mugabe, who shortly became the greatest despot on the continent. In just a few years, he not only established a totalitarian state that quashed human rights, but he converted one of Africa's most fecund lands into a nation of hunger, despair, and hyperinflation.

The Bushes' journey through Africa wound next through Zambia and Kenya, but its climax was a bizarre and disturbing visit to Zaire, today called the Democratic Republic of Congo.

Sunday, 21 November 1982

As we came in to land at Kinshasa, the verdant hills east of the capital caused everyone to exclaim about the beauty of this country. The city was known as Léopoldville in 1960, when the Belgian Congo became independent. There followed years of insurgencies, coups, and foreign intervention [ending with the seizure of power by Joseph Mobutu in 1965.] The prime minister welcomed the VP at the foot of the ramp, and a teenaged girl came forward with flowers to recite a well-rehearsed speech in French that concluded, *"Vive le Président Mobutu! Vive les États-Unis d'Amérique! Vive l'amitié Zaïroise-Américaine!"*

My room at the InterContinental Kinshasa has a sweeping view of the Zaire (ex-Congo) River and of Brazzaville in Marxist Congo on the other side. Clumps of water hyacinth, which came to leaf hundreds or even thousands of kilometers in the interior, floated lazily toward the Atlantic. It isn't especially beautiful, but it is impressive, this river that drains the entire midsection of a continent. I read the embassy's information packet and admired the tawdry invitation from President Mobutu to tomorrow's yachtboard lunch.

Monday, 22 November 1982

Ben Payton and I shared a car down to the dock where President Mobutu's yacht, *Kamanyola*, was moored. It is a former Congo River steamer with four decks and a broad area aft where Mobutu lands his helicopter. This he does for security reasons, we were told. Indeed, Mobutu left his meeting with GB and arrived on board by chopper while his guest drove.

When he landed, I shook hands with Mobutu. He is called the president-founder of the Mouvement Populaire pour la République (MPR), Zaire's sole political party, to which every *citoyen* and *citoyenne* belongs by birth. A soldier with an upraised Uzi brushed past Lou Sullivan and me, and we stepped back to accommodate him. On the fo'c'sle a sailor raised the President's personal standard: a leopard rampant on a field of red, fringed in gold. Mobutu's trademark is the leopard-skin hat he wears at a cocked angle; no others are permitted to affect this style.

Once the Bushes' motorcade arrived, *Kamanyola* got under way. On our two-hour cruise upriver, we were never alone: three small patrol boats brandishing machines guns escorted us, as did Mobutu's helicopter. I stood at the rail and delighted at the Conradian scene that passed before us: river steamers and houseboat barges, the rusted hulks of steamers that didn't make it, warehouses and customs houses, and ever more water hyacinth. We proceeded to Stanley Pool, a broad spot in the river, at which time we were shown to the paneled dining saloon. There was a huge but not especially appetizing array of both Zairian and continental fare. I played it safe and took a lot of rice. Joan Abrahamson [an aide to Admiral Murphy], Wayne Welch, and I sat at a small table with the minister of economy and his wife. Joan and I both used our French to talk with them, but the man was no conversationalist and the madame even less. Mobutu delivered his toast standing under his omnipresent official portrait, which doesn't flatter the way he looks now.

Toward 3:00 we edged toward N'sele, the site of President Mobutu's private demonstration farm (run by Israelis) and of the MPR's national headquarters. We were greeted by young dancers and singers who chanted praise of the great *président-fondateur*. Art Fletcher joined in the dancing, to the merriment of all. The VP and Mobutu went off to the President's favorite fishing hole, so small and overstocked that fish practically leapt onto the hook, happy to escape. Other Zairian officials sped on to the next event, running over a child en route.

We official party folk were to proceed to the People's Palace, an enormous structure built by the Chinese, for the welcoming ceremony. But Jennifer peeled off to go shopping, and other cars bypassed the palace for the hotel. So two embassy officers and I impersonated the entire US delegation. We stood on the steps of the palace, facing thousands of Zairians bused in for the occasion.

There we waited and waited till Mobutu decided to stop fishing and come on over—he by helo and GB by motorcade. That's when I formed the notion of Mobutu as bully of the playground, forcing all the other kids to play the games he wants—and who has the keys to the toy store, too. Without warning, he took GB on a *bain de foule* (literally, a crowd bath, or walkaround) that made the Secret Service go bananas. After this, they mounted a red-carpeted platform below where the embassy guys and I stood, now joined by Mrs. Bush. The troops and band of the presidential guard made a snappy pass in review, goose-stepping in their leopard-skin vests. Then Mobutu escorted GB inside to look at the conference hall. It held the aroma of China, like the guesthouse in Beijing.

With that, the madcap unreeling of a motorcade took place. Joe Hagin— asserting "I've had enough!"—and I barely managed to get in a vehicle with advanceman Rick Ahearn. As our driver plowed through a mob of Zairians finally able to head home, Rick said, "I have never been happier to leave a fucking site in my life!"—and he was at Ronald Reagan's side at the Washington Hilton on 30 March 1981.

Chapter 22

Job Hunting in the (Semi-)Gloom

Tuesday, 23 November 1982

When AF2 lifted off from Kinshasa at 10:00 a.m., Art Fletcher waved at the Zairians and said with a sardonic sneer, "So long, brothuh!" It was a six-and-a-half-hour flight back to Cape Verde, during which we passed close to a special geographic spot: 0°00' longitude east–west and 0°00' latitude north–south—where the prime meridian meets the equator in the Gulf of Guinea. The Admiral stood next to me, getting something out of his briefcase. I said softly, "I'd like a few minutes with you to talk about something that's been on my mind for a few months." He said he'd do it. A couple of hours later, the Bushes invited the Ruppes into the cabin to have lunch. This freed the seats next to the Admiral, and with Jennifer elsewhere, he nodded to me.

Well rehearsed, I made my short and simple statement that "it's time for me to move on and look for a job in an agency with responsibility, etc." The Admiral's initial reaction was to indicate the VP's cabin and say, "It'll be a shock to him, because he relies on you so much." But he added, "You're thinking the right way," inasmuch as there is nothing of substance on our staff. I said I'd like something in Defense, where I could get both management and national security experience. He thought aloud that I could get a deputy assistant secretaryship in one of the services. With his Pentagon background, the Admiral's thinking such a thing is possible was both surprising and gratifying.

Several hours later, after another combination refueling-and-official-visit to Cape Verde, I hurried out to the plane to be ready when GB came aboard. As soon as he had changed into casual togs and was repacking his suitcase, I asked if I could speak with him for a few minutes sometime during the fight to Bermuda. He said I could have it right then. I made my "short and simple" declaration again. Caught by surprise, GB settled into his chair and said,

"First of all, I think you're smart as hell to want to do it," adding he has long felt that people should be in staff jobs only till they can get something better. He absolutely endorsed my desire to get some management experience and asked what I'd like. He was somewhat less encouraging about DOD than was the Admiral, but he said I can count on his support and (more important) his active help in pursuing an appointment. GB worries about competition from defeated members of Congress, and I said I am well aware this project will be long and tough.

In talking about who will fill my political duties on staff, GB said he's become "philosophical" about 1984, musing that he would have the same problem Mondale has in being tied to an unpopular president. He even said he was "philosophical" about being kept on the ticket, though I think he's guaranteed that. All this suggests GB fears (as I have all year) that the question is not so much who will be the Republican nominee for president in 1984 as whether the Republican nomination will be worth anything.

Not wanting to prolong my conversation with GB, I thanked him and once again got his strong offer of backing. I could not have asked for more.

Sunday, 5 December 1982

I was at the White House this afternoon when Jim Baker, just back from South America with the President, came in for an NSC meeting. He showed me a copy of the letter ex-Reagan political aide and press secretary Lyn Nofziger sent to the 1980 Reagan leaders, calling for a meeting tomorrow to discuss 1984. The key portions read: "I think it is important that the next presidential election be a Reagan-Bush campaign, not a Bush-Reagan campaign. . . . [We must] try to get hold of the campaign organizations. Frankly, while I'm confident that the President is going to run, I'm not confident that the campaign will be run by Reaganites." It was a clear slap at Jim, who told me he asked the President, "How long do I have to work for you before I'm a Reaganite?" RR assured Jim he considered him one. At JAB's behest, the Nofziger meeting will be boycotted by every addressee who is in the government (e.g., Secretary of Transportation Drew Lewis, Office of Personnel Management director Don Devine, and Lee Atwater).

I was brief, knowing that Jim wanted to get home. When I told him I am ready to take a responsible job in a department or agency, he was as instantly sympathetic as GB had been. "You're smart to do it," he said. "I was wondering how long you'd want to stay on here." With a smile he added, "Of course, I'm one to talk, since I'm in a staff capacity, too." The comparison is inexact, but it betrayed what the press has speculated: that Jim Baker also wants to move on. As for a DAS [deputy assistant secretaryship] at Defense, Jim said, "We can sure do it and hopefully get something you like." He said he will call Helene von Damm [director of presidential personnel],[1] perhaps as soon as tonight, to mention my interest. With the vice president and the chief of staff already enlisted in my behalf, Helene ought to be cooperative. I have the potential to surround a position at DOD. Such is the advantage of "working the inside game" as I can.

Tuesday, 7 December 1982

Congressman Tom Evans (R-Delaware), defeated for reelection, came by to see the VP, probably about a job. While GB was in the discussions between President Reagan and President Zia of Pakistan, I kept Evans company. He was astonished that as a Reagan original he wasn't on the list for Lyn Nofziger's celebrated meeting yesterday to plan for 1984. Both he and Holmes Tuttle, California millionaire and longtime RR backer, told GB how much they object to what Lyn put in his letter. Today, Lyn sent the VP an apology (or explanation) that praised both him and Jim Baker but still spoke of mysterious "Bush people" who want to turn the '84 race to their own ends.

Wednesday, 8 December 1982

Helene von Damm was (and continued to be) signing letters when I was announced. She already knew that I am entering the job rumble, concentrating on DOD. After exclaiming "Ve haf received 300 rézumés since der election!" she said I should work with Ron Mann on her staff. She also advised me to "use your own contacts. You're [politically] cleared, zo dere's no problem vid us. It's chust a matter of finding somethink." It was Helene's way of saying that if I do find something, it's mine. On the other hand, I didn't detect any sense of mission on her part to help me, despite Jim Baker's intervention.

---

1. A native of Austria, Helene was Ronald Reagan's longtime personal secretary and one of his most zealous advocates. As personnel chief she rigorously promoted those who had supported him over Bush. She would be ambassador to her homeland from 1983 to 1986.

Finally, Helene inquired into my replacement on GB's staff. Perhaps think-ing she was being helpful, she recommended that we look for my successor through someone on her staff "who knows your people." She just can't seem to forget 1980.

Thursday, 9 December 1982

At 3:00, I had an appointment with Ron Mann, who is in charge of DOD, State, and other national security agencies for Helene von Damm. Ron is an agreeable fellow but very much in the mold of personnel placement of-ficers. I told him what I wanted, which he quietly contemplated a long time before asking the classic question: "Where do you want to be ten years from now?" I groaned inwardly, but without betraying what I'd *really* like to be doing, said I would like to be known as an expert in national security. Then, Ron said, I should work for a senator and become his foreign affairs and de-fense specialist. Irritated but polite, I reminded him I've already worked for a vice president. Eventually, Ron got around to saying that, yes, a DAS in the "manpower" field at Defense is a possibility, because manpower is the kind of thing a generalist can handle, whereas international security affairs usu-ally demands someone with academic credentials or think-tank experience. When I specifically mentioned the Navy, Ron suggested I talk with John Herrington, the assistant secretary for manpower and reserve affairs. I got to know John when he preceded Helene as director of presidential personnel, bringing order out of chaos. "He's a straight guy and will level with you if he has an opening," Ron said.

Mann's suggestion that I go to work for a senator was aggravating but wise. In ad-ministrations of both parties, Hill staffers with defense expertise are regularly tapped for Pentagon positions. By the end of the Reagan Administration, for example, two former staffers of Senator Tower (chairman or ranking Republican on the Armed Services Committee) had become secretaries of the Navy and Air Force. If Tower had been confirmed as secretary of defense in 1989, another former aide would have headed the Army Department as well.

Friday, 10 December 1982

At 11:30, I told Barbara Hayward that I was "going over to the other side." Normally this means the VP's suite, but today my EOB destination was a conference room where there was a training session for presidential appointees at the subcabinet level. When it broke for lunch, I spotted John Herrington,[2] and we moved a ways down the corridor to talk. I told him of my interest in working in Navy manpower, and John's response was instantaneous: "I'll hire you in a second. I've seen your work. I want you." I was astounded at the rapidity of the sale. John took out a pen and drew a box chart of his office on an unsanded palette leaning against the wall. He tapped at a box and said he wants me there if he can lose the incumbent in a staff reorganization he hopes to execute within ninety days.

Quite delighted, I went back to the West Wing to scratch down notes on the conversation just ended. There's no other agency of the government in which I'd rather work, even in a higher-level job, than Navy. John's enthusiasm for me creates enthusiasm of my own—to be at Navy, to work for him, to prove my mettle, and to learn bureaucracy from the inside. Up there watching would be [Secretary of the Navy] John Lehman, a good man to tie to. And further up there would be ex-Navy pilot George Bush, pleased that his former executive assistant is doing a substantive job. If things go well, I might credibly hope to become an assistant secretary or to return to the White House as assistant to the president for presidential personnel.[3] For now I'm happy to be in a groove that leads to the Pentagon.

Saturday, 11 December 1982

Today brought the funeral of ex-Watergate special prosecutor Leon Jaworski in Houston. He died Thursday of a heart attack while cutting wood on his ranch. Aboard *AF2* (the C-9 we used so often during the midterm campaign) were Jim Baker and Justice Lewis Powell, a tall, spare, elderly Virginia gentleman who, like Jaworski, had been president of the American Bar Association.

When we landed at Ellington AFB, we went immediately to the First Presbyterian Church on Main Street. Baker and Justice Powell joined the other pallbearers, which included a frail-looking Oveta Culp Hobby. Aside from paying tribute to the man I got to know last year when I was his point

---

2. A former Marine, John twice headed Presidential Personnel for President Reagan and served him as secretary of energy from 1985 to 1989. He and his wife, Lois, then an assistant attorney general and later a California judge, became good friends of mine.

3. This is indeed what happened.

of frequent contact with the White House, I relished today's event as a chance to underscore my identification with Houston. I shook hands with the senior partners of Fulbright and Jaworski, and upon leaving gave a wave to Governor-elect Mark White. If this all seems self-serving and political, all I can say is that Colonel Jaworski not only would have approved, he would have been doing the same thing.

Wednesday, 15 December 1982

Jennifer and I went with the VP into the Roosevelt Room for a meeting with such national black leaders as Dr. Benjamin Hooks of the NAACP and Dorothy Height of the National Council of Negro Women. The purpose was to give a briefing on our trip last month to Africa. Time and time again the leaders praised GB for taking black Americans with him—and blasted the Administration for having so few blacks in foreign policy positions. It was clear that GB himself is held in great esteem. That same popularity may be the only thing that prevents a tide of black and brown votes from drowning the Reagan Administration in 1984.

Thursday, 16 December 1982

Tom Pauken, director of ACTION [and a fellow Texan], was my guest for lunch. GB had wanted me to sound him out on various things. A twenty-year veteran of conservative causes, Tom said the VP "has done nothing" to erase the feeling by conservatives that he is an Eastern Establishment liberal. What more can he do than what he's done? I asked, citing the number of trips and campaign appearances Bush has made in two years. Tom had no ideas, saying only that it was a mistake for GB to have joined the Trilateral Commission in 1977. Pauken is also troubled by an administration that exalts "credentials" over conservatism in making personnel selections. This sounds ridiculous to me, having felt the resistance to our credentialed recommendations, but Tom sees it everywhere. He said no less than three times, "If it's this bad in a Reagan Administration, how much worse would it be in a Bush Administration?"[4]

---

4. Pauken's distrust, if not downright dislike, of father Bush extended to the son. As chairman of the Texas Republican Party in 1996, Pauken made himself, not Gov. George W. Bush, head of the state delegation to the national GOP convention. Neither the governor nor his chief

Friday, 17 December 1982

The VP met at 2:00 with Charlie Dougherty, defeated for reelection to Congress last month, and Bob Hurst, president of Philadelphia's Fraternal Order of Police. Hurst, who looks like a priest or a debt-haunted businessman, is a veteran of the department's "granny squad" of decoys, portraying elderly men and women, nuns, pizza delivery guys, and winos in the hope of apprehending lawbreakers in the act of assault or robbery. To our astonished ears he said he's been mugged 238 times, shot four times, stabbed 11 times, and hospitalized 58 times—rushing to reassure us "that's over a ten-year period, though." Hurst further said of himself, "I don't fight worth a damn, but I can take one hell of an ass-whipping."

Sunday, 19 December 1982

At 2:00 there was a Christmas party for White House staff and families held on the richly decorated State Floor. When not nibbling the small pieces of holiday cakes, served with a citrus punch and spiked eggnog, I wandered around talking with people. One of them was Wendy Borcherdt, formerly of Presidential Personnel and now an appointee herself in the Department of Education. "Everybody in the White House should spend two weeks working in an agency to see what it's really like out there," Wendy said. She is distressed about the morale of all our political appointees, whom she said never get invited to receptions such as the one we were attending. Because of the drop in morale among "the people who got us here," she fears for RR's reelection.

Rumors of the President's arrival sent people streaming from room to room till the Reagans appeared to make a handshaking sweep. An image of this (semi-)gloomy Christmas of 1982 is of a beaming, ruddy-faced RR and a red-suited, radiant Nancy standing on the landing of the grand staircase, waving vigorously and wishing everyone a happy holiday.

Monday, 20 December 1982

The Bushes gave a jolly staff party at the Naval Observatory. The Army Chorus sang full-voiced Christmas songs, but the highlight was the staff choir.

---

political aide, Karl Rove, forgot this when Pauken ran for state attorney general two years later. He finished an ignominious third in the GOP primary.

They did a spoof on "The Twelve Days of Christmas" written by Peter Robinson and deputy counsel Frank Blake, who had solo parts. The burden of the lyrics was: "On the——day of Christmas, the VP gave to us . . . One admiral from the Sixth Fleet . . . two bouncing Boydens . . . three chaste Chases [delivered with an upraised index finger, my symbol] . . . five kilos of confiscated coke [cocaine] . . . seven African countries . . . nine trips to Bismarck," and so forth.

Tuesday, 21 December 1982

I spoke on the phone with Art Kelly, [a Texas political friend of longstanding] who is now press secretary to Richard Viguerie, conservative direct-mail specialist and publisher of *Conservative Digest*. When I joked that I hoped my call wouldn't endanger his employment, Art replied in total seriousness, "We have finally realized that the enemy is not George Bush or even Jim Baker. It's Ronald Reagan who is soft on Reaganism."

Friday, 31 December 1982

New Year's Eve in Houston provided the occasion to record gloomy thoughts about years past and future.

1982 Concludes

This year, like 1981, was wrapped up in my job with GB. As such it was even bigger and more lustrous: the trips more frequent and exotic, the public events (like Brezhnev's funeral) more exciting, and my role more comfortable. But it was also a time of increasing determination to find a less glamorous but more challenging job elsewhere in the federal government. By 10 December I had the prospect of such a job at Navy, and that's what I want out of 1983. I also feel I need to do this right away, out of a growing conviction the GOP will be tossed out of power next year.

It is doubly sad—sad for the country and sad for the GOP's lost opportunity—that economic conditions got grimmer and grimmer as 1982 progressed. We could brag about inflation and interest rates coming down, but the specter of unemployment and business failures overwhelmed any joy for the (temporary?) vanquishing of these old foes.

But I greet 1983 with gratitude that I amassed a lot of memories to tide me over in leaner years to come.

Sunday, 2 January 1983

At a dinner in Washington for Steve Bartlett, the new Republican congressman from Dallas, Jim Oberwetter[5] asserted that GB's "preppiness" still hurts him at the grassroots, and I agree. The very elegant informality (summering in Maine, jogging, tennis, and lounging in orange nylon trousers) that makes GB so charming also strikes people as frivolous. One of Reagan's biggest image problems is a blithe personality that permits him to don jodhpurs and go horseback riding while people are laid off from their jobs. I told Jim that one can be of the elite, as were Franklin Roosevelt and Henry Cabot Lodge Jr., and still appeal to ordinary voters if the aristocrat-politician presents the better qualities of the breed, such as confidence, resolution, stability, kindness, and strength. If GB becomes president, he would act with much more sobriety and firmness than he displays now as VP, but like Rich Bond I doubt he can alter his nature.

Wednesday, 5 January 1983

As soon as he arrived, GB phoned to ask whether he should call Congressman Phil Gramm to congratulate him on becoming a Republican. This was a nonsurprise that came after the House Democratic Caucus finally removed Gramm from the Budget Committee for being such an enthusiastic Reagan supporter in 1981. Gramm has also resigned from the House, forcing a special election on 12 February, in which he expects to win as a Republican and dispose of the party-switching issue. I admire Gramm's brains, but he has an obvious lack of fidelity to party. When GB called Gramm, he offered his help but conceded it's probably best "for us at 1600 Pennsylvania Avenue to leave you alone." Gramm agreed, saying he wants the special election to be "between my people and me."

Gramm won the "special" against ten opponents without a runoff. Propelled by his triumphant act of principled defiance against the Democrats, Gramm easily won the 1984 Republican primary and general election to succeed Senator Tower. He was a leader in Congress on economic issues until his retirement in 2002.

---

5. A Bush stalwart in Texas since the 1960s, Oberwetter would become George W. Bush's ambassador to Saudi Arabia.

Friday, 7 January 1983

Tonight, my date and I were guests of Secretary and Mrs. Weinberger in the presidential box at the Kennedy Center for a National Symphony Orchestra performance of "The Best of Broadway." During the intermission, while pouring little bottles of champagne, SecDef asked me about the VP's forthcoming European trip. We sat together during the second half, and when the cast did "The Jets Song" from *West Side Story*, I leaned over and said to the budget-bedeviled secretary, "They're not singing about the F-18." Weinberger started and then said, "Oh ho. Yes. Right."

Saturday, 8 January 1983

President Reagan today announced in his weekly radio message that GB will travel to western Europe to consult with our allies on responses to recent Soviet sallies on disarmament and a nonaggression pact. He will go to West Germany, Belgium, Netherlands, Britain, France, and Italy (including the Vatican).

Wednesday, 12 January 1983

The VP asked the Admiral, Pete, Jennifer, and me to remain after the staff meeting. He mentioned the reports that [majority leader] Howard Baker will retire from the Senate next year to be ready to run for president if RR retires. GB alerted us that this will cause Bush supporters around the country to agitate for an active response. "I'm still convinced that the best politics is no politics," he said. He also believes that Baker is far more popular with the DC press corps than with rank-and-file Republican voters. There are few "Baker people" in the country and almost no Dole people. Nevertheless, Baker has useful contacts in New Hampshire like Sen. Warren Rudman, enough to make GB think he ought to do some event there this year. I suggested a fundraiser for [Rudman's freshman colleague] Gordon Humphrey, who has a tough reelection race in 1984. And I said, "There is some powerful New Hampshire campaigning you can do right here in Washington, and that is the romancing of Gerry Carmen." GB is committed to his friend Hugh Gregg,[6]

---

6. Gregg served as governor of New Hampshire from 1953 to 1955. His son Judd became congressman, governor, and US senator.

who dislikes Carmen. But Gerry is winnable, and it would be terrible if for any reason he went over to another candidate like Baker.

Thursday, 13 January 1983

Ed Rollins is convinced RR will run again, based chiefly on what longtime California political sage Stu Spencer related from private conversations with the President. But we both can't figure out why Reagan won't simply say so and thus forestall the Howard Bakers and Bob Doles from ginning up their own contingency campaigns. Ed will soon travel extensively through the West and Lee Atwater through the South to check the GOP's Electoral College base. He reports that longtime Reaganites voluntarily tell him of their regard for the VP's loyalty to the President.

Saturday, 15 January 1983

On the C-9 flying to Atlanta were a notable group of black Republicans, including Thadd Garrett, Steve Rhodes [of the President's staff], and Lionel Hampton. Also with us was the Rev. Ralph David Abernathy, successor to Martin Luther King Jr. as head of the Southern Christian Leadership Conference. In Atlanta we went to the relatively new MLK Jr. Center for Nonviolent Social Change, a combination museum and headquarters for Coretta Scott King's social and political activities—in large part funded by the federal government. Mrs. King earlier this week escorted Walter Mondale through the center, and today GB's hosts were the late Dr. King's sons. About twenty protestors chanted "Go Home, Bush, Go Home!" as the dignitaries stood before the tomb of MLK, placed on an island in the middle of a lighted pool.

Later there was a dinner that, with extra speakers and extra time for scheduled speakers, ran an hour and twenty minutes behind. The black elite of Atlanta and all America were there, as were such celebrities as actor-director-producer Sir Richard Attenborough and the new governor of Georgia, Joe Frank Harris. The Governor won a standing ovation by pledging his support for making MLK's birthday (today) a state holiday. The audience of course wants it made a national holiday, and that was the only message they directed at the VP—no pleas to help the jobless, the sick, the old, the uneducated, or the homeless. It was almost as if 1983 were a year of unparalleled prosperity for black America, such that its leaders could focus their attention on a holiday.

The value for us Anglos in going to such affairs—and I've gone to far more than most Republicans—is to feel the pulse and hear the heartbeat of black Americans, to appreciate their sense of community, of achievement, and of struggle, their pointed sense of humor, and their genuine religious fervor. I can also claim to be one of few Republicans who ever heard Dr. King preach—at Memorial Church at Harvard in January 1965.

Monday, 17 January 1983

To a small group after the staff meeting, GB voiced his concern that the crescendo of press comment on the European trip may create unrealistic expectations on both sides: on the left, among those who want him to bring back the days of détente, and on the right, among those who are sure he will be soft.

Tuesday, 18 January 1983

Richard (Rick) Burt, Assistant Secretary of State–designate for European Affairs, briefed the VP and senior traveling staff on what we will find in Europe. A protégé of Al Haig, Burt has long been under attack by Senator Helms for using classified material while he was a reporter for the *New York Times*. Though smart, Burt is conceited and surely not indispensable, but State will fight hard for his confirmation. This afternoon, sitting before a cozy fire, Burt said our allies have a crisis of confidence—in themselves and in the US—without parallel in thirty years or more. There is still a strong image of "Reagan the cowboy," out to achieve military superiority over the Soviets (a stated goal in the 1980 Republican platform) and intent on placing new missiles in Europe so the next war will be fought there rather than in the US. Burt wants the VP to emphasize American steadfastness yet willingness to negotiate. As a polished, experienced, and respected statesman, GB is perhaps the best man in the country to sell this line.

GB again worried about "excessive expectations" from the press and thoughtful citizens about the trip. He also worries about doing or saying something that would hasten the defeat of the Christian Democrat Helmut Kohl in the German elections 6 March. All it takes is one verbal slip that confirms attitudes about the "reckless" Reagan Administration, and Kohl is *aus*.

Wednesday, 19 January 1983

GB met with Helmut Sonnenfeldt, a foreign policy specialist often called "Kissinger's Kissinger" in the old days. Reviled by the right as a softie, Sonnenfeldt says the US should not be forced by allied public opinion to retreat on RR's bold "zero-zero" intermediate-range nuclear missile plan.[7] We must show consistency of and confidence in our own policy, he said.

Thursday, 20 January 1983

At 1:45, the VP left for the DAR [Daughters of the American Revolution] Constitution Hall a couple of blocks from the White House. In the holding room we chatted with the current president of the DAR, who urged us to look in the middle of the ceiling when President Reagan came on stage. Jennifer, Sue Cockrell, and I were shown to our box in the auditorium as Secretary of the Interior Jim Watt was speaking—really, preaching—to the "Executive Forum" of Administration appointees. Held on the second anniversary of the Inauguration, it was a veritable pep rally. Barely containing his religious fervor, Watt evoked rebel yells of approval when he closed with, "Let Reagan be Reagan! Let Reagan be Reagan!"

This famous incantation was more or less directed at White House chief of staff Jim Baker, sitting just a few feet away. Unlike my old school chum Art Kelly of Conservative Digest, many conservative leaders couldn't bring themselves to blame Ronald Reagan for what they saw as the Administration's deviation from ideological purity. They preferred to blame Bush and Baker instead.

Watt was a tough act for GB to follow, and indeed the VP didn't give a performance equal to his campaign best last fall. Peter Robinson at my suggestion inserted a definition of the vice presidency from Lyndon Johnson, who compared the job to being a steer, "someone who has lost his standing in the society in which he resides." Since neither Peter nor Chris Buckley nor other Yankees knew what a steer is, the text said "neutered bull."

When Bush sat down, the Marine Drum and Bugle Corps marched in to beat and blast away "When Johnny Comes Marching Home Again" and "The Battle Hymn of the Republic." Then the Marine Band, on stage, broke into "Hail to the Chief," and a weary-looking RR came slowly out from the

---

7. It was to spur the Soviets to agree to a mutual ban on such weapons (called "the zero option" or "zero-zero") that Reagan called for the deployment of Pershing II missiles in NATO countries. He sent Bush to Europe to persuade certain allies to accept the missiles and to applaud others that had already agreed to do so.

wings, noticeably grayer than ever and not waving or beaming his broadest, rosy-cheeked smile. As he stood at the rostrum, the Drum and Bugle Corps performed "The Stars and Stripes Forever." Upon the crescendo, an enormous flag suddenly appeared from the ceiling, just as the DAR president had hinted. The President got laughs by saying he had had "one big lesson in how to be an anticlimax." Subliminally proving how rough the past two years have been and how grim the next two will be, RR's voice was without conviction as he spoke of "a new beginning" and "a new confidence building in America." Yet the audience, few of whom ever see the President even though they are his missionaries in the bureaucracy, was totally thrilled.

Thursday, 21 January 1983

Barbara Bush and I had a wonderful hour together at the VP's Residence, eating a light lunch on trays in an upstairs sitting room. I had requested the get-together because our times to talk are so fractured and so few, frequently over the noise of a helicopter engine. I'm glad she was just as enthusiastic. BPB said her "new philosophy is to do your job the best way you can. Don't be defensive, don't explain all the time. And when you're done, you can be satisfied that you did what you could." This was undoubtedly inspired by the 1982–83 mood of the Reagan Administration and of politico-journalistic Washington toward it. In our wide-ranging talk, we also discussed my job search. "Promise you won't go off and forget us," she said, with eyes fixed on mine. "Remember you're a part of our family. And George will miss you—he says he will." I made that promise, a bit amused that anyone could "forget" the Bushes or the events of the past two years.

Tuesday, 25 January 1983

Jennifer and I rode with George and Barbara Bush in the limo up Pennsylvania Avenue to the gloriously illuminated Capitol for the State of the Union Address. In the ceremonial office off the Senate lobby we had wine and cheese and studied BPB's changes in the decor: she had a thick white carpet removed to reveal the original tiled floor, which unfortunately makes the small room ring with echoes.

GB went into the Senate chamber to lead his charges over to the House side. Jennifer, Joe Hagin, and I waited to join the procession of peacocks, two by two, at its end. This made for a stellar parade under the Rotunda and through Statuary Hall. GB had left word with the House doorkeeper to let his aides in, and Susan Alvarado took us to stage-left of the Speaker's dais. We had to stand throughout the proceedings to come, but it was a privileged position.

The doorkeeper announced the arrival of the Joint Chiefs, the Supreme Court, and the Cabinet. Then, right at 9:00 p.m., he cried out, "Mr. Speaker: The President of the United States!" All rose to give RR a hearty welcome, gratifying in these days of partisan and media sniping about his leadership. Throughout his forty-minute address, the President played heavily on a theme of bipartisanship. He called for a freeze on federal spending, a freeze on all federal pay increases, and standby taxing authority for fiscal year 1986–87. Standing where I was, I could look past the President at the Democrats. They sat quietly through all the applause lines. But, obviously primed for a particular passage in the advance text, they all instantly rose in cheers when the President said, "We who are in government must take the lead in restoring the economy." The puzzled Republicans didn't know how to react. RR was ready with a quip: "I thought you were all just reading the paper."

Wednesday, 26 January 1983

At the Pentagon, I met with John Herrington, assistant secretary of the Navy for manpower and reserve affairs. He has a wonderful office on the river side decorated with signed photos, flags, and models. A colored relief map of the world covers an entire wall—a popular item in the Pentagon.[8] After a Marine orderly brought us coffee, John dropped a bombshell: he is leaving his job in about two weeks to become head of presidential personnel, succeeding Helene von Damm, who gets her not-so-secret wish to be ambassador to Austria. In perhaps the key promise of a generally promising conversation, John said that he will work to get me an assistant secretaryship once he's in charge of presidential personnel. As 1983 wears on, and as questions are raised as to the reelectability of the Administration, it will be harder to get people from outside DC to take such jobs, he said, and therefore people already in place will have some excellent opportunities. "Then, if there's a second term, you're set," John said, adding, "The VP will run for president someday, probably in 1988. He'll need you, and by then you'll have a lot of experience."

---

8. The office would be mine from 1984 to 1988.

Thursday, 27 January 1983

I went to the EOB auditorium for GB's session with reporters from the countries he'll be visiting plus US reporters covering foreign affairs. Bush stressed that his trip won't be for negotiation but for consultation. The reporters vigilantly tried to get him to say the Reagan Administration won't insist on the "zero-zero" formula. GB kept returning to the point that RR's plan is equitable, stabilizing, and moral—and that the Soviets still haven't come up with anything that meets those criteria. I wish I could leaven GB's trademark enthusiasm with a bit more dignity. That's all that keeps him from being credited with "brilliance" in foreign affairs instead of mere knowledge.

Chapter 23

Mission Most Important

Sunday, 30 January 1983

On the flight to Andrews, GB was up but edgy, a reflection of the tremendous worldwide attention being given this trip. At last night's Alfalfa Dinner, for example, Sen. Sam Nunn (D-Georgia) gravely told him it was the most important vice presidential trip in a decade. The *Washington Post* editorialized today: "This is a remarkable day in the Reagan Administration's foreign policy. Two senior officials, Vice President George Bush and Secretary of State George Shultz, are flying to opposite points on the globe. [Shultz is going to China to try to patch up relations there.] . . . The Vice President seems to us just the right man—positive, experienced, political—to satisfy the allies' real craving for a strong and sensible American lead." There was also a good piece in the *New York Times*.

Aboard *AF2* were Rick Burt of State and thirty-five-year-old Cdr. Dennis Blair, the European specialist on the National Security Council staff. Heavily laden with fuel, SAM 86970 lifted off at 8:45 a.m. on our tenth foreign trip in only nineteen months. We crossed the icy wastes of Canada and a cloudy Atlantic, headed for Germany.

Toward 10 p.m. local time, we landed at the airport serving Cologne and Bonn. Amb. Arthur Burns, white-haired and pipe-puffing, came aboard with the German chief of protocol, a gentleman with the theatrical name of Count von Finckenstein. Then we descended to TV lights and a welcoming party led by FM Hans-Dieter Genscher. He heads the minority Free Democratic Party, whose defection from a coalition with Helmut Schmidt's socialists to join the CDU-CSU conservatives led to Helmut Kohl's installation as chancellor last October.

Monday, 31 January 1983

At 9:00, Jennifer, Dennis Blair, State Department interpreter Harry Obst, and I walked to the modernistic chancellery building just across Adenauerallee from our hotel. Harry said that [former chancellor] Konrad Adenauer chose Bonn as the capital of West Germany [in 1949] because it was a short distance from his home in Cologne—exactly like another father of his country who had a plantation on the Potomac. We stood on the edge of a red carpet facing a blue-uniformed honor guard. Chancellor Kohl came out of the building and took a salute saying, "*Guten Morgen, Soldaten!*," to which they replied in loud chorus, "*Guten Morgen, Herr Bundeskanzler!*"

A few minutes later, GB's motorcade entered the courtyard and stopped before the TV cameras. Kohl and FM Genscher sprang forward to greet him. "These guys are fighting for their political lives," the DCM [deputy chief of mission] at the US embassy said out of the corner of his mouth. "Every thirty seconds they get on TV with the vice president of the United States is worth another 5,000 votes to them." GB introduced the members of his official party to Kohl, a strapping man who is slightly taller than Bush. Mrs. Bush followed with Frau Hannelore Kohl, an attractive and vivacious woman whose broad jaw and red hair recall Margaret Heckler.[1]

The Chancellor and VP took their places on the reviewing platform as the band rendered stirring versions of both anthems. Then the two leaders went inside the chancellery for talks. Jennifer and I followed to have some strong coffee and take a look at the place. We were both amused at the official portrait of Chancellor Willy Brandt (1969–74), a warm-colored abstract with no facial features.

We later got a car that took us into the neighboring community of Bad Godesburg, dominated by a medieval castle on a hill. At its foot is La Redoute, a pretty Italianate house of the eighteenth century where Mozart once performed. The West German government uses it for official entertaining, such as this afternoon's luncheon for VP Bush. In his toast, Chancellor Kohl spoke of the warmth that exists between Germany and America and of what West Germans owe to American generosity after the war. It was a campaign speech, of course, in which the Chancellor also called for both "defense and détente" and a US-Soviet summit.

When *AF2* took off for Berlin, it carried a distinguished passenger list headed by Chancellor and Mrs. Kohl. Those who wish to take that as a sign that Kohl is our boy may do so, and they won't be wrong. But RR gave then-Chancellor Schmidt a lift to Berlin in *Air Force 1* last summer. When we

---

1. Heckler, defeated for reelection to Congress from Massachusetts the previous fall, was the new secretary of health and human services.

landed at Tegel Airport at dusk, we were met by Richard von Weizsäcker, the governing mayor of West Berlin,[2] who gave some stirring words in faultless English. GB paid the obligatory respects to what Berlin means to the Free World, after which the motorcade swept us into the city.

At dinner, GB gave his long prepared speech, knocking down, point by point, the anti-NATO arguments one hears among the German young. The ending was a surprise: GB pulled a piece of paper from his pocket and said it was "an open letter from President Reagan to the people of Europe." It called on Yuri Andropov to meet him anytime, anywhere, "to sign an agreement banning intermediate nuclear weapons from the face of the earth." The audience applauded after both Bush's own words and the translation. It was a deft propaganda coup, good until the Soves try their inevitable counterplay.

In my hotel room, I checked *Das Telefonbuch von Berlin (West)*. It contains not one Untermeyer!

Tuesday, 1 February 1983

On a windy gray morning, we proceeded down 17 Juni Boulevard through a broad tunnel of leafless elms toward the Brandenburg Gate. Before the gate we turned off to a section of the infamous Berlin Wall where observation platforms have been erected. The VP mounted one, the press another, and the staff a third. Someone had written "Bush Fuck Off" on ours, but that was the only visible protest of our visit to Berlin. The *Polizei* kept an estimated 5,000 demonstrators well out of our sight. The view was of a vast ugly scar through the center of what once was the heart of Berlin, Potzdamer Platz. In the no-man's-land between the actual walls are barbed wire, tank barriers, dog runs, guardhouses, and all manner of other discouragements. An embassy officer pointed out a mound of earth. It was the site of Hitler's bunker.

Air Force 2's next stop was the Netherlands, another first visit for me.

Our ride to Den Haag (The Hague) was lovely in the Low Countries way: a serene green plain fringed by feathery trees and now and then stippled by windmills. No longer in use, they stood ironically still on this blustery afternoon. In the town of Wassenaar we passed through nineteenth-century

---

2. Von Weizsäcker served as mayor until 1984, when he was elected president (head of state) of West Germany. He became the first president of a united Germany in 1990.

houses, many with tiled roofs and gazebos, before arriving in Den Haag. We are staying in Kurhaus, a huge seaside hotel in the calliope style of the 1880s, a Dutch cousin of the Hotel del Coronado near San Diego. Out our windows the North Sea was whipped into churning froth by the winds. The filtered sunlight, the pale blue sky, and the gritty beach all were the same as in Dutch and Flemish paintings of the Golden Age.

Tonight's grand event was dinner in the Bushes' honor given by Queen Beatrix of the Netherlands. Our motorcade entered the grounds of Huis ten Bosch, Her Majesty's official residence, its seventeenth-century façade lighted for the occasion. Doormen doffed their top hats as they opened our doors. We signed the guestbook and mounted a narrow old stairway to an assembly room hung with trompe l'oeil paintings of cherubs. Ladies- and gentlemen-in-waiting to the Queen thoughtfully introduced us Americans to Dutch guests, who were cabinet ministers, industrialists, and burgermeisters of the major cities of the nation. Then we were led into a hall where Her Majesty, dressed in a blue gown with puffed Philippine sleeves, stood to greet us. Beside her stood the Bushes, her sister Princess Margriet, and Margriet's husband. (Beatrix's consort, Prince Claus, seldom appears in public due to a mental condition of some sort.) We took drinks in a reception room hung with portraits of eighteenth- and nineteenth-century rulers of the House of Orange-Nassau.

Members of the court next led us into the spectacular Orange Room, a bell-shaped chamber, every square meter of which is richly painted in the exuberant style of Rubens (though not by the master himself). A history professor told me the work was done by several painters as a memorial to the first *stadhouder* of Holland, the man who built Huis ten Bosch. The walls and ceilings were so entrancing, especially by candlelight, that it was irresistible to keep looking up.

Footmen with military precision marched in and out to serve us a fine French meal of tender venison. The toasts were exchanged early. The Queen with perfect English diction spoke with great warmth of Dutch-American relations. The VP's response included some political issues that jarred with Beatrix's higher-toned remarks on mutual values, freedom, and the like. The waiters passed demitasses and cigarettes, served on trays with lighted candles. When the Queen and the VP rose, we followed them back into the reception room for brandy and cigars. (I took two, which I later gave to a Secret Service agent and to the VP's traveling physician, Dr. Ed Yob.)

GB found Jennifer and me and brought us over to talk with the Queen, who showed us the guestbook, completely made by nuns. It feature illuminated crests of Beatrix, Claus, and the eldest of their three sons, Crown Prince Willem. (The lads, all blond and smiling, appeared after dinner to greet the Bushes.) When the Bushes left, the rest of us followed in a great wave. Thus ended an elegant and friendly evening in the Dutch manner.

Wednesday, 2 February 1983

At 11:35, I left by car with the administrative counselor of the embassy for Catshuis, the official residence of Prime Minister Ruud Lubbers, who gave a friendly and informal luncheon for the VP. A charming country place, Catshuis was named for its builder, a man named Cats (= Katz). It has a goose-filled pond in front and a peacock-strolled lawn in back.

We ate in a long paneled dining room whose leaded windows looked out onto the lawn and through which sunlight came in, Vermeer-like, to illuminate a centerpiece of yellow roses.

The vice presidential entourage continued on to Brussels, Conrad's "sepulchral city," followed by Geneva.

Friday, 4 February 1983

The Bushes are staying at Château de Bellerive, the residence of GB's friend Prince Sadruddin Aga Khan. Tonight "Sadri" and his princess gave a reception and buffet dinner for their special guests, to which they invited *la crème* of Geneva society, Swiss government officials, and diplomats. Jennifer helped plan the affair, but she pulled another of her I-won't-go acts tonight, claiming that our sightseeing walk this afternoon had exhausted her. Prince Sadruddin greeted me with his diplomat's warmth and asked where Jennifer was. I gave her excuse of exhaustion. This was received as illness, and His Highness went immediately to phone her. Of course by then Jennifer had gone out to dinner with fellow staffers. I quickly disappeared.

Chris Buckley's parents had come down from Gstaad with other socialites. As he and I stood talking, I pointed out Viktor Karpov, chief Soviet negotiator at the strategic arms talks. "Do you want to go talk with him?" Chris asked brightly, answering himself, "Let's." We introduced ourselves to Karpov and his deputy, Aleksei Obukhov, a tall, debonair fellow who spoke perfect English—probably KGB. Karpov used an intense young man as interpreter, obviously not aware of who we were but certain he hadn't see us in his meeting with the VP this afternoon. "Are you optimistic about the talks?" Chris asked as an opener. Speaking in a strange squeaky voice, Karpov said, "We must always believe, as the proverb says, 'All's well that ends well.'"

"Then I propose a toast," Chris said, carrying on an act I later accused him of practicing for years while shaving. "May all end well!" We drank. Karpov asked Chris whether he is optimistic about START [the Strategic Arms Reduction Talks]. "I am an optimist; I am an American," Chris replied assertively, cribbing the line from RR's inaugural address. It became my turn to talk, and I asked Karpov, based on his experience, how frustrating is it to be a negotiator when the real decisions are made elsewhere. He said arms talks should be conducted like the election of a pope. Communists always get attention when they speak of anything vaguely related to religion. When I asked what he meant, Karpov said that negotiators should be locked up and put on diminishing rations until they reach an agreement. Ah, but the analogy isn't quite apt, I found myself blurting, because cardinals are princes of the church and don't have to answer to masters outside the walls. "Good point, Chase!" Buckley exclaimed, as if I had just scored on Karpov in a ping-pong match. The Karpov-*Americanski* talks ended soon thereafter.

Chris's mother, Pat—tall, soignée, and irrepressible—took a liking to me and invited me to join them at the buffet. We went into a room lined with cases containing Prince Sadruddin's flawless collection of Persian and Indian miniatures. We sat at a table in the corner with other Gstaad émigrés. The couple to my right were Brazilians, who also live in New York, London, Paris, and Marrakech. Marty Feldstein [chairman of the President's Council of Economic Advisors] later said he learned, "You don't ask them what they do. They don't *do* anything. They *spend*. They might well have said to me, 'You write about the economy. We *are* the economy.'" I got to meet the great William F. Buckley, but he was too far and the Brazilians too close to talk. I made a break to get Mrs. Buckley a selection of desserts, returning to find that George Bush had taken my seat.

Saturday, 5 February 1983

With Rick Burt, I rode to the US mission to the UN agencies in Geneva, where GB held a press conference. He reiterated the United States' strong support for the zero option as "a moral position. . . . The only argument I've heard against it is that the Soviets don't like it." When asked to balance this comment against his equally strongly stated desire for disarmament, Bush said, "Our view is that what goes in can come out." It was a neat and quotable way of saying that the US and its allies can proceed with deployment of INF

[Intermediate-range Nuclear Forces] this December without closing off any opportunities to sign an agreement later with the USSR.

The next hop was to Nuremberg, where the VP visited with US Army forces in Germany, and on to Rome for a rare day off. Despite a steady rain, I spent my first visit to the Eternal City walking its sublime streets.

Sunday, 6 February 1983

Nine o'clock came, and, not having heard from anyone about a dinner outing, I started out on my own. By great good fortune, I ran into Dennis Blair, who suggested we go together. I was delighted to get to know Dennis better. He is a highly impressive fellow: US Naval Academy '68, Rhodes scholar, now on the NSC staff, and soon to be commanding officer of a DDG [guided missile-armed destroyer]. He is a third-generation Annapolis product and a sixth-generation naval officer. I can easily see him one day as an admiral—perhaps CNO, chief of naval intelligence, or even superintendent of the Academy.[3] Over dinner, however, Dennis expressed doubts about the value of a Naval Academy education, which sounds like heresy. He thinks the Navy could do just as well if Annapolis were a postgraduate rather than undergraduate outfit.

Monday, 7 February 1983

At 10:45, the motorcade pulled out of the Villa Taverna, the splendid residence of the US ambassador, crossed the Tiber, and proceeded up a boulevard into the welcoming arms of Bernini's colonnade at the Città del Vaticano. Tourists hurried over to see who it was, and the pigeons went in the opposite direction. We entered through the Arch of Bells, passed around the apse of the great Basilica of St. Peter, and motored through more archways and courtyards, each with its own name, till we reached the larger Cortile di San Damaso, right below the papal apartments.

A line of Swiss guards with their pikes, plumed helmets, and candy-striped uniforms came to attention as GB emerged from his limo. He was

---

3. Blair rose to be a four-star admiral and commander of the Pacific Command and director of National Intelligence.

greeted by a half dozen gentlemen-in-waiting to His Holiness the Pope. Prosperous Romans who work as volunteers, these elderly, good-humored men wore white tie, tails, gold chains, and whatever papal and military decorations they merited. [When I expressed curiosity about a particular medal on the lapel of one of these men, he replied with some hesitation that it was for service in Mussolini's Ethiopian campaign in the 1930s.] We took an elevator that opened onto a loggia with a ceiling painted by Rafael. Passing through one superb audience chamber after another, we came to the Sala Clementina, where we waited while the Pope and the VP had their forty-five-minute tête-à-tête.

At last we were lined up in rank order and led into the Pope's library. John Paul II, dressed in satiny white, waited alongside GB and BPB (in a mantilla). He was every bit as kindly and beatific as he appears in pictures, but I was rather surprised to find he is not a big man—only about my height [five feet eight]. But John Paul projects great strength and vigor, and his role as a tireless moral leader and the embodiment of resistance to communism marks him as special among all recent popes.

Our audience was simple: as we filed past, GB introduced each of us to the Holy Father, who smiled and murmured an indistinct word of greeting. Catholics such as Dr. Ed Yob and Admiral Murphy knelt to kiss his ring. We then formed a semicircle for a group photograph, after which the Pope and VP came forward to examine their gifts to each other. His Holiness gave a book of paintings by Rafael, and the VP presented a Steuben glass sculpture representing peace. [This gift had first been given in error to the prime minister of the Netherlands, who was much amused at being mistaken for the Pope.] A papal aide then stepped up with a silver tray stacked with white boxes covered with what seemed the same shiny textile as the Pope's garments. As we in the party filed past again, the Holy Father gave each of us one of these boxes, clasping our hands in a gesture of farewell. Women received rosaries, and men received gold medallions specially struck for the fourth year of John Paul II's reign. It was all over in a few memorable minutes.

Upon taking leave of the Pope, the party was led this way and that down more immaculate marble hallways and stairways to the offices of the Vatican secretary of state, Cardinal Casaroli. As the VP met with him, BPB had a private tour of the Sistine and Pauline chapels, led by an Italian professor involved in the decade-long restoration of the great frescoes. Other visitors in the Sistine Chapel tried to puzzle out who the white-haired lady and her burly male companions were.

At 7:30, in evening clothes, we went to the Villa Madama, another fine house (ceilings again by Rafael) used by the Italian government for state occasions. Tonight's dinner for Vice President and Mrs. Bush was hosted by Prime Minister Amintore Fanfani, one of the eternal wizards of Italian politics. He is a mite of a man, and his stylish wife looks twice as tall as he. At dinner, I was seated next to Antonio Badini, *consigliere diplomatico* (or foreign affairs advisor) to the prime minister, formerly posted in Washington. I told him that Rome's long and apparently successful struggle against leftist terrorism is "another great Italian contribution to western civilization," a phrase I thought worthy of George Will.

Afterward, during coffee, Jennifer and I spoke with an old fellow who was once minister of finance, is now a liberal (that is, conservative) member of the Italian Senate, and who speaks English with an Oxford accent. He told wonderful stories how Italian families like the Borgheses and Farneses would build great *palazzi* and move to Rome right after a kinsman was elected pope. "Then Uncle Pope—or sometimes even Daddy Pope—would take care of them." He spoke of a beauteous Farnese whose corporal charms obtained the keys of St. Peter's for her brother, an achievement heralded in the many nude portraits of her in the Farnese Palace, now the French embassy.

The final stops were Paris, where the Mitterrand government was pro-INF, and London, also friendly but nervous about Reagan's bellicose image. At the historic Guildhall in the City of London, Bush gave the most important speech of the trip, delivered to members of the Royal Institute of International Affairs. The text was written by Chris Buckley, who before the VP's arrival strode the aisle like a nervous playwright on a Broadway opening night.

Wednesday, 9 February 1983

At 5:30, a functionary in a red-and-white sash asked that "we all be upstanding" for the Vice President, US ambassador John Louis, and Lord Harlech, former British ambassador to the US and today's chairman. The VP's speech was clear and resolute but not warlike. He delivered it the best I have ever heard him read a speech, and his handling of the Q&A afterward was masterful. Challenged on the nuclear freeze issue by Bruce Kent, general secretary of the Campaign for Nuclear Disarmament, GB replied with great sincerity and almost Churchillian majesty: "Do you think we feel less than others about nuclear war? We want peace, and we want to keep the peace." Asked about the 300 or so demonstrators outside the hall, GB said, "I had no feelings of anger. I could see my own sons out there." The Guildhall speech more than anything established him as the premier spokesman on American foreign policy in Europe; he was presidential tonight. (*Time* says in its current issue, "Bush faced his European challenge with all the zeal of a man who would like to be president.")

Chapter 24

Moving On

Demonstrating the full range of duties required of an American vice president, Bush's next trip after successfully selling INF to the European elite was to Florida to wave the green-and-white starting flag at the Daytona 500 NASCAR race.

Sunday, 20 February 1983

We landed at Daytona around 11:00; the raceway is next to the runway. We staffers rode in a van, and along with the other cars in the VP's motorcade actually went onto the two-and-a-half-mile track. We rode on the level lane, amazed at the 31 degree banked lanes that rose to our right. To our left in the infield was a small city of RVs [recreational vehicles] whose owners and occupants were finishing off a meal and mounting the roofs to watch the twenty-fifth running of the Daytona 500. Confederate flags fluttered in plenitude, reminding me of Lee Atwater's great definition of NASCAR: "Woodstock for rednecks." That truth was underscored when the motorcade broke and we staffers were driven through the crowds into the stadium area behind a police vehicle with flashing lights. At close range we could see the celebrants: people with stern, weathered faces, most—male and female—wearing red gimme caps advertising both the race and Winston cigarettes. Peter Robinson turned to Boyden Gray, scion of a rich North Carolina family closely connected with R. J. Reynolds Tobacco, and asked, "Boyden, does this awaken any feudal feelings in you?"

The time of constant trip-taking with the vice president of the United States was drawing to an end. I was closing in on my desired job at the Navy Department, and the final stop was a meeting with the man who would dominate the next four years of my official life as George Bush had done the previous two: Secretary of the Navy John F. Lehman Jr.

Friday, 25 February 1983

A staff car delivered me to the Mall Entrance of the Pentagon. With a few minutes to spare, I looked at portraits of former Army chiefs of staff before taking the escalator two flights up to where SecNav [the Secretary of the Navy] dwells. In the early-American waiting room I was greeted by Cdr. Dan Murphy Jr., the Admiral's son and staff secretary to Secretary Lehman. A short while later, a remarkably young four-striper [Capt. Paul David Miller, Lehman's executive assistant] led me into the Secretary's office. John Lehman stood just inside the doorway, buttoning his jacket. He took me to a seating area and apologized for the short meeting, saying he had a lunch with "Cap" [Weinberger].

Lehman looked at me with a stare that was both casual and intense, his blue eyes fixed on me as he commenced a monologue in a Philadelphia drawl. "First of all," he said, "we want to have you here at Navy in the sort of job you want. We don't want you to slip away." He spoke of my working on procurement matters with the assistant secretary for shipbuilding and logistics, George Sawyer. He made unmistakable that the job would be a DAS. He also talked of my possibly going into OSD [Office of Secretary of Defense] to fight "the McNamara creeps" who have been chopping up or shooting down Navy programs.[1] Lehman said several times that such work would be "noticed." But we both concluded it would be better for me to get grounded in the Navy before considering a move elsewhere in the Pentagon.

A ship's clock sounded eight bells; lunchtime had arrived. Lehman rose and escorted me to the door. It had all been exciting, but there is an obvious catch: I have never dealt in procurement, contracts, or contractors, which ought to give a George Sawyer pause when considering me for his staff. I believe my analytical skills and hard work would enable me to do the job, but there would be billions of dollars at stake and very experienced (even tricky) people with whom I'd be dealing. It is a proper challenge, and it isn't mine yet. But, as [DOD political personnel chief] Marybel Batjer told me, "This is something Lehman wants to do, and it will be done."

Later, GB told me he was very excited and "proud" at what seems to be

---

1. This was a reference to OSD bureaucrats who still hewed to the "quantitative analysis" method of weighing weapons acquisition programs, made popular during the reign of Robert S. McNamara, secretary of defense under Kennedy and Johnson. Though I never went to OSD, it was classic Lehman to plot the infiltration of a Navy sympathizer within its ranks.

shaping up. Lehman owes GB a favor, since he (Bush) pushed for Lehman's selection as SecNav. I suggested that Lehman is "thinking of the future as much as the past in wanting a Bush connection."

Today may not have been as portentous as was 2 December 1980, but time could prove it so—the day I truly met John Lehman, my generation's best bet to become SecDef (or better) in a later Republican administration.

Lehman never became secretary of defense. His brilliance and success in pushing Navy programs earned him powerful enemies who, beaten by him again and again, would wait to exact their revenge. Worse, at the time George Bush became president a close associate of Lehman's was under federal investigation (and later conviction) for bribery. This made Lehman too risky a choice to replace Bush's nominee for defense secretary, John Tower, when the Senate voted him down. Instead, Bush chose the noncontroversial and widely respected Congressman Dick Cheney of Wyoming. Speedily confirmed, Cheney proved an able Pentagon chief during the Gulf War, but I consider John Lehman the greatest secretary of defense that America never had.

Monday, 28 February 1983

Jennifer and I were guests of DC lobbyist (and ex–assistant chief of protocol) Bill Codus for a salute to retired Adm. Hyman Rickover, "father of the nuclear Navy," at the Sheraton Washington hotel. On the dais were former presidents Nixon, Ford, and Carter; Senators Henry (Scoop) Jackson, John Warner, and Strom Thurmond; and of course the eighty-three-year-old Rickover. Of all the exes, Carter looked the best: handsomely gray, relaxed, his famous smile warm rather than appliqué. Ford looked fit and tanned. Nixon resembled the cartoonist image of himself, with a trapezoidal head and a somber, jowly expression, except when he chose to turn on a campaigner's smile. He spoke the best of the three presidents, albeit with a slurring of his words.

Senator Thurmond got the biggest laugh when he observed, "The Admiral and I both decided to marry young women. We figured that our age it's better to smell poifume than linnyment!"

Rickover read his remarks, the most fascinating of which were about his father's emigration from Czarist Russia in 1906. An immigration officer on Ellis Island almost rejected the senior Rickover but ultimately let him enter. "Many a defense contractor has had reason to curse that officer ever since,"

Rickover told us. "I served longer than any naval officer in our history. I followed every order that I agreed with."

A huge cake was brought out, and Richard Nixon himself sat at a piano to bang out (badly) "Happy Birthday," followed by "God Bless America." I happily joined in the singing; it isn't often that one has a former president of the United States for an accompanist.

Thursday, 3 March 1983

Ron Mann, who handles Defense for [the Office of] Presidential Personnel, was showing his Sunday school class around the West Wing. He said George Sawyer had called to ask how fast I could be cleared for appointment as DAS, and Ron said as fast as Sawyer could get the papers to him. This was the first word that I have been hired at Navy.

Friday, 4 March 1983

Visiting family in New York, I called Liz Grundy for messages. All could wait till Monday–save one, from George Sawyer. The assistant secretary was businesslike: "Chase, we'd like to put a request into the system for you to become deputy assistant secretary for installations and facilities." He listed the chief items this would cover: property management, military construction, environmental affairs, and occupational safety and health. "I think you'll find it fulfilling," he said. Sawyer *didn't* say anything like "I think you'll do a great job" or "I really want you to work with us." Oh well, if he has doubts about me, then so do I. My task will be to eradicate these, one by one.

So now it's done, approximately three months after beginning the job hunt. I note the lack of heart-thumping excitement when Sawyer called. This is chiefly due to uncertainty about the job and how I'll handle it. Would I have come to Washington in 1981 to do this? My initial reaction is to say no; I would have wanted something at the assistant secretary level.[2] But it's the kind of highly responsible job that, sitting in an endless session of the Legislature later on, I would have regretted passing up. I'll save all the excitement for later, when I score great triumphs.

---

2. An assistant secretaryship is a presidential appointment requiring Senate confirmation. A DAS position is filled by a Cabinet secretary with White House concurrence.

Wednesday, 9 March 1983

GB asked me for "any news" on my job search. Unable to get an appointment with Admiral Murphy to tell him first, I gave up on following the chain of command and told all. GB thinks the assignment is superb, "just right for you." The fact he's thrilled means that if I do well, he'll be all the prouder. He said it is excellent preparation for unspecified bigger jobs later on. "It won't last forever," he said, adding that if things don't work out, "feel free to come out to Massachusetts Avenue, put your feet up, and tell what's not going right, and maybe we can do something."

I appreciate his fatherliness and the sincerity of his offer. But while it's nice to have such an insurance policy made out to me, I intend to throw myself into being DASN [deputy assistant secretary of the Navy, pronounced "Dassin"] without a look backward. My future colleagues, particularly those who think of me as "Bush's boy," will probably be surprised at the utter absence of signed pictures and other memorabilia in my office.[3] And I won't talk about the past two years unless talked to. If something better comes, I'll take it. But my aim will be, as always, to do well by doing good.

Thursday, 10 March 1983

At the 8:45 staff meeting, I made a general announcement about becoming DASN. The VP picked up on it to say how glad he is that I have such a big job, and he made the point of saying I got it on my own, "with very little assist" from him. Then he expressed a deep-seated concern over "rumors among secretaries around the water cooler" on my successor—a direct reference to anti-Jennifer stories leaked to the press. He called this "the same sort of sickness that has helped destroy the president of the United States," namely indiscriminate talking to the press.

At noon, Lee Atwater and I had lunch in the Mess with Horace Busby, originally a Texas newsman who went to work for Lyndon Johnson before the 1948 Senate election and remained with him for years. [He now has a political newsletter.] A short, slow-speaking man, Busby has a knack for political analysis and the larger view of history. When not kicking political

---

3. In Washington, the place for such souvenirs is called a "power wall" or an "I-love-me wall." I flaunted my connections by *not* advertising them, decorating my Navy offices instead with ship models, historic prints, and paintings from the department's extensive art collection.

opponents in the nuts, Lee is a political scientist, so he listened eagerly as Busby described a new era of bipartisanship and moderation, forced on the country by the "dual lock" of Republican control of the White House and Democratic control of the House through the end of the century. "There is no [presidential] race next year," Busby said flatly. With the South, Southwest, and West's electoral votes firmly Republican and with the Democrats' propensity to pay primary attention to grabby interest groups, he predicts a Reagan sweep. Both he and Lee believe there is "a natural majority out there" of something like 60 percent of the electorate, only it's not so easily defined by party or ideology.

Alone among soothsayers during the winter of 1983, Horace Busby foresaw the great Reagan victory in 1984 with nearly 60 percent of the vote. But his popular theory of "a Republican lock on the presidency" lasted only through George Bush's election in 1988. The theory presumed that the "sunbelt" states of California, Texas, and Florida would remain solidly Republican, but California started voting Democratic in 1992, and Florida went for the Democrats in 2008 and 2012.

Jim Baker, leaving his solitary lunch, shouted, "Congratulations!" Busby asked what the chief of staff meant. When I told him I am doing what Bill Moyers did in 1961, "leaving a vice presidential staff for a job in the bureaucracy," he said, "That's the smartest thing I've heard in Washington for a long time!" Not only is it healthy to get away from the White House, Busby said, but "if you come back, [the VP] will look upon you differently than he does now."

Friday, 11 March 1983

At 3:00, gagwriter Ray Siller arrived with Peter Robinson to say hello, followed a few minutes later by BPB. She hugged me, and when I asked if she knew my news she said, "Know it! George was so excited he couldn't talk of anything else."

John Herrington had an appointment with the VP so that GB could introduce Jennifer as the new liaison to Presidential Personnel. I sat in on this fascinating little discussion. John said, "I've worked for Ronald Reagan since 1966, but as far as I'm concerned, this is a Reagan-Bush administration, and I want you to keep your organization intact" through the personnel process. Till he takes over from Helene von Damm around 1 May, John is conducting a management audit of several White House staff offices, especially Communications, which David Gergen heads. Gergen has a big reputation and a lot of friends in the press, but for two years I have failed to see any genius in shaping RR's public image. On the contrary, it's been consistently botched. I am glad John sees his charter as telling Jim Baker bluntly how and why the present arrangement doesn't work.

GB thanked John for helping get me placed at Navy. John then said what he's been telling me, "Chase probably should be in a higher spot than he is, and I look to moving him up as soon as there's an opening." I rushed to cushion the compliment by adding, "on good behavior."

Saturday, 12 March 1983

This afternoon, Jim Baker and I talked about my new job. He thinks it is excellent, but he said—twice, without provocation—"Don't stray too far away from him," motioning toward GB's office. "He'll need you one of these days."

Sunday, 13 March 1983

At 8:00 p.m., with no clinched heartstrings, I walked out of the West Wing for the last time as executive assistant to the vice president. I view the morrow [when I start work as DASN] with doubts but much more eagerness. In other words, it's not like the previous two occasions in my life when I left GB's staff for the Navy.

This terse valedictory referred to my pained departure from George Bush's congressional staff, first in 1967 for Naval ROTC summer duty and then in 1968 for the fleet as a newly commissioned ensign. As I had wisely resolved during the 1980–81 transition, when the time came to leave the West Wing it was with anticipation for the future, not with pining for the past. I had what I wanted, a substantive job in a major center of action during the Reagan Administration, away from staff grumbles and gnawing guilt for being a grand supernumerary on ninety-nine domestic and foreign trips.

As Barbara Bush had hoped, I would not and could not forget the two great years spent with her and GB all over the world. It may have been "a diet of whipped cream," but it nourished me sufficiently until the time came to return again with them to the White House.

Afterword

Why Things Went Right

Looking back after thirty years with the perspective not allowed the nightly diarist, how might one say "things went right" in the United States under President Ronald Reagan and Vice President George Bush? The reasons I submit below characterize their entire tenure but were of particular value during their first two years in the White House.

Optimism. Like Winston Churchill's steely confidence in the worst days of World War II that Adolf Hitler would be defeated, Ronald Reagan's sunny optimism during the long, rough economic troubles of 1981–83 that his program would achieve sustained prosperity for the American people spurred his appointees, high and low, to keep plugging away at his agenda. The story he told on the first anniversary of his inauguration ("There's got to be a pony in here somewhere!") was one he frequently repeated, for nothing better illuminated his outlook on life.

Clarity of purpose. Reagan had only a few items on his agenda, but they were the right ones: a limited government, lower taxes, fewer regulations, and a strong and resolute national defense. He never wavered from these goals and never tired of stating them again and again until the American people knew what was in his heart and what he was determined to achieve. No one ever needed to take a poll into the Oval Office to determine what the President felt about a given issue.

Boldness. Nothing better illustrated this trait than Reagan's staunch belief that American might, resolution, and readiness would push "the evil empire" into the scrapheap. The acquisition of new missiles and aircraft, the drive toward a 600-ship Navy, the use of this revived force in selected cases (against Grenada in 1983 and Libya in 1986), and his determination to achieve strategic missile defense persuaded the Kremlin that Reagan meant business. He was therefore able to reach agreements with the USSR to eliminate intermediate-range nuclear weapons and reduce strategic systems, achievements that the muddle-headed proponents of a mere "nuclear freeze" never dared dream.

Humor. Reagan was always ready with a quip, one that appeared to poke fun at himself but which in reality poked back at his detractors. The press, though scarcely on Reagan's side, had to publish or show him making these cracks, because they were just plain funny. Once, in a press conference, a reporter told the President he always blamed the Democrats for national problems; didn't he ever blame himself? Reagan swiftly said, yes, he did blame himself: "You see, I was once a Democrat." Or the time he ran down the list of his accomplishments in office, paused, and then noted, "Not bad for someone who only works half-time." Unfortunately, many conservatives, then and now, are too dour, viewing humor as trivializing serious matters, whereas in Reagan's hands it was a devastatingly successful weapon.

Willingness to work across the aisle. In our time, the political parties in Washington are so polarized they cannot imagine working with those they consider philosophically and morally repugnant. Republicans call Democrats "socialist"; Democrats call Republicans "fascist." If mere physical proximity is deemed abhorrent, then sitting together to achieve compromises is out of the question. While patriots, they no longer have reverence for the Congress, for their individual houses, and much less for the United States government. These past touchstones of loyalty bound members and motivated them to work together. Games like golf or poker, and not a little alcohol, allowed members from different parties to get together on evenings and weekends and even to like each other. Today, when senators and representatives routinely fly home on Thursdays, they no longer have time, let alone the desire, to develop such friendships.

Partisanship was not unknown in the 1980s, and the Democrats' attack on Reagan was unrelenting. The saw him (in the words of Washington fixer Clark Clifford) as "an amiable dunce," and that was when they felt they should be respectful. But Reagan had a useful deafness when hit by questions from obnoxious reporters and by criticism from the loyal opposition. As he famously said of his relations with the Democratic speaker of the House, Tip O'Neill, a fierce foe, "We're friends after six o'clock."

Willingness to compromise. Steadfast dedication to achieving his goals did not prevent Reagan from making adjustments and compromises along the way, as long as he continued to make progress in their direction. For example, when the historic tax-cut bill was moving through the US House (then controlled by Democrats) in 1981, Reagan wanted to reduce the rate on unearned income from 70 percent to 50 percent in order to stimulate investment. But to get this he had to agree to cut personal taxes by 25 percent instead of 30 percent. In his diary that night, Reagan wrote: "H—l, it's more than I thought we could get. I'm delighted to get the seventy down to fifty." (Reagan censored his own expletive.)

Today, many conservatives who claim to be faithful followers of Ronald Reagan view any compromise as a betrayal of principle and ample reason to root out any Republican who engages in it. They, like those who in 1983 cheered James Watt's cry "Let Reagan be Reagan!," imagine him to be what he never was. Unable to discern (or admit) this truth, many at the time blamed deviations from dogma on evil influences, specifically George Bush and James Baker. This always struck me as odd, for these supposed Reagan devotees were in effect saying the same thing as his most vicious foes, namely that Reagan was a witless actor who merely recited lines others had written for him.

The late Clymer Wright, a Houston conservative leader, wrote an open letter accusing Baker of undermining and sabotaging Reagan's program. The President promptly wrote him: "Yes, there is undermining of my efforts going on, and, yes, there is sabotage of all I'm trying to accomplish. But it's being done by the people who write these articles and columns, not by any White House staff member and certainly not Jim Baker. . . . I'm in charge, and my people are helping to carry out the policies I set. No, we don't get everything we want and, yes, we have to compromise to get 75 percent or 80 percent of our programs."

A belief in competence. Reagan did not see competence in making government work as in any way in conflict with conservative principle. Quite the contrary, he put people in power who not only shared his philosophy but who could also move his agenda. Loyalists were horrified when President-elect Reagan chose Jim Baker—who had led Gerald Ford's and George Bush's campaigns against him—as White House chief of staff. But Reagan recognized Baker's gifts as a strategist and a cool administrator. Doctrinaire conservatives assailed Baker for betraying Reagan; yet it was he who got Reagan's historic legislative program through Congress in 1981. Likewise, Reagan saw the value of George Bush's experience, extensive domestic and foreign contacts, and tireless service in choosing him for vice president and in making him a key member of the White House team. Elsewhere in the administration, principled and competent leaders like Caspar Weinberger, George Shultz, Drew Lewis, Lynne Cheney, William Bennett, John Lehman, and Jeane Kirkpatrick carried the good fight into the bureaucracy with great success.

Modesty. A sign on his desk in the Oval Office said it all about Ronald Reagan: "There is no limit to what a man can do or where he can go if he doesn't mind who gets the credit." Reagan knew that as president he would receive history's accolades for the success of his entire administration—and its condemnation if things went badly. But, amazingly for one who was truly the focus of all eyes, and even more amazingly for one who had been a Hollywood star, Ronald Reagan was a modest man. This was at the base of his appeal to all segments of the American people and why they twice trusted him with their highest gift.

It is no surprise, therefore, why things went right when Ronald Reagan was president; it was because all was right with him.

Notes on Sources

The primary source materials for this book are the Journals of Chase Untermeyer, Volumes 106 through 118 (covering 3 September 1980–6 May 1983, inclusive).

Also consulted for occasional facts and quotations:

Baker, James A., III. *"Work Hard, Study . . . and Keep Out of Politics!"* New York: G. P. Putnam's Sons, 2006.

Bush, Barbara. *Barbara Bush: A Memoir.* New York: Charles Scribner's Sons, 1994.

Bush, George. *All the Best, George Bush: My Life in Letters and Other Writings.* New York: Scribner, 1999.

Cannon, Lou. *President Reagan: The Role of a Lifetime.* New York: Simon & Schuster, 1991.

Mann, James. *About Face: A History of America's Curious Relationship with China, from Nixon to Clinton.* New York: Alfred A. Knopf, 1999.

Noonan, Peggy. *What I Saw at the Revolution.* New York: Random House, 1990.

Reagan, Ronald. *An American Life.* New York: Simon & Schuster, 1990.

———. *The Reagan Diaries.* Edited by Douglas Brinkley. New York: HarperCollins Publishers, 2007.

Rove, Karl. *Courage and Consequence.* New York: Threshold Editions, 2010.

Websites

Biographical Directory of the United States Congress, 1774–Present (bioguide .congress.gov)

US Department of State, Office of the Historian (history.state.gov)

Wikipedia.org

About the Author

CHASE UNTERMEYER has held both elected and appointed office at all four levels of government: local, state, national, and international. A diarist since the age of nine, he went to Washington, DC, two weeks before the inauguration of Ronald Reagan in January 1981 to work for the new vice president, George Bush. He remained over the next twelve years, closely observing two presidencies. This he did as executive assistant to the Vice President, as an assistant secretary of the Navy, as director of presidential personnel for the first President Bush, and as director of the *Voice of America.* He would later serve the second President Bush as United States ambassador to Qatar.

Untermeyer is a 1968 graduate of Harvard College with honors in government. During the Vietnam War he served as an officer in the United States Navy aboard a destroyer in the western Pacific and as aide to the commander of US naval forces in the Philippines.

Upon his return to Texas, Ambassador Untermeyer was a political reporter for the *Houston Chronicle* for three years before becoming executive assistant to the county judge (chief administrative official) of Harris County, Texas, the jurisdiction surrounding Houston. In 1976, he was elected to the first of two terms as a member of the Texas House of Representatives, resigning this office to go to Washington.

He is married to the former Diana Cumming Kendrick of Sheridan, Wyoming, whom he met when they were both on the White House staff of the first President Bush. Their daughter, Elly, is a student at Stanford University. The Untermeyers live in Houston, where he is an international business consultant and a member of the Texas Ethics Commission.

Index

Abbreviations